The Sense of Sociability

How people overcome the forces pulling them apart

LORNE TEPPERMAN

OXFORD

UNIVERSITY PRESS

Oxford University Press is a department of the University of Oxford.
It furthers the University's objective of excellence in research, scholarship,
and education by publishing worldwide. Oxford is a registered trade mark
of Oxford University Press in the UK and in certain other countries.

Published in Canada by
Oxford University Press
8 Sampson Mews, Suite 204,
Don Mills, Ontario M3C 0H5 Canada

www.oupcanada.com

Copyright © Oxford University Press Canada 2010

The moral rights of the author have been asserted

Database right Oxford University Press (maker)

First Paperback Edition published in 2011

Library and Archives Canada Cataloguing in Publication

Tepperman, Lorne, 1943–
The sense of sociability : how people overcome
the forces pulling them apart / Lorne Tepperman.

Includes bibliographical references.
ISBN 978-0-19-543929-8 (bound). — ISBN 978-0-19-544168-0 (pbk.)

1. Social groups—Canada. 2. Social interaction—
Canada. 3. Community life—Canada. I. Title

HM716.T45 2010   302.0971   C2009-906331-X

Cover image: © iStockphoto/James Steidl

Oxford University Press is committed to our environment. This book
is printed on paper which contains a minimum of 50% post-consumer waste.

Printed and bound in the United States of America.

1 2 3 4 — 15 14 13 12

Contents

Acknowledgements

I want to thank several people for their invaluable help in creating this book.

First, thanks go to David Stover, president of Oxford University Press (Canada) and a friend in publishing for over twenty years. David encouraged me for over five years to write this book, read several false starts, and finally was there when the book took off in its present form. He offered kind words and useful criticism at every stage, even taking time to edit the book closely when all the chapters were in place. It is no exaggeration to say that I wouldn't have written this book but for David's cajoling and help; so thank you, David.

A selection of people whose sociological judgment I value highly also read and commented on the book, and I paid a lot of attention to what they said, almost invariably making the changes they suggested. Without fail, their suggestions improved the book. These readers were Patrizia Albanese, Nina Gheihman, Jack Veugelers, and my wife, Sandra Wain. Thank you for your time and wisdom, select readers!

Three undergraduate students at the University of Toronto—Sarah Fox, Jason Jensen, and Len Liu—did much of the background research that helped me write the bibliographic essay at the end of the book. They are outstanding young people, and I predict a great future for each of them. Thank you, guys!

Finally, and certainly not least, I want to thank Jennie Rubio, my editor and friend in the Trade Division at Oxford University Press. Like David, Jennie read and edited every chapter, making numerous changes and suggesting improvements. Her comments were always interesting, provocative, and insightful. Jennie and I have come to know each other around a variety of book projects in the last two years, and the result has been stimulating, a lot of fun, and some good books published (only some of them my own).

I'm really glad I wrote this book. It has given me the chance to bring my own thoughts together in a new way, and I like the result. I hope you do too.

Preface

This book is about people's social relations and the ways people live, work, and play together in the twenty-first century, with a particular focus on Canada.

I begin with a brief discussion of the natural and social backdrop to our social relations. Against this backdrop, we should all be able to live "happily ever after," just like people in fairy tales. Yet the reality is that this turns out to be harder than you might think. The main reason for this is social inequality. In the second part of the book, I consider a range of social inequalities and the conflicts to which they give rise. Finally, I look at social arrangements that help bring people together to solve these problems. Sociologists don't know all the answers to the problems of living together, but sociological research has brought us part of the way, as you will see.

In writing this book, I've tried to come as close as possible in tone and style to the introductory sociology lectures I give at the University of Toronto. I like to think those lectures sound like the lectures John Coltrane would give if he were still alive and if he performed sociology, not tenor saxophone: somewhat rehearsed and somewhat improvised, a bit raucous yet interestingly complex and sometimes surprising. So, I dedicate this book to John Coltrane and the other creative artists who do everything they can to get our heads into conversation with our hearts, and vice versa.

Introduction

Sociology emerged as a distinct field of study about two hundred years ago. Some say that it evolved alongside the new social problems arising from industrialization and urbanization, and together with political revolutions in France and other parts of Europe. People needed new ways to think about the societies that were being created. Others think sociology was a direct result of changes associated with the Enlightenment: the rise of science, skepticism about religious belief, and a general questioning of tradition.

Whatever its origins, sociology was likely fertilized by the growth of international trade and exploration. Whenever people have encountered other civilizations, they have wondered about them, and reflected back on their own. Even Herodotus, said to be the father of history, devoted a great deal of attention to the differences he observed between the Egyptians and Persians, two dominant powers that came into conflict during his lifetime. In addition, Voltaire, that great Enlightenment thinker, devoted an entire work to differences between the English Protestants and French Catholics. No wonder, then, that sociology began with important cross-national comparisons. Sociology's main founders—Marx, Durkheim, and Weber—were all familiar with and interested in the variations between societies.

Differences and comparisons always lead to questions. Why do *we* do things this way while *they* do things that way? Addressing such questions promotes a sense of cultural and moral relativism, a feeling that perhaps it is just as right or legitimate to do things a different way, if people accept both ways. Therefore, sociology—and social science more generally—probably arose out of a desire to explain differences and find patterns in people's social relations, in their ways of doing things and their ways of living together. As it turns out, there are many different ways of living together, although given different conditions, some clearly work better than others.

In that sense, sociology was always oriented to problem solving: to finding better ways of living together, given the visible difficulties associated with industrialization, urbanization, poverty, political upheaval, and so on. In periods of dramatic change, such questions are characterized by a sense of both urgency as well as fascination. What took place during the nineteenth and twentieth centuries was the attempt to develop a language that could describe the problems of living together and theories about the nature of these problems. Like every science, sociology as it matured spent additional time developing more precise language, theories, and methods of research.

Sometimes, because the topics of sociology are so familiar, it seems as though we are just relabelling the obvious, to make it seem more complicated or mysterious. However, that's not quite right. All science—all knowledge—involves three processes: *labelling* (or naming or classifying) the real world, so we can foreground it for discussion; *measuring* what we have foregrounded; and *linking* the foregrounded objects in some kind of causal theory. So labelling (or relabelling) the obvious is very important. In fact, how we label something often shows how we conceptualize or think about it, and how we intend to link it to other things.

For example, it makes all the difference in the world if we relabel frequent gambling as an "addiction" or silk panties as a "sex fetish" or a certain joke or attitude as "racist." This labelling implies a linkage with other things labelled the same way. It also implies that similar theoretical linkages can be used to explore newly labelled phenomena. So there will be a lot of relabelling and linking in this short book. However, we will leave issues of measurement, which can get complicated, to another book.

In this introduction, I consider a few of the key concepts in sociology, and some interesting ironies and paradoxes that sociologists have encountered.

Key Concepts

STRUCTURE AND PROCESS

The subject matter of sociology, social structure, is interesting because it is invisible; yet, like gravity, it controls everything.

In human society, everything is changing all the time. Below the surface, relations are constantly fizzing, flashing, and humming. But sometimes these changes are hard to see. The Greek philosopher Heraclitus said that you could never step in the same river twice because it is always renewing itself; it is always a new body of water even if that renewal is invisible to our naked eyes. Likewise, other things change so slowly that we do not perceive the change taking place: consider the conversion of forests to deserts over centuries, even millennia. The same is true of human societies. Some changes take generations or even centuries to complete. From the point of view of the present, societies in the Middle Ages changed imperceptibly; compared to the Roman Empire which preceded them and the industrial societies that followed, they evolved only by tiny increments. What defines a modern society is precisely the opposite characteristic: technological, economic, and social change taking place at a comparatively rapid rate.

Yet even in modern societies, some things change very slowly. From day to day, most people seem to behave the same way and follow the same predictable routines. "Social structure," this relatively unchanging feature of lives and societies, is the central subject matter of sociology.

Take the average university sociology class. In important ways, one introductory class is pretty much like another. They all have the same broad features, and after years of experience, I know how they are going to behave. The most dedicated students will sit at the front of the room, ask questions, answer questions, take notes, and even record lectures. They will introduce themselves personally or by email; often they will ask seemingly unnecessary questions, just to make contact. By contrast, the students who are least dedicated, most alienated, or part of a group that wants to *seem* alienated from the learning process, will sit together at the back of the room. By their inattentiveness, tardiness, relaxed body language, and often even by their form of dress, they will let me know they are not seriously interested in what is going on.

This classroom "drama" is predictable, from one course to another, as though someone had scripted it and hired professional actors to play the parts of students. No wonder I feel a sense of déjà vu whenever I walk into a new class and give my first two or three lectures.

But it is not only relative permanence that characterizes social structure. All social structures have three other things in common, as illustrated by the classroom example. First, they *control* us, so we act pretty much the same way in a given situation, despite personal differences. University classrooms are socially different from, say, bars, churches, or bedrooms. They invisibly force us to conform to unwritten norms of behaviour. For example, while in a classroom, we avoid casual conversation, eating, dancing, making love, or praying. In this fashion, classrooms—in fact, all social structures—make us behave like one another. Second, social structures *change* us, so we behave differently in different situations, despite our more or less fixed "personalities." Outside the classroom, my students may be noisy, dreamy, or self-absorbed. Inside the classroom, they form a relatively undefined mass of listeners and note-takers, with the avid ones down front and the alienated ones in back.

Third, social structures resist the efforts of individuals to bring about social change and yet they also produce social change. This fact is far harder to discuss briefly; we will examine it throughout the book. The point is, social structures—classrooms, families, businesses, empires, and so on—all have lives of their own that resist outside pressures for rapid change. But over the course of time, they do change, and when some of their parts start to change, other parts change too.

Social structures are like ecosystems in which many seemingly independent, complex pieces make up the whole. Their mechanisms of change are called "processes," and we will discuss these throughout the book as well. Let's start with deviance and conformity.

DEVIANCE AND CONFORMITY

What mechanisms preserve social order? Or, stated otherwise, why do people behave in orderly, predictable ways? Trying to answer these questions makes us realize the importance of the concepts of deviance and conformity. All social institutions and groups are imposing rules on us all the time, but why do we "choose" to obey? Why do we conform to their rules? And, since we do not always obey society's rules, we might instead ask: under what conditions are people likely to obey society's rules and under what conditions break them?

These are very broad, general questions, and people have been trying to answer them for centuries. Criminologists focus on the reasons why people break laws and the ways police, judges, and jailers try to reduce the likelihood of crime. Political sociologists focus on political movements, rebellions, and revolutions; they study the factors influencing the breakdown and re-establishment of political order. Medical sociologists study the conditions under which people deemed "ill" play the patient role, a role that releases them from the duty to conform to normal rules of social activity.

A key point is that all societies allow a margin of tolerable or invisible deviance—deviance that will go unseen, or if seen, unpunished. This allows people to "blow off steam" without derailing either themselves or the social order. We have all taken advantage of this margin of safe nonconformity at one time or another. Conformity is easier knowing there are occasional opportunities to break the rules.

Since sociologists are mainly interested in deviance and the persistence of social order, they study deviance differently from psychologists and draw different conclusions. Psychologists typically focus on individuals and the factors that influence them in a social context. For example, a social-psychological approach to the Holocaust might focus on the ways charismatic leaders create unwavering obedience among their subordinates. Note how this perspective stresses the party follower and his or her cognitions, not the entire National Socialist (Nazi) party as a social group or the political ideology of German society.

Psychology, and especially pop psychology, takes the position that deviance is the usual behaviour of abnormal people; that people who are bad or crazy commit crimes, and the reasons for such crimes are often unknown or unknowable. Crimes are due to some personality defect. By contrast, the stance of sociology is as follows, depending on the particular theory in question:

- Deviance is the *unusual* (i.e., occasional) behaviour of normal people.
- Deviance is the usual behaviour of normal people in *deviant roles*.
- Deviance is the usual behaviour of normal people in *abnormal situations*.
- Deviance is the usual behaviour of people who violate *unreasonable rules*.
- Deviance is the usual result of *unequal opportunities* to conform to rules.
- Deviance is the usual result of *deviant learning* (e.g., imitation of criminals).
- Deviance is the usual result of *defective social connection* (e.g., lack of control).

The sociologist looks for answers *outside* the individual actors. He or she wants to understand why society is pathological and, at times, inhuman. Sociology wants to improve societies, not individuals—indeed even to "cure" problems in society, not individual members of society.

Social structure requires conformity. So perhaps the relevant question is this: why do people conform? And here again, there are many theories and many approaches. I will discuss some of these in the last six chapters of this book when we examine such integrative forces as socialization, education, religious belief, and social exchange, among others. Simply, people learn to behave in conforming ways, and they feel rewarded for continuing to do so. We ask ourselves this: is it more remarkable that people conform most of the time? Or that people sometimes deviate—disobey or break the rules? Both conformity and deviance are normal, universal, and continuously present; so we need theories to cover both. However, they are two sides of the same coin.

Note, finally, that all living systems—including social systems—are constantly in a state of decay. The bonds of attachment and obedience are always losing their "charge" and always in need of renewal. Sociologists must develop theories about the ways people renew or refresh their commitment to society and the institutions within it: the ways they recommit to their family, their workplace, their course of education, and so on. Often this recommitment occurs in a social context, as for example, through the social processes associated with "charismatic leadership." In the end, we all need good, strong, emotional—as well as rational—reasons for conforming to the rules. Social structures provide these.

CATEGORY AND COMMUNITY

Nowhere is this conformity-production more evident than in communities. Communities, defined sociologically, are people who interact and communicate frequently with one another, share common interests, common values, and common goals. Often these people live together. Most important, they identify themselves as members of a community—often their community even has a name—and identify one another as members. Membership in the community is very important to these people, almost sacred. In many communities, people will do just about anything, and conform to almost any rules, to stay in good standing. People dread exclusion or expulsion, they are shamed by gossip about them, and they push one another to live up to community ideals.

A community is made up of individuals, but these are individuals who have submerged their personal identities in the community enterprise. True, these individuals have individual characteristics. As individuals, they belong to statistical categories: some are men, some women; some are young, some old; some are rich, others poor; and so on. Some of the things they say, do, and believe will reflect their "membership" in these statistical categories. However, statistical categories are not the same as social communities. People within these categories may not communicate or interact with others in the same category simply based on membership. What's more, people are less often aware of, and less likely to identify with, the statistical categories to which they belong than they are to identify with the social communities to which they belong. Therefore, statistical categories are of less interest to sociologists than communities—until and unless they mobilize and become communities.

That, of course, is what the women's movement was about, what the gay rights movement was about, and what Black Power was about. In each instance, through consciousness-raising, interaction, communication, and political action, a statistical category—woman, homosexual, black—became a social community, with an identity, a membership, a point of view, and a fierce commitment. Statistical categories are only of interest to census-takers and marketers. However, social communities are of interest to sociologists because they are social structures. They constrain and change people's behaviour, demand conformity, and punish deviance.

Role and Identity

Does conformity originate inside or outside the conforming person? That is, do we experience conformity as a type of imposed servitude?

Or do we experience it as voluntary subordination to a set of rules we largely agree with?

Of course, the answer is "both." Sometimes, when we obey the rules of a social situation, there is nothing we would like better than to leave, or at least voice our disapproval of what is going on. Few people have not been bored, irritated, or even outraged by a teacher and a classroom routine. In the workplace, sometimes we have all had to suffer foolish, irritating bosses, idiotic colleagues, and work that seems meaningless. We keep our mouths shut and do what we have to, because we fear the punishment of doing otherwise or desire the reward for conforming: the gold star, the high grade, the pay raise, the retirement package.

At the same time, most of us are *not* in a state of constant irritation, frustration, and disappointment about the social rules we obey. Somehow, we come to tolerate them and take them for granted. More than that, we often come to embrace them, as though we had chosen them or invented them ourselves. Somehow, we find meaning and value in the social rules and rituals that control us. Karl Marx might have called this "false consciousness." Most sociologists would say it takes place through a process called "internalization." We take the rules into ourselves. They become part of who we are and what we believe. Obedience to the rules becomes obedience to ourselves. This happens because we enter and play social roles, and these roles become our identities.

Take an example. An idealistic young person wants to become a doctor, to cure sick people. This is a person of high ethical standards and real dedication. To become a doctor, she needs to study hard and get good grades. Finally, she is admitted to medical school and then the professional "socialization" begins. Of course, she learns the names and features of many bones, organs, and illnesses. She also learns professional norms of behaviour (for example, "Do no harm," the first of the many rules invented for doctors by the father of medicine,

Hippocrates). She also learns to act in ways that some people might consider unethical: for example, when to tell the patient the whole truth, a half-truth, or a white lie. She learns when to take chances, when to call for a second opinion, how to cover small mistakes, and so on. Medical education, indeed *any* professional education, is moral as well as technical training.

The process of professional socialization is long and hard; often it is nerve-racking and upsetting. However, at a certain point, the student stops feeling like her teachers are "they" and starts feeling like the teachers are "we"—as in, "We doctors do such-and-so." As the student learns to play the role of doctor, and then gradually embraces the identity of doctor, the rules that apply to doctors, as well as to medical students, come to seem natural, sensible, and—most important—worthy of obedience.

The same happens in all our social activities. The longer we perform a particular role, whether as husband, mother, teacher, friend, lawyer, or child, the more likely we are to adopt and internalize the identity associated with that role: to identify with it and embrace its values. When we do, we are freely conforming to rules that other people invented. In fact, we are all constantly embracing, inventing, and refreshing all of society's rules.

POWER AND AUTHORITY

Related to conformity is the topic of compliance: why do some people do what other people tell them? Why do some people get to make the rules while other people have to follow them? Why are some people seemingly more in command than others?

This brings us to the topic of power, which is the ability to get your own way, or force another person to do what you want. Sociologists have spent a lot of time studying power, as have political scientists, anthropologists, and psychologists. Obviously, people use many varied techniques, tools, and strategies to get their own way. Some use round-about methods: trickery, seduction, and deceit, for example. Others use methods that are more direct: a raised voice, a loaded gun, a threat of violence, and so on. Gangsters, schoolyard bullies, and political dicta-tors are among those who specialize in using naked power or brute force. What is interesting for sociologists is that most of the time, in most social affairs, brute force is not needed. Often lies and deceit are enough. Even more frequently, compliance is gained through the exer-cise of authority.

Authority is what we might call "legitimate power": power that is exercised in what seems to be a justifiable way, by people who we think have the "right" to exercise it. For example, police authority confers the right to carry and use a firearm. Other people—ordinary civilians—do not enjoy this right and can get into serious trouble if they use a gun to compel other people's behaviour. Along with the military, the police hold a monopoly on the right to use armed force on behalf of society. The elected government has the authority to demand that we pay taxes. The courts have the authority to send us to prison, to deprive us of our liberty, for a failure to obey the laws of society.

The sociologist Max Weber rightly pointed out that authority is a key concern of sociologists. Not only does an understanding of author-ity provide us with insight into the questions of social order, con-formity, and the exercise of power—all matters of great practical and theoretical interest. It also leads us to ask important questions about the source of authority: how and why societies come to grant authority to particular people under particular conditions.

Weber identified three main sources of authority in history that he labelled traditional, rational-legal, and charismatic. Weber usefully pointed out that the large social change we call modernization was associated historically with the change from traditional to rational-legal bases of authority—from mere repetition (for tradition's sake) to reasoned, even debated, consideration. This meant placing new importance on scientific (empirical) investigation, the rule of law, and democratic decision-making. Weber also pointed out that throughout history, major social upheavals have been associated with a shift from traditional to charismatic authority, associated with the leadership and teaching of so-called charismatic figures like Jesus or Muhammad (and more recently Gandhi and Hitler). These emotional and moral upheavals—often with profound social and political consequences—always give way (in time) to a stabilizing process that Max Weber called the "routinization of charisma."

Thus even social upheavals have a regular, predictable pattern. We could probably say that no society will avoid revolutionary upheaval completely, and no revolution ever results in permanent upheaval. It always gives way to new, stable social patterns.

Key Paradoxes of Social Life

PEOPLE ARE BOTH FREE AND UNFREE

As you will have seen already, there is a complex and delicate link between the roles people play and their personal identities, between what the community or another source of authority commands and what people feel willing to do. People are the ultimate source of all social order, conformity and compliance, deviance, and resistance, and they have the freedom to do "what they want"; yet seemingly, what they want often falls into predictable patterns. Why?

This question necessarily brings us to the topic of free will—that old, unresolved, and seemingly never-ending debate in philosophy. Why, you may ask, are we embarking once again on this ancient journey-without-end? The answer is this: because the quest for freedom is an enduring goal and an enduring tension in all social life. The tug of war between freedom and constraint is never-ending, the source of all social stability and change, co-operation and conflict.

This discussion, though old, is far from dead; sociologists continue to worry about it. I recently received a mass email from the president of the International Sociological Association, promoting the next international conference. The message read:

> Determinism is dead in the social sciences. Despite a strong interest in social structures, social mechanisms, [and] forms of reproduction, we are all aware that human beings are not completely dominated by them. The world changes and this change to a large extent depends on human action and imagination.

The president's message, however opaque it may seem to "outsiders," signals that the stance of sociology today emphasizes the agency of humans as social actors, not mere objects of action; as survivors and not mere victims of oppression; and as resisters, not mere slaves to authority or routine. All people seemingly have the ability to act, survive, and resist, and also to imagine, propose, create, and challenge. Therefore, we sociologists cannot presume to make deterministic theories about people as though they were physical objects: electrons, atoms, molecules, chemical compounds, or even lower organisms (amoebas, fruit flies, or bees). Even pigeons, rats, dogs, and chimps make choices and, in that sense, exercise free will.

Of course, as sociologists we understand that history never repeats itself exactly or literally, which is why Max Weber was unwilling to see sociology as a predictive science—or perhaps even as a science at all. Sociology's other founders, Karl Marx and Émile Durkheim, were less hesitant on this score; they believed we *could* make general theories about people, and perhaps about history. Much of twentieth-century sociology, and especially American sociology, believed this to be true. Lately, however, we have seen a sea change in the thinking of sociologists about this matter. Though the goal of sociology is still to interpret and explain social life, few are courageous enough to actually *predict* social life. Perhaps that is why the president's statement—"Determinism is dead in the social sciences"—seems clear enough to some sociologists.

This is no place to go into the history and politics of sociology. Let us simply note that there are contending schools or approaches to sociology, and they use somewhat different methods, hold somewhat different assumptions, and ask somewhat different questions about reality. Happily, they tend to arrive at the same results when they ask the same questions and examine the same data, but they differ in their views about the goals and purposes of sociology. This may seem puzzling and disconcerting to people like chemists, accountants, and engineers who study inanimate objects, but it is the dominant fact of life for sociologists.

Paradoxically, then, people are both free and unfree. The job of sociology is to explain and interpret social life within the context of competing freedoms and compulsions.

RULE-BREAKING CAN BE CONSTRUCTIVE

Nowhere is this paradox of freedom-coupled-with-unfreedom more evident and impressive than in the study of deviance. Here's why.

If you adopt a strictly deterministic approach to understanding human behaviour—the belief that people are pushed around by social forces—you are hard-pressed to explain why people break social rules. As we have said, people typically learn social rules; over time, they come to embrace these rules, with the result that social order is more common and enduring than social disorder. People obey the rules because they consider the rules legitimate, they support the community that gave rise to these rules, and they identify with the roles they play in a society guided by these rules (among other reasons). So from a deterministic perspective, one would not expect to see much rule-breaking.

Yet in reality people break social rules all the time. You have only to step outside your door or read a newspaper to know this. A great many explanations of this rule-breaking have been put forward. First, the rule-breakers may have been improperly or incompletely trained as children to obey the rules. Second, the rules people are asked to obey may conflict with one another, creating what sociologist Robert Merton called a state of "anomie," which amounts to moral confusion about the proper course of action, or blocked opportunities to do the right thing. Third, the rules themselves may be in doubt because of a rapidly changing culture, or because of conflicts between the main culture and competing (for example, ethnic) subcultures.

Ironically, as sociologist Émile Durkheim pointed out a century ago, not only are deviance and crime common, they are universal—found in every society, at all times. This led Durkheim to the interesting speculation that perhaps deviance and crime are *necessary* and that societies could not survive without these challenges to the social order. If so, it might be useful to think of crime and deviance as something like forest fires that also serve a fundamentally essential purpose for the forest ecosystem. Sure, forest fires are dangerous, but they also clear away dead underbrush, nourish the soil, and leave more space for new trees to grow tall and strong. Though usually unplanned and uncontrolled, forest fires serve the long-term good of the forest nonetheless. Without occasional destruction, healthy new trees could not develop and the forest could not survive.

Likewise, there is perhaps some irony in the fact that, while sociology is the study of social order, a key component of this is the study of destruction, conflict, deviance, and crime. These are all universal and inevitable, and as we will see throughout this book, they also help to cleanse, preserve, and change the social order. Deviance, in point of fact, is an essential aspect of our efforts to live together and co-operate.

CONFLICT CAN BRING PEOPLE TOGETHER

We don't have to go far before meeting another irony of social life: not only is deviance constructive, but so is conflict. Usually we think of conflict as harsh and unhealthy, a source of stress and misery. Often we think of conflict as separating people and setting them at each other's throats. However, consider the possibility that not only is conflict, like crime, normal and universal, but it is also healthy for society.

New ideas that produce conflict today may not do so tomorrow, once we are used to them. Conflict helps a society to voice, to debate, and to define emerging ideas that may lead to useful changes. Conflict serves notice that current ideas and arrangements are not working well and need review or change. In effect, conflict completes a range of useful functions. Arguably, it serves all the same "social functions" as crime, if you want to take this Durkheimian approach.

And while this is happening, conflict unifies people around particular positions: pro and con, for and against. For those who share the same view, conflict is not the opposite of co-operation: it *is* a form of co-operation, a way of intensifying social cohesion. Thus conflict can be integrative as well as divisive. Of course, on many issues, most people are indifferent or undecided (for example, on the question of developing wind power, sending troops to Sudan, or electing the Canadian Senate). On other issues, opinions are strong and, often, strongly divided (think of issues such as assisted suicide, legalization of marijuana, public funding for religious schools, or support for the Israelis or the Palestinians).

Like crime, which clarifies the social boundaries between right and wrong, conflict clarifies the boundaries between people who take one position and those who take another in a debate. And like punishment, which (according to Durkheim) intensifies social cohesion among the law-abiding members of society, conflict intensifies social cohesion among people who share the same point of view. This it does by dramatizing the difference between the two opposing groups. Conflict, then, contributes to changing society at the same time as it contributes to strengthening social bonds and clarifying important social issues.

EFFORTS TO INTEGRATE CAN REPRODUCE SOCIAL DIVISIONS

One of the key challenges in helping people to live together, as we will see, is that often inclusion and exclusion are opposite sides of the same coin. As we saw above, people pull together most effectively when they are locked in conflict with another group. However, they do this largely by drawing group boundaries that have the effect of excluding and distancing members of the "enemy" group, reducing any kind of friendly communication and interaction. So in the long-term, conflict—though integrative for one group—divides the larger community.

Nowhere is this more evident than in high schools, where people form hostile cliques. Members of clique A (the jocks, say) are hostile to or contemptuous of people in clique B (the social leaders), who in turn are hostile to or dismissive of people in clique C (the nerds). All of them ignore or ridicule people who aren't in any clique at all. The stronger the boundaries that separate the cliques from one other, the more socially and emotionally linked are the members of each clique. Only a disaster affecting all the students—for example, a school shooting or explosion—stands much chance of breaking through these limits on cross-group communication.

This is an enduring problem all societies face. Every effort, whether peaceful or violent, to draw people together runs the risk of dividing people around new or existing lines of division. Émile Durkheim, in his classic work *The Division of Labor in Society* (which, incidentally, was one of two doctoral theses he had to write as a student), tries to understand this problem. Durkheim argues that, very gradually, societies develop new forms of cohesion based on common interdependency. In a modern market society, he argues, we all depend economically—if not socially and psychologically—on one another's efforts. Teachers rely on car mechanics to keep them moving, bakers rely on truck drivers to deliver supplies, shopkeepers and factory workers rely on customers to buy merchandise, and writers rely on readers to buy their books.

This interdependence is evident in any well-functioning market. However, when the market starts to collapse, as in the recent recession, it is hard to repair these links and hard to restart the flow of goods and services. The same is equally true of intergroup relations. In most societies, members of different racial or religious groups, for example, get along fine for centuries. However, when this starts to break down—say, through the perpetration of hate crimes by a few or, even worse, through a series of genocidal acts by a political party—the trust and co-operation between these groups may be lost forever. A few societies have tried to repair the harm done by racial conflict. Germany has tried hardest, perhaps, and the Truth and Reconciliation strategy adopted in South Africa has a lot to teach us. However, few societies have succeeded in mending these intergroup relationships.

Even when strategies or technologies are expected to reach across group lines, they often merely reproduce existing social divisions. Take the Internet: many expected it to break down social divisions. In large part it has; certainly, the Internet has increased the sheer volume of communication across distances, spanning regional and even national boundaries. However, many note that access to computers and computer literacy are still influenced by traditional social barriers—by advantages and disadvantages rooted in social class, for example. This is to say, then, that social class boundaries are not quickly erased by a wider use of the Internet.

As we will see later, a similar observation is sometimes made about the educational system. Formal schooling, which has the potential to unite all young people through shared communication and interaction around a common set of themes, falls short of unifying people completely. Some believe it even justifies continued inequality and blames the victims for failing to study hard and move up the ladder. In the end, formal schooling tends to perpetuate divisions between the poor, the middle class, and the rich. Sometimes it also perpetuates the differences between males and females, whites and blacks, and other groups, be they advantaged or disadvantaged.

Victims Can Be Perpetrators

Many people, faced with paradoxes like these, feel great frustration and want to blame someone. These paradoxes are not normal "system properties" of societies, they might say; rather they are the result of some group's malevolence or drive for power. They are a result of efforts by the rich to subordinate the poor, for example, or of efforts by whites to subordinate visible minorities. In fact, we are all inclined to seek fault when we encounter seemingly impossible problems, problems that repeatedly resist an easy solution.

This book, however, is not about finding fault. One reason is that although every individual has agency and free will, at the same time, every individual is also constrained and manipulated. We all live in a world we didn't make, according to rules we didn't agree to. Civilization, as Freud said, is always based on the repression of our personal desires, which is why conflict, mental illness, crime, and addiction are so common and ineradicable. We are all frustrated and irritated some of the time (and some of us are irritated and frustrated much of the time).

Another reason for not setting out on a fault-finding mission in this book is that everyone is to blame for something, to a greater or lesser degree. Everyone who lives in the developed nations of the world benefits from the oppression, the low wages, and the grinding poverty of workers in the less developed nations. Everyone who enjoys the seeming natural bounty of cheap energy, clean water, a house and backyard in the suburbs—a high level of material consumerism generally—benefits at the expense of future generations whose natural non-renewable resources we are using up. Everyone who drives a used Ford is likely to ask how others can afford to drive a new Camry, and the Camry drivers are likely to wonder how others can afford, or justify, their Jaguar, Hummer, or Cadillac Escalade SUV.

Closer to home, we are shocked by the incidence of (often hidden) domestic violence. Usually it is violence directed by adult men against their wives and children, or even by adolescent males against their girlfriends. We are shocked by the incidence of bullying—both physical and cyber—in our schools and neighbourhoods. And we are shocked by the amount of aggression young men express toward other young men in bars, on roads and highways, and on city streets. None of this behaviour is morally defensible, nor is it safe or socially acceptable.

Yet when we study the victims and perpetrators, we often learn an interesting fact: most perpetrators have histories of victimhood. Men who beat their wives, or parents who beat their children, are likely to have been beaten in childhood or forced to witness the beating of their own mothers and siblings. People who bully others are disproportionately likely to have suffered or witnessed domestic violence, to have been bullied themselves, or to be the current victims of bullying. And men who are the most likely to assault or attack others—to pick fights—are more likely than other men to be attacked.

There are a number of implications. One is that all violence tends to have a ripple effect, spreading out in society and infecting many secondary targets. In turn, these secondary targets, blameless victims, spread the infection of violence to others, in this way becoming perpetrators themselves. The only way to stop this chain of events is to get to the root of the problem: the underlying causes of violence in our society. Blaming is not enough. Second, and following this train of thought, we must avoid looking for psychological and psychiatric explanations for anything that appears to be a widespread social problem. To look for psychological explanations is to blame the victim and ignore the root social causes. Throughout this book we will look for root causes—social causes—of depression, anxiety, addiction, ill health, unhappiness, violence, and crime. This is not a quick-fix, self-help book; it provides no chicken soup for your soul.

Third, we should focus on a variety of problems and a variety of "symptoms," given that no single symptom is enough in itself. Our method of investigation is the literature review. We ask: what does the field of sociology—that body of published work that by now numbers hundreds of thousands of articles and books—tell us about the sources of human misery? Happily, there is a lot of agreement about the findings reported in this book; where there is such convergence we can feel confident about the validity of our results.

People Find Happiness in Hardship by Lowering Expectations

One of the biggest problems we face as sociologists is gaining valid information about the types and extent of problems people face. In sociology we are often stymied by the problem of studying other human beings in their natural surroundings. For example, you might imagine that people are open and forthcoming about their concerns, worries, and troubles. Well, perhaps some people are, but most North Americans are not. They prefer to put a happy face on their lives, to minimize or deny their troubles, or to explain their troubles in non-social ways.

First, since people in our society are supposed to pursue and find happiness, many of us often feel embarrassed if we fail to feel happy. We feel like losers, and wanting to avoid appearing like losers, we avoid revealing unhappiness to others. Likewise, we don't want to seem like complainers, whiners, or bores, and may report more happiness with relationships, jobs, homes, and so on. than is really the case. And since many others are lying about their own lives and their own feelings, most people have no way of judging what reality looks like.

So, second, they may adjust themselves by lowering their expectations. They may think, "Well, I'm a loser but there isn't much I can do about it, so I will just settle for my marriage, my job, my home, my children (and so on) as they are and make the best of it." No wonder elderly people and religious people are reportedly happier than anyone else. Elderly people have had ample opportunity to adjust their worldly expectations downward as their incomes and physical health have dwindled. Religious people, by contrast, have sought and found meaning in life by believing that, in another world, they will be rewarded for their suffering and deprivation in this world. Even people in poor countries are said to be happier than people in rich countries, perhaps because they expect little from life and take pleasure in what they can get, however meagre by Western standards.

Finally, in some societies, and to some degree in our own, people "somatize" their unhappiness: that is, they develop, experience, and report physical illnesses as a response to their woes. This is evident in a variety of forms, including chronic pain, indigestion, headaches, irritable bowels, skin disorders, and so on. In societies (or groups or communities) where people are not permitted to criticize their lives or relationships—as for example, women in patriarchal Arab marriages—people gain sympathy and support by being sick. Some might call this hypochondria, but again, I want to avoid undervaluing this social problem by suggesting that it is "merely" a personal psychological problem.

The implication of all this is that we sociologists cannot always rely on what people tell us. People reporting on feelings of happiness and satisfaction, or unhappiness and dissatisfaction, are notably unreliable indicators of their actual experiences. By contrast, physical and mental illnesses, addictions, crimes, and other dangerous behaviours—taken together—are relatively reliable indicators of human experience. Show me an unhealthy, crime-ridden community of people who are suicidal, depressed, and addicted, and I will show you a community—a society—that isn't working. This is why we should all be concerned about the plight of Canadian Aboriginal peoples on reserves.

Blaming Is Not Explaining

To say "I will show you a community—a society—that isn't working" is at once to make a two-hatted statement. What are my two hats? First, I am a sociologist. To say sociologically that a society or community is "not working" is to say that, even by its own standards, the community is failing to meet the needs of its members. There is no known community that actively embraces sickness, crime, suicide, depression, and addiction: so I feel confident, as a sociologist, saying that evidence of these symptoms is indicative of a massive problem for that community, by its own standards.

My other hat? I am also a citizen and a human being. I am concerned about the misery and suffering of other people, so I study it and teach about it. If I were not socially concerned, I would have gone into a different line of work; indeed, so would most sociologists and other social scientists. Perhaps we could have all become "financiers" like some people on Wall Street and stolen billions of dollars. So I would like to see sociology help the world. As a citizen, I want to encourage good social behaviour and discourage bad social behaviour. I would like to help society move toward something that is more ideal (in my mind), where people co-operate and respect one another.

Sometimes, when talking or thinking, I accidentally slip into my citizen hat when I shouldn't. There is no place for moral outrage or blaming—for example, railing at Wall Street "financiers"—when we are wearing our sociologist hats. This is not because there is nobody to blame. It is simply that blame is a moral concept, and sociology is not about morality; it is not about *why* people behave badly. Religion is about morality. Ethics is about morality. Sociology is about explaining people's behaviour, whether as citizens we like the behaviour or not. When this behaviour breaks the rules of society, we sociologists study it not because we disapprove of it but because we are interested in deviance and control, the social conditions under which people obey and break rules.

The failure to maintain a clear boundary between explaining and blaming leads to bad sociology. As researchers, we may become cowards and fail to speak out against the powerful, or become too concerned with "political correctness" and fail to say what needs to be said about disadvantaged groups that behave badly. It is our job, as sociologists, to speak truth to power and also to speak truth to the powerless. In short, our job is to speak the truth about how society works, as best we understand the truth. As we do so, we must keep in mind that all truth is always tentative, given our understanding of the research to date and pending the appearance of research that forces us to adopt different views.

I am cautious—even nervous—when I use the word "must," as in the sentence above: "We must always keep in mind that all truth is tentative." "Must" sounds like a citizen word, a moral word, a word outside the sociologist's professional vocabulary. But in this case, it isn't. The rule that we must keep in mind is that the tentativeness of truth is a professional academic guideline. All scholars—and particularly all scientists—live by the rules of peer review. In becoming researchers, we agree to learn the research findings of others and seek the judgment of our colleagues about our own findings. We don't just make things up—creating fantasy worlds like novelists for example (or financiers, for that matter). To be a doctor, one must follow the professional rules of doctoring: do no harm. To be a sociologist, one must follow the professional rules of sociology: read the published research literature and contribute to a theoretically consistent, scientifically defensible picture of society, regardless of your personal beliefs. And when the evidence demands it, we must change our theories.

This is what I have undertaken in *The Sense of Sociability*. This book represents my best understanding of how our society works and why it faces the problems it does, based on many years of thinking about this topic and reading the research literature.

This book provides a wide-ranging outline of sociological findings referring mostly to Canada, secondarily to the United States, and sometimes to other countries. I embed this survey of findings from various branches of sociological research within an overarching theme: the antagonism between conflict and co-operation. Simply put, I argue that conflict is bad for human life and find that there is too much of it. Co-operation is better and is attainable, through intelligence and hard work. That said, I find plenty of evidence of co-operation already. Without wishing to be unrealistically optimistic, I see evidence of many opportunities and initiatives toward co-operation, and they all involve civility and awareness of interdependence.

Saying so doesn't mean closing our eyes to the ample evidence of inequality and injustice in the world. Indeed, I highlight inequalities and injustices as major obstacles to co-operation. But inequality and injustice are widespread, perhaps even natural, though not necessarily inevitable.

It is difficult and risky to make summary statements about the world and its historic course. Leaving aside the sheer immensity of the task, the difficulty is because some things change slowly: popular beliefs, superstitions, prejudice, the prevalence of religious strife. Other things change slightly more quickly: secularization, demographic patterns. And some things can change very quickly indeed: regime (via revolution), access to higher education, universal suffrage. Because it is difficult to separate these change processes according to their different rhythms, our overall sense of the rapidity of social change is blurred. In his classic work on the Mediterranean world in the time of King Philip II, French historian Fernand Braudel distinguishes usefully between macro (or "deep"), meso, and micro levels of history—to be measured in centuries, decades, and years (or less), respectively. If this book were much longer, I would try to root my analyses in this useful distinction.

The approach to social science I embrace, known as positivism—prevalent through much of the nineteenth and twentieth centuries—has taken a beating of late. Yet I feel something of value is to be salvaged from this approach, and what I present here is my own brand of systemic, positivistic sociology. I come to this book a student of population (and populations), ready to recognize the complicated network of relationships in the natural and social worlds. In the book I draw attention to interrelationships between sets of elements that contribute to an outcome of particular interest: namely, co-operation. This approach also points to feedbacks, the possibility of equilibrium, and the idea there are no perfect solutions, only trade-offs between costs and benefits.

In the end, I am trying to apply to society as a whole the reasoning many demographers have used to great advantage in studying populations. Although I recognize that positivism has not delivered what we expected (and some of the work of my most notable teachers has fallen out of favour), I remain convinced of the benefits that come from viewing societies as systems of interrelated parts.

I *do* see societies as social systems of interrelated parts. In fact, I see the world's population as a social system. By that, I mean simply that everyone is directly and indirectly connected. Also, every event has multiple causes and effects; many of them are unexpected, unplanned, and unintended, and some of them are even random. And, because of the many vested interests, there is a tendency to inertia: a tendency to oppose change that would equalize societies, for example. Much of the global system resists planned change, though the system is changing in unplanned ways all the time.

But as the great American sociologist C. Wright Mills remarked, we sociologists are trained to see the connections between large public events and small personal issues, and between history and biography. It is our job—our calling—to see the systemic links between people, events, and institutions, and to understand our place in history. That is the "sociological imagination." From this standpoint, the greatest sociologists have been system thinkers.

"System thinking" doesn't mean believing that peace, order, and good government are natural outcomes. It doesn't mean believing that everyone is treated well or satisfied with life. It certainly doesn't mean there is an invisible hand that yields the best outcomes—a free market in justice and well-being—when everyone behaves in the most self-interested way. This thing I am calling the social system isn't guaranteed to produce consensus and co-operation, equilibrium and tidiness, or even happy endings. On the contrary, it is vast, messy, sometimes chaotic, and rarely kind to most of humanity. It always favours the powerful. Inequality and conflict are common (perhaps natural, in some sense) and far more common than equality and co-operation. To gain co-operation, we have to fight unwarranted, excessive inequalities, but to do so, we have to co-operate.

Unregulated, a social system produces the kinds of inequality and conflict I discuss in this book. That is why humanity will have to struggle to achieve justice and equity, co-operation and civility. They don't come easy or cheap. Living together co-operatively is an accomplishment—whether in a household, community, nation, or world—and humanity has yet to accomplish it. We may be a few steps farther ahead in Canada than elsewhere, but there is no reason for complacency.

My personal beliefs (the ones I engage when I am wearing my citizen hat) shape where I begin: what questions I ask and what personal biases I may have at the start of any research project. However, they do not affect the ways I act when I put on my sociologist hat to write this book.

True, this book represents my own personal desire for a more peaceful, co-operative, and civilized world. Others might have different, even loftier goals: for example, universal equality. I applaud them. However, my goals are my goals, and I consider them realistic. Here, I like to recall what Thomas Malthus said two hundred years ago to critics—utopian critics—who urged him to endorse social policies he thought were unrealistic:

> A writer may tell me that he thinks man will ultimately become an ostrich. I cannot properly contradict him. But before he can

expect to bring any reasonable person over to his opinion, he ought to shew the necks of mankind have been gradually elongating, that the lips have grown harder and more prominent, that the legs and feet are daily altering their shape, and that the hair is beginning to change into stubs of feathers. And till the probability of so wonderful a conversion can be shewn, it is surely lost time and lost eloquence to expatiate on the happiness of man in such a state; to describe his powers, both of running and flying, to paint him in a condition where all narrow luxuries would be contemned, where he would be employed only in collecting the necessaries of life, and where, consequently, each man's share of labour would be light, and his portion of leisure ample.

I feel the same way. We must take humans as we find them and study how they create and maintain social relationships, and how they act as members of society. Philosopher Immanuel Kant wrote, "Out of the crooked timber of humanity, no straight thing was ever made." As sociologists, that's where we begin the analysis.

So with this in mind, thinking ahead I wonder: how can humans live together more happily and effectively? How can we overcome the obvious obstacles, the selfishness, aggression, and distrust among others? Are people naturally unfit for human society? Are the nastier aspects of social life inevitable (the inequality, the injustice, the prejudice, and the discrimination), or can we change them? Are suspicion, abuse, and violence the inescapable conditions of humanity, or can we prevent them? Are people naturally antisocial, so they need to be controlled by a despotic ruler or totalitarian system of rules to keep from tearing each other apart?

On the other hand, if humans *are* potentially able to live together in human society, through what mechanisms can they achieve this goal? This book will investigate this question, but before doing so, I will need to prepare the groundwork.

ONE

Social Life: The Material Backdrop

In the movie *Radio Days*, Woody Allen recalls that his parents were always arguing. They even argued about which ocean was better, the Atlantic or the Pacific. This kind of irresolvable argument is characteristic of dysfunctional families—and also academic disciplines. Nineteenth-century philosophers endlessly debated whether ideas are primary or secondary to the material world. Karl Marx, philosopher, economist, and sociologist, believed he had triumphed when he stood the idealist philosopher Hegel's theory on its head; he declared that the material world clearly came first and the world of ideas was secondary—mere "superstructure."

Well, every journey to Winnipeg has to start somewhere and whether it starts at the Atlantic or the Pacific is arbitrary. In sociology, whether we start with the material conditions of life or, like many sociology books, with the realm of ideas (with culture and socialization, for example) is ultimately unimportant, since we will end up talking about both.

In an equally arbitrary vein, I start with a look at the material setting of social life. The reason for this is that I want to end by discussing integrative processes that largely rely on transmitting ideas. Here I consider the material settings of human life as a backdrop for the dramas of conflict and co-operation that are the topic of this book.

Populations

The single most important fact about societies is that they are made up of people: they are collections of human beings. Human beings are flesh and blood, they need food, and they occupy space. Since in every important sense people possess materiality, we need to say something about ourselves as material beings. Different disciplines would do so from different angles, such as evolutionary history, biochemistry, or neuroscience.

A sociologist might begin with the observation that people live in populations. People are rarely solitary; in almost all cases, they are social. Perhaps, there is an inherent need for sociability. We seem to need company, even if we don't get along very well with our fellows. So if there were a built-in need for sociability, we would have trouble explaining how people as a species can be so selfish, individualistic, aggressive, and often hostile to one another. People are far less co-operative than ants and bees, for example. But for whatever reason, most people live in collections or communities. In early human history, human populations were small—sometimes no more than a few dozen, at most a few hundred. Even today, hunter-gatherer communities remain small. By contrast, modern cities are large, containing millions or even tens of millions of people. What this shows is that people can adapt to living in communities of widely varying sizes.

There is a field of social science called demography that studies human populations; many sociologists are familiar with demography and some even contribute to research in that field. The kinds of questions we might ask, as demographers or demographically informed sociologists, include the following: first, does it matter socially whether a human population is large or small? Second, does it matter socially whether a population is densely concentrated in space—that is, if the population is crowded? Third, does the makeup or composition of a population (for example, its age structure, ratio of males to females, or mixture of skills) matter? Fourth, does it matter whether the population is mainly healthy or unhealthy, and whether the lifespan is short or long? And fifth, related to this, does it matter whether people pass through the population quickly or slowly?

The answer to all these questions is, "Yes, it matters." So we need to consider the significance of these population features: how and why they serve as important indicators of the material conditions of social life. We also need to ask whether changes in the population lead to, or result from, changes in other societal processes. Here again, the answer is, "Yes, they do." Rapid population changes can change societies dramatically, even drastically; understanding why this is so gives us important insights into the evolution of society.

Population size is important for several reasons. First, a large population puts more pressure on the natural environment than a small population. (I'll explore this later in this chapter.) Second, a large population is likely to innovate—to invent new technologies and develop new ways of producing food and wealth—or else break into smaller populations. Generally, large populations (and this is especially true of large, rapidly growing populations) require the systematic production of food. There are no hunter-gatherer societies with large populations, and in industrial (mainly post-agricultural) societies, the growth rate typically slows down dramatically, until the population starts to shrink. This observed connection between population size and food production, as the first demographer Thomas Malthus explained, is due to a problematic relationship between population increase (which he said was always exponential) and food increase (which he said takes place on a linear scale).

Third, large populations are usually dense or crowded, and often they live in cities. So as the human population began to grow rapidly over the last few hundred years, it also became mainly urban. Urban communities, housed vertically in tall buildings, can hold many more people than rural communities, and this vertical increase results in more crowding. Urban life is clearly a different experience than rural life, and I will also look at this feature later on in this chapter. The important point to remember is that as humanity grew in size, transient hunter-gatherer lifestyles gave way to settled agriculturalists, then to urban industrialists and post-industrialists. The connections between population size, location, and type of economic production are not accidental, though they are too complex to discuss thoroughly in a few sentences.

Fourth, populations that are large and dense tend to invent new social and economic roles, or as Durkheim said, they divide the labour of society in specialized ways. Productive tasks are broken into smaller detailed tasks, and this requires training. Increasingly, social roles are distinguished not only by age and sex but by other characteristics associated with skill, aptitude, and interest. And within any set of social roles, the population composition makes a difference. For example, it makes a difference whether a population of 20,000 people is composed of 95 percent men or only 50 percent men. The first (95 percent men) is typical of a frontier town—say, a mining or mill town—with many single transient young men who often behave in disorderly ways. The second (50 percent men) is typical of a settled family community, which includes children and old people. Here, disorder poses much less of a problem.

Sex ratio clearly makes a difference, as does age composition. It makes a difference whether the population is "young," where half the population is under the age of fifteen, or "old," where half the population is over the age of forty-five. A young population demands a good deal of spending on education; an old population needs pensions and health care. Other things being equal, a young population is unruly, creative in certain kinds of ways, and up to date with the latest technology; an old population is more sedate and conservative. So politics and popular culture vary between younger and older societies.

The health and longevity of a population also affect how a society works. A healthy, long-lived population is likely to contain a higher level of "human capital"—skills gained through lengthy education and on-the-job experience. Other things being equal, this will contribute to higher productivity and increased prosperity. As well, leaving aside immigration, a healthy, longer-living society will have a lower rate of population turnover. As a result, people will develop stronger loyalties to the community. And with population stability, the social networks on which people rely for information and support will remain intact for longer periods.

At the same time, an older, longer-living society will rely more on immigration to provide needed population renewal by way of new skills and human capital that the community is unable to provide for itself. Population turnover has both a positive and negative effect: on the downside, it continuously undermines traditional culture and existing social networks. But from a more positive angle, it continuously reinvigorates the culture and introduces new social elements that may enrich our social networks through diversity. In Canada, demographically an aged and aging society, this is especially important since many of the people who immigrate are young parents of young families.

Note, finally, that such changes—consider for example a sudden rejuvenation of the population through an increase in child-bearing, as occurred during the baby boom—have a huge effect on culture, politics, and social institutions. Even a dramatic aging of the population (through decreases in child-bearing) has a huge effect. Such changes in the age structure all lead to dramatic shifts in the relations between the generations; we will come back to this topic later, too.

THE NATURAL ENVIRONMENT

Today, compared to a generation or two ago, we are all much more aware of the natural environment in which our society is situated. This is due in large part to the important work of environmental and climate scientists, as well as campaigning scientists from Rachel Carson (author of *Silent Spring*) to David Suzuki. Equally, organizations like Greenpeace have raised our awareness of deeply problematic issues, from Alberta's tar sands projects to the accumulation of plastic in our oceans. Senator Al Gore's prize-winning film *An Inconvenient Truth* drew international attention to climate change.

The global ecosystem is a key feature of social life, and sociology must keep this in mind. We need to remember that people throughout history have had a closer, more intimate relationship with their natural environment than we do now; with regards to the natural environment outside our homes, shops, and offices, we are probably the least informed humans ever. So let us start at the beginning.

By natural environment, I mean all of those conditions that affect us as animals with survival needs that are similar to those of other animals. First is food and water: concerns about the food supply and clean water are essential. This is why Thomas Malthus was interested in the relation of food supply to population growth and why Karl Marx was interested in the plight of the wage worker, forced to sell his labour in order to purchase food. And this is also why sociologists study corporate agribusiness: increasingly these giant corporations control our access to reliable quality food.

Second, humans compete with other species for survival. We have developed tools and strategies that provide key advantages over these species. For example, we invented weapons—spears, knives, guns— to hunt some animals for food and keep the larger predators at bay. We learned how to domesticate and harvest food animals—chickens, cows, pigs—and are constantly improving our efficiency at doing so. We learned to understand and control many biochemical interactions, creating pesticides, herbicides, fungicides, antibiotics (and other medicines). We are increasingly able to manage our relationships with problematic species, from bacteria to protozoa, mosquitoes to cockroaches, invasive plants to cereal rusts. Currently, it looks like this war is at a standstill: the possibility that we could ever fully eradicate our smaller competitors seems unlikely (not to mention profoundly unwise, given the complexity of the biosphere). But we do usually keep them under control. Now and then, however, an epidemic like SARS, H1N1, or HIV/AIDS reminds us that even our best efforts can fail.

Third, to survive in the natural environment—to produce enough food, housing, and warmth, for example—and develop the tools we need to protect ourselves against other species, we need to harvest and process natural resources. Modern medicine depends on modern pharmaceuticals, which in turn rely on minerals and plants. The same is true of modern agriculture, which relies on fertilizers, based on naturally occurring sources of nitrogen, phosphorus, and potassium. To heat our homes and transport our food we are still dependent on petroleum-based fuels. The plastics used for food transportation and storage also rely largely on petroleum. To meet our needs for shelter, we need wood from trees; granite, limestone, and sand for concrete and bricks; and iron ore and bauxite for steel and other metals based on steel. Clearly our most basic needs depend on natural resources: water, minerals, plants, and petroleum. And of course we also crave luxuries, from televisions and iPods to cars and home furnishings: again, all derived from natural resources and all requiring an input of energy to manufacture, a process that itself almost always requires water.

Most of these resources are non-renewable or hard to reuse: water, petroleum, natural gas, iron ore, and wood. When we have extracted it all . . . well, we do not yet know how to finish this sentence. One possible answer is recycling. Another is to invent alternatives (for example, nuclear energy) to harness renewable alternatives (such as wind and solar power). A third answer is to find another planet to inhabit, or perhaps to look for new resources in currently inaccessible places (e.g., under the sea, at the centre of the earth; we are told that water has recently been found on the moon). A fourth answer is to reduce the rate at which we consume these resources—although it is worth noting that this is a short-term answer, since it only slows down the inevitable disappearance of resources.

When thinking about the natural environment, we also need to think about location. We live on the earth's surface, whenever possible near the resources that we need. The location of populations influences the environmental problems they create and the resources that will be available to them. Thus the study of human geography, the study of locations of population, is also important to sociological analysis.

Where do people live, and why? And how does location affect people's social lives? One answer is that historically people have lived near bodies of water. In addition to the immediate biological necessity, water is also traditionally part of our communication and transport networks, sanitation, and irrigation. Well, many people still live next to a body of water—an ocean, river, or lake. In large part, that is because bodies of water make travel, communication, and commerce relatively easy. They also supply fish for food and, in the case of lakes and rivers, they supply water needed for drinking, irrigation, sanitation, and other uses. Other people locate away from major bodies of water: mountains are an example, with both advantages and disadvantages. Mountains provide enough local water from streams and enough local food from grazing and light agriculture. Minerals can often be sourced in mountains (coal for example), as well as timber and stone for housing. Another important feature is that mountains are easy to defend and difficult to attack; often, they are also hard to travel through, so they are good for those who want relative privacy.

There are many other natural environments we might discuss—plains or prairies, forests and jungles, or deserts—which all provide different opportunities and challenges to people trying to secure food, shelter, transport, and communication. And that leaves aside the importance of climatic variations: the differences between living in a hot climate (near the equator) and a cold climate (further from the equator). The combinations of geographical location with consequent climate variation and local terrain provide a wide variety of human experiences, natural resources, and interspecies competitions.

At the risk of sounding like a geographic determinist, it is possible to say that these factors, like population, exercise an influence on human cultural and social relations. Take one simple example: because people who live on water—whether on the Atlantic Coast or the Mississippi

River—have more encounters with travellers and strangers, they are more likely to develop a tolerant, cosmopolitan, and changing culture. Consider New Orleans, put where the mighty Mississippi River empties into the Gulf of Mexico. No wonder New Orleans, a port city populated by traders and sailors who spoke French and Spanish and English, and by slaves from Africa, was the birthplace of Creole food, Creole language, and jazz, a new kind of music with both African and European roots.

By contrast, people who live in the mountains—in the Ozarks, Albania, or Afghanistan—have few contacts with outsiders and, as a result, are much more likely to preserve a traditional culture. Of course, these comments do not apply readily to the people of Switzerland, who live in the shadow of the Alps. Clearly other factors are involved. For example, Switzerland, though mountainous, is at the crossroads of three important European empires, bordering Italy, France, and Austria. Sociologists need to devote some effort to explaining how Switzerland succeeded so admirably in its socio-economic development where (most) other mountainous societies have failed.

And what of people in deserts? They tend to live in small bands, hunt or gather their food, and have low rates of reproduction. With little material surplus, there is little social differentiation among these people: no social classes and no luxuries. Yet to judge from the Kalahari Bushmen, desert nomads seem to lead healthy, happy lives. They occasionally meet other tribes and even trader caravans travelling across the desert, but by and large, they lead an inward, self-sufficient life based on family and community.

Without doubt the natural environment deeply influences our social relations. Similarly, when the natural environment changes, this alters our relations. We have yet to see how global climate change, for example, will affect social lives. Current thinking maintains that it will inundate coastal settlements around the world (and flood the New York subway system, for example). It will be interesting to see how new modes of transportation and communication affect the importance of geographic location, and how new types of medicine and public health affect our historic competition with other smaller species.

BUILDINGS AND CITYSCAPES

Buildings and cityscapes provide a built human environment that interacts with, and intervenes between, humans and the natural environment. So, for example, we can think of houses as tools for heating and protection, roads as constructed "rivers," and cities as planned human ecosystems, not unlike beehives.

Cities have existed for thousands of years. Likely they developed gradually and without planning, as neighbourhoods and villages grew together near certain key roads and waterways. Cities were always centres of commerce and administration, locations for trade and government. The rise of cities coincided with the rise of markets and states. Generally, cities have relied on other regions for the supply of food, importing most of their food from rural areas, so the growth of cities was only possible when surplus food was available from outlying districts. This means that cities could not come into being until the rise of settled agriculture and the development of systematic farming techniques: ploughs, irrigation systems, crop rotation, and so on.

That said, cities have always had troubled and sometimes conflictual relations with their rural and semi-rural neighbours. Cities provide markets for the neighbouring rural communities, and the surrounding areas provide commuting workers as well as food. But this division of roles has also meant a differentiation of activities, morals, and wealth. Cities have often been the richer, more powerful neighbours of farming areas, a fact that often caused envy, irritation, and hostility. Cities have also developed more varied, cosmopolitan, and "civilized" social practices, for which they have been chided by their more traditional rural neighbours. The tension between culturally tolerant city populations and more traditional rural (and small-town) populations has proven a constant source of political tension in North America, spawning Prohibition in the US, Social Credit in Alberta during the 1930s, the Moral Majority in the 1980s, and so-called Culture Wars in the 1980s onward. To a large degree, the recurrent political conflicts over abortion, capital punishment, decriminalization of marijuana, and gay marriage have all followed this urban-rural dividing line.

Today, most people in North America live in or near cities. A large fraction lives in what demographers call census metropolitan areas—urban, semi-urban, and suburban areas centred on older downtown areas. Many live in the surrounding "bedroom communities" and commute downtown to work every day. The commuter revolution of the past fifty to one hundred years has been made possible by the building of high-speed roads for automobiles and tracks for trains and subways. The conquest of distance, and the increased connection between town and country over the last hundred years, has relied on innovations in transportation and construction.

Cities have changed dramatically in the last five hundred years, in several important ways. First, as mentioned, they have gobbled up ever-larger portions of their surrounding semi-urban and suburban surroundings, and the purely rural populations have accordingly shrunk. Second, new cities have grown up all around the world. These new population centres often comprise many millions of people, and in recent decades, the populations of cities such as Mexico City and Tokyo have swollen far beyond the ten-million mark. Third and more important, cities have to an increasing degree been planned and zoned, to achieve a consistency of building standards and styles. In planned cities, to take an example, commercial districts are distinguished and regulated differently from residential districts.

Even the oldest cities have changed over time, becoming more subject to planning. Some cities like Paris were drastically re-engineered in the nineteenth century to allow an easier traffic flow (in the case of Paris, this was to ensure the easier movement of troops to quell political protesters). Other cities—for example, Washington, DC, and Brasília (Brazil's capital)—were built from scratch according to idealized urban plans. These "invented" cities characteristically incorporate regular parallel streets that meet at right angles or empty into circular beltlines; such features are rarely found in the world's more ancient cities (in, say, Florence or Cairo). Such invented cities not only facilitate traffic flow: they also embody ideas about what city life should be about—easy movement, improved communication, simplified commerce, and the rapid movement of police and firefighters, among other things.

Above all, cities were invented to promote political freedom and commerce. As the medieval European rule had it, *Stadtluft macht frei* ("city air makes you free"). This saying originates with the eleventh-century custom that a serf who escaped his rural lord and master was, once settled within the city walls, free to pursue a new life as a "citizen." And in the words "citizen," "civility," "civilization," and "cosmopolitan" we have the roots of the English or Latin words for "city." For the last five hundred years, Western cities have been self-governing places that supported a larger measure of freedom and tolerance than could be found in rural areas, dominated as they traditionally were by landed aristocrats and other landlords.

Because of both their location and their special legal status, cities were havens and refuges for travellers, migrants, fugitives, and the ambitious. As sociologist Louis Wirth pointed out, cities—and especially twentieth-century cities—developed a unique cultural profile. Their vast size made them places where, most of the time, people encountered strangers, with all the potential excitement and danger that implies. No wonder both police forces and social distancing practices (for example, practiced inattention to other people, such as lowered eyes) were perfected in cities! More important, cities provided economies of scale that allowed the development of businesses and activities that were impractical elsewhere. Because of their size, wealth, and social variety, many cities can afford opera companies and orchestras, specialized bookstores, high-end restaurants, and sex clubs—facilities that are impractical or unprofitable in smaller population centres.

Because of its size and turnover, Wirth points out, a city population is diverse and mobile. Faced with this, city people simply have to develop a tolerance for one another, for other cultures, and other ways of living. Traditional moral prescriptions cannot be defended in cities: a ban on Sunday shopping disappears, for example. People in cities perambulate the streets in all manner of dress and undress, acting and talking in all sorts of ways that are more or less familiar, and more or less irritating. They move quickly and honk their horns; they are in each other's face. As a result, people in cities are forever developing new etiquettes for public behaviour; no written rules apply well enough, yet without rules chaos prevails. For example, we are still figuring out where and when it is proper to speak loudly on a cell phone in public places.

Cities continue to develop, but not only through the spread of commerce and rapid transit. They also continue to rely on other forms of new technology, for cities are truly built environments: human-constructed ways of living together and separating ourselves from the natural environment. In the effort to improve and enlarge our built environments, innovations in various realms continue to be critical. Ask yourself, what does it take to build and occupy a tall condominium, apartment, or office building—the kind of building that characterizes most cities today? Start with strong, durable, relatively lightweight, and readily available building materials and combine these with building techniques that use these materials together in easy, cheap, reliably engineered ways.

However, the regular use of any tall building demands elevators as well as stairs, reliable heating and cooling, complex electrical wiring, and developed communication technology so people on the thirtieth floor of one building can contact people on the fiftieth floor of a building ten kilometres (or ten thousand kilometres) away. This means there is a need for telephones, computers, BlackBerrys, fax machines, and so on. Human messengers and snail mail are no longer good enough. (Well, that isn't entirely true: large cities like New York functioned perfectly well using human messengers and pneumatic tubes to carry messages for more than a century before BlackBerrys arrived—some would say functioned far better than today. At a certain point, however, pneumatic tubes outlived their usefulness.)

Therefore, technological innovation in the past few centuries has largely been driven by the needs associated with building and living in an urban environment. Today we take these features of the built environment for granted, until they (occasionally) fail; for example, when the power-grid in one or another portion of the country overloads and shuts down all our ability to function in our complex, crowded social network.

The built environment—and our reliance on it—has put a huge pressure on the natural environment, well beyond what one might expect from numbers alone. North Americans use a disproportionate share of all the world's energy and mineral resources—much more than our population size would predict. That is because our quality of life and the amenities we expect rely on the environment humans have built through their ingenuity. But today, we need to use our ingenuity to solve the problems we have created in building this environment. Think of the greenhouse gases and air pollution emitted by commuting auto vehicles alone. We also need to solve the problems of garbage disposal, as we are starting to drown in our own waste. No longer can we afford to simply ship garbage somewhere else, dump it into the nearest body of water, or propel it into the atmosphere as burnt residue. We're stuck with it on (and around) planet Earth, one way or another.

The history of cities, and of construction and transport, all point to the huge social importance of our built environment. All our life dramas—at school, work, on public streets, and so on—are played out here. As the level of comfort of our built environments evolves, and the range of choices that they offer increases or decreases, our social lives will consequently become richer or poorer.

Technology and Tools

As we have already noted, the creation of a built environment calls for tools and technology. Today, you can't build a city without tall buildings, and you can't build tall buildings without precision engineering and precision-engineered materials and building techniques. And, as we have already noted, occupying this built environment means relying on heating, cooling, computing, and other technologies that humans have invented and continue to improve.

Where did these tools and technologies come from? When and how did they make their first human appearance, and why are humans so much better at making tools than our nearest animal relatives? The answers to some of these questions are lost in prehistory. Likely, our first tools were sticks and stones: sticks to help us walk, to reach for high objects, or to fend off wild animals, and stones to stun edible animals or knock coconuts off high branches. Eventually, of course, sticks and stones became much more useful: the right stick, used with the right stone, can form a lever that greatly extends the strength of the user. The invention of the lever has been incredibly important; our earliest forebears could certainly have invented it with the materials at hand.

Similarly, the later invention of the wheel was also hugely important. Most of pre-twentieth-century (that is, pre-electronic) technology was based on the use of wheels—to move heavy objects forward or as toothed gears in machines or clocks. Even today, our automobiles and many other forms of transportation rely on wheels. Yet, the wheel is a cognitively simple discovery, needing little prior technology. All you need to do to make a wheel is cut a slice off a (cylindrical) tree trunk.

In practice, however, that is harder than it sounds. Cutting a slice off a tree trunk means you need a saw, and this in turn means you need metallurgy, a strategy for finding, refining, and crafting minerals. What is a saw but a piece of hard metal with sharp, regular teeth? But how do you convert buried minerals into a sheet of metal that is harder than the tree trunk you are trying to cut, and how do you then shape that piece of metal to give it handles and sharp teeth? These were questions our earliest ancestors must have solved before they could make wheels and then undertake major construction or transport projects.

Of course, some would say that the real turning point is a shift from mechanical to electronic devices. Transistors are critical, because they're more compact than tubes and have made electronic devices more portable and convenient; so a crucial step in human development was the invention of the vacuum tube. But no one will deny the importance of the wheel—especially if you ride a bicycle to work, as hundreds of millions do.

It seems probable that these problems were solved slowly and anonymously, building on accumulated knowledge over generations. Early knowledge about metal craft and other activities like wheel-making was likely passed along by word of mouth, across lifespans and between communities.

In this gradual, unheralded, and painstaking way, man the tool-maker (*Homo faber*) invented his world and laid the foundations for a built environment. As anthropologist V. Gordon Childe says, "man made himself" through the invention of tools and technologies and, in that way, created what Marx called "the means of production." Each new tool further separated humanity from its animal forebears and from the natural environment. Each tool gave humanity a greater advantage over less technologically advanced animals.

Why did humans catch this break? This question is impossible to answer, but we can speculate that humanity enjoyed a few natural advantages. One was the opposable thumb, which allows people to grasp and manipulate tools more precisely than other animals. Another was erect posture, which gave humanity a different, less grounded, perspective on the environment and more rapid mobility. Humanity also suffered disadvantages that made the invention of tools necessary. Relatively weak and slow, lacking sharp teeth and claws, humans had no choice but to capitalize on their toolmaking abilities. These tools became their shields and swords, and gave them protective housing and secure food supplies; humanity could flourish.

What is not clear is whether humans enjoyed certain genetic advantages that allowed them to think better than other animals. All animals had access to sticks and stones, and some animals (for example, chimpanzees) even used them as weapons or projectiles. These same animals were nearly erect in their posture too! Did humans have other latent abilities—thinking or speech abilities—that will only become known to us through further genetic research and brain imaging? Perhaps complex speech and communication is part of why our brains developed the way they did—they enable us to manage the complex relationships needed in larger groups. And did the invention and use of tools lead, evolutionarily, to transformations of the brain or genetic structure that gradually increased the distance between what animals and humans could do? Some believe that using tools regularly meant hands were employed and could no longer be used in social networking (grooming, for example), so language arose to fill the gap, and now our brains are specialized in this respect.

We do know the development of technology gave humans control over other animals, and it also gave them control over other humans. Repeatedly throughout history, superior technology has triumphed over inferior technology. Weapons technology is particularly important here: much of human history involves organized warfare; ongoing arms races involving ever bigger, better, and more deadly weapons; and strategies that use the new weapons more effectively than the old ones. The history of imperial conquest is the history of more technologically advanced nations conquering less technologically advanced nations—even though the latter nations may have other apparent advantages.

Even religious history has a military, and therefore technological, aspect: ideas have often spread on the ends of swords. Islam and Christianity did not extend around the world merely because of their spiritual merit: they were circulated by armed zealots (for example, during the Crusades). Military concerns have also been instrumental in developing tools and technology with uses in civilian life and have also contributed significantly to the improvements of medicine and health. Wars and technology are an integral feature of human history.

Advances in technology have come at an ever faster rate in the last two centuries. In part this is due to the increased importance of technology for warfare, industry, and global commerce. Everywhere, machines have come to supplement and even replace human labour. This rapid growth in the importance of technology was also a result of significant social and cultural change. First, it reflects capitalism's central concern with profit-making, which is often maximized by improving the mix of human labour, capital, and technology. Second, the growth of technology reflects the secular culture's concern with material improvement—with building bigger and better "toys"—and leading more efficient, effective lives.

Finally, advances in technology have come about because of the scientific revolution that began in Europe five hundred years ago. These advances rest on empirical, often experimental, research that obeys the "norms of science" identified by Robert Merton as "CUDOS." This acronym draws out the important processes that have moved science forward: Communalism (the results of science are public and free for anyone to use); Universalism (the evaluation of scientific claims is based on universal criteria not specific to the researchers themselves); Disinterest (scientific knowledge is pursued and presented without hopes of personal reward or advancement); and Organized Skepticism (active and critical evaluation of claims; postponement of judgment until sufficient reasons for or against a claim have been presented).

Without these scientific norms, and the social institutions (like peer review) that enforce them, technological advances would have been slow, gradual, and haphazard. In Canada many complain there has been too little technological advancement, due to a relative absence of research and development work here, but compared to pre-industrial societies, technology has always been a force for Canadian development.

Arts and Artifacts

Harder to explain in this inventory of material settings for social life is the role played by arts and artifacts, by the cultural phenomena such as music, writing, painting, sculpting, and fashion. Along with these are the material objects these activities produce, a list which would include songs, books, paintings, statues, clothes, and an array of beautified practical objects: artful embroidery, colourful woven rugs, complex decorated pottery, elaborate jewellery, elegant home furnishings, luminous glass containers, and so on.

There is no known society that has lacked arts and artifacts; yet unlike tools and technology these have no obvious practical value. The decorated pot or amphora is useful as a container of oil, wine, or water, but decorations do not contribute to its usefulness. Likewise, though people need to communicate information, it can be communicated in plainspoken sentences, not by necessity in artful songs, verses, or stories. So, what is the social or evolutionary advantage conferred by beauty and artistry? What role does art, through material artifacts, play in the making of a society?

Many have argued that artistic expression is spiritually uplifting. Art can give people hope and meaning, and the creation of art in any form can be intensely pleasurable and entertaining. Music, dance, and the other arts, perhaps, are just plain fun. Some people even promote art therapy, believing that different kinds of art and art-making can give people valuable insights into their relationships, their troubles, and their aspirations. Likely, one reason why popular songs are so popular is because they give voice to feelings and sentiments that may be otherwise difficult to express.

Before the Industrial Revolution, most art was amateur and collective. It was done alongside other people. People sang together, performed music together, danced together, quilted together, painted and decorated objects together. True, some artists were better than others; some even made a living from their artistic and artisan activities. But the social role of art, for much of human history, was to preserve and express group traditions, and to give people opportunities to celebrate these traditions together. Only with the rise of Romanticism during the nineteenth century did art come to be considered the unique product of gifted creative individuals expressing their personal insights. Beethoven, for example, was very different from Mozart and Haydn in seeing himself and his art in this individualistic, self-aggrandizing way.

Accordingly, in the last two hundred years, arts and artifacts have changed in two main ways. First, the trend in arts toward individualization and innovation has continued. Artists today are expected to produce new and unusual objects, not to repeat traditional themes in traditional ways. Related to this, non-artists are expected to appreciate and revere artists, and to see themselves as consumers, not participants in the art process. The development of art markets has been helped by the rise of art dealers and art critics, who promote the best new artists and interpret their work to consumers.

A second important trend has been the mass production and reproduction of art objects: for example, the mass reproduction of images through photography and the mass reproduction of music through recording. This process has commodified artistic production, turning art objects into yet another consumer good. No longer social, spiritual, or unique, now art in its various forms is little more than another item for sale. As well, the process has often also alienated the artist from the product of his or her labour and has put a cash exchange between the producer and the consumer. How different that is from the experience of, say, ancient Greeks listening to Homer or another bard around a flickering fire as he improvised verses of the Odyssey in live public performances, night after night.

Today the arts play far less of a significant a role in creating social cohesion than they did in pre-industrial societies. However, they do continue to play a social role that is probably as old as societies themselves: namely, providing groups of people with emblems of themselves. (They largely do the same for social classes, as we will see.) The best-known and best-loved artistic products continue to signify national groups to themselves and to others. The English continue to think of themselves as the people immortalized by Shakespeare, while the Germans have similar feelings about Goethe, and the French about Molière. Every self-aware society has its own signature poems, novels, songs, dances, and symphonies that preserve traditional memories and represent the group to outsiders.

Which leads us to ask: what are Canada's signature poems, novels, songs, dances, and symphonies? And why do we have such difficulty answering that question? Likely, French Canadians would have less difficulty here than English Canadians; the francophone Quebecois have made a point of preserving and passing on their artistic culture. English Canada has done much less of this, for various reasons. One has been the disruptive effect of American culture on Canadian art and artisanship. It is hard to compete with a neighbour who is ten times as large, much richer and more powerful, and creates in the same language. Another reason has been the disruptive effect of high rates of immigration and the official policy of multiculturalism, which appears to favour the preservation of immigrant ancestral traditions over creating new Canadian traditions.

Yet there is an indigenous Canadian literature, celebrated by Margaret Atwood in *Survival* and by Noah Richler in *This Is My Country, What's Yours? A Literary Atlas of Canada*. Some would say there is also an indigenous Canadian painting tradition, as represented by the Group of Seven, for example. And one should not forget the singular importance of Aboriginal painting and sculpting as a distinctive national art form. It is less clear whether there is an indigenous Canadian musical or playwriting tradition.

Has this relative lack of distinctively Canadian arts and artifacts hurt Canadian society? Some believe it has: the argument has been made that most Canadians don't know or value their own history or support their own artists. As a result, Canada is culturally, socially, and politically disunited and unable to offer leadership on the world stage, or even to resist the cultural incursions of American popular culture.

Does change in a society's arts and artifacts change that society? In other words, do arts and artifacts affect social relations as strongly as the other factors we have discussed in this chapter? I am thinking here of population, the natural environment, the built environment, and tools and technology. The answer is that probably they do, but the effects of cultural artifacts on social cohesion and identity are subtler, less visible, and less immediate than other factors. There are continuing crises in the Canadian arts, a result of inadequate funding to symphonies, ballet companies, writers, painters, and playwrights. Would Canadian society improve significantly if the arts were better funded and better appreciated? It's impossible to say. Perhaps we need to run that experiment, although some believe we may have done so in the 1950s and 1960s.

One thing we can say with confidence is that the products of human creativity—the arts and other more commercial variants like architecture, advertising copy, logo designs, interior decoration, and musical jingles—are increasingly all treated as commodities. In an information- or knowledge-society, products that grow mainly out of human insight and ingenuity are more likely than ever to be marketable. No wonder that artists and other creative people are among the main drivers of economic growth in urban communities.

Last night, I smelled the neighbourhood skunk again. It must have been skirmishing with one of the local raccoons, or maybe with a cat. My wife says she thinks it shelters in our neighbours' garage or under their deck. I'm thinking it isn't much fun being a wild animal in downtown Toronto, especially during the winter. My friend David disagrees, saying that skunk is probably a lot happier and better fed than if it didn't live in an urban area.

Sometimes when I am doing sociology at home, I look out the window of my second-floor den and see animals on the roof looking in my window. Squirrels are common visitors and sometimes even raccoons come by to bask in the sunshine. I wonder what they think when they look inside. Do they imagine I am a prisoner, trapped behind the glass windows, surrounded by all those books, seemingly chained in front of a strange machine (my computer) for hours on end (and without a scrap of food in sight)? Meanwhile, they are free to come and go as they please.

Our cairn terrier Maisie probably thinks she has the best of all possible worlds: easy access to the backyard, daily walks in the park, and a secure food supply—plus a loving family life inside our warm household. Sometimes she goes out to bark at the squirrels; she is intimidated by the raccoon's size, so she does her barking at it from indoors. There's no doubt about it: she has been drawn into our domestic routine.

As for me and all the people I know, we have separated ourselves from nature and, most of the time, we view it through the windows of our home, office, or car. We do what is needed to keep non-domesticated animal species out of our way, and we live inside all the secure luxury we can afford and technology can provide. Occasionally, we spend time at a cottage or camping "in the wild," but we always return to the material environment our ancestors so gradually and painstakingly built for us. For it is only within this secure environment that we can carry out the "higher" tasks that set humanity apart from raccoons, squirrels, skunks, and other animal species: activities that include writing sociology textbooks, listening to Beethoven's piano music, playing jazz, reading newspapers, and pondering current events.

Whether these uniquely human activities really are "higher" is beyond the scope of this book. But clearly humanity has set itself socially and culturally apart from the rest of the natural world, and it has built a unique material stage for this uniquely human drama. In the next chapter, we discuss the forms that social relations take in front (or inside) of this material setting.

Two

Social Structures

In the last chapter we discussed the material backdrop for our social relationships: all those factors just outside human society that influence how we get along with one another. In this chapter we will discuss some of the human factors that influence our social relations. In particular, we will discuss what I here call social scripts and forms.

By "social scripts" I mean those culturally constructed, socially enforced practices that we are all expected to follow when we interact in social situations. Each situation has its own script in a given community or society, and the majority of the adult members of society are aware of that script. They have learned it through many years of observation and practice. Within a given situation, certain scripted deviations are permitted: for example, women may be expected to act somewhat differently from men, or adults from children. However, people who deviate too far from their proper script are criticized, sometimes even punished. At the very least, they will likely lose respect and credibility within the community.

By "social forms" I have in mind social arrangements arising out of interactions that are often below the cultural radar. People may not always know about them and they are not socially enforced, but they nevertheless appear regularly and influence our behaviour. The sociologist whose name is most associated with social forms is Georg Simmel, who wrote roughly a hundred years ago in Germany; since then, many sociologists have developed and extended his insights.

As we will see, these scripts and forms constrain the ways people relate to one another in social situations. These are the human social factors that influence how conflicts arise and co-operation is negotiated.

Roles and Role-sets

Social scripts are most closely associated with the dramaturgical approach to sociology popularized (and systematized) by sociologist Erving Goffman (who was born in Canada, but spent his professional career in the US). Goffman showed that we can think about social life more fruitfully if we treat it like a stage production, with costumes, scripts, roles, and audiences. Of course, social life is *not* a scripted play. We noted earlier that everyone has some freedom to act as they choose in social life. What's more, no written script completely covers any social situation. Improvisation is always needed. Situations and the people in them are too diverse to allow for complete scripting, even if we wanted it.

So it's clearly a metaphor to say that social life is a scripted drama; however, it is a useful metaphor, allowing us, for example, to predict how situations may unfold. It also helps us explain the sheer fact of social structure: that predictable, enduring feature of social life that is the subject matter of sociology. In fact, this metaphor helps us understand why people behave the same in introductory sociology classes in the year 2010 as they did in 2008 or 2003 or 1998, and why they behave differently in a classroom from the way they behave in a club, sports stadium, or bedroom. Why such a range of behaviour? Because performances in university and college courses are scripted differently from performances in clubs, sporting events, and bedrooms.

The dramaturgical approach also helps to account for other features of the situation that are play-like: for example, the fact that we use costumes and makeup to prepare ourselves for performances in particular situations. We dress differently for church, say, than for Sociology 101 or for a romantic occasion. We also make important distinctions between backstage and front stage (where we are on display).

Even more convincing is the observable fact that people in socially scripted situations behave like actors in plays when someone fails to perform as expected—in effect, when they step out of character or forget their lines. When such flubs occur, people feel embarrassed, even disoriented. They don't know what to say next or how to get the interaction back on track. They will do almost anything to ignore the flub and keep the interaction moving along. At best, they experience confusion and upset until someone figures out a way to resolve the dilemma. Sometimes they just laugh and walk away, or someone makes up lines to patch over the silence. At worst, there is anger and resentment about the ruined scene.

Take an example. You're Sarah. Andrew, this guy you like, meets you at school. You are with some friends, and you've planned to go out and do something special—maybe something fun and romantic. You've dressed up for the occasion; you like Andrew and you want him to think you look fantastic. Maybe you're falling for him. So Andrew arrives, stares at you, gets a worried look on his face and whispers, "Sarah, are you okay? You look terrible—kind of bloated. What's wrong with you?" Well, Andrew's show of concern is well intentioned, of course, but it wasn't scripted. This is not how boyfriend-girlfriend conversations are supposed to go, especially during romantic dates. What do you say then, Sarah? Or Andrew, seeing Sarah's embarrassment or shock at his words: what does he say then?

The social scripts we follow are usually sketchy: they give us the general outlines of what we can say and do, but not the details. We need some social skills and insight (qualities Andrew is clearly lacking) to be able to deduce what can properly be said or not said to a new girlfriend on a date. The seeds of such a script are contained within roles and role-sets.

We all know generally how young men are supposed to act, how young women are supposed to act, and how people in general are supposed to act if they want to communicate a romantic or sexual interest in each other. We also know how we should act when other people are around, when we are in a public, rather than private, setting. With all these clues, it should be possible for Andrew to construct, or remember, a workable script for the situation, but he blows it. And under no circumstances should Andrew's (or anyone's) script include the words, "you look terrible—kind of bloated." (Those may be the six words in the whole English language that are least likely to result in sex.)

Many roles and role-sets are even better defined than this. Role-sets like husband-wife, parent-child, or teacher-student are all well defined, in the sense that we all have a clear idea how people in these roles are *supposed* to act toward one another. Other imaginable role-sets, however, are completely undefined: for example, plumber-lawyer, father-waitress, or prostitute-ballet dancer. That doesn't mean we can't invent or imagine scenarios that people in these roles might play, face-to-face with each other. (If we did, we would likely focus on important age, sex, or class differences and similarities.) It just means our culture hasn't defined particular scripts. In our culture, there is no "right way" for plumbers to talk to lawyers, or prostitutes to talk to ballet dancers. Therefore, we have no expectations about these interactions and no surprise or embarrassment about anything that transpires.

A classic role-set first discussed by the American sociologist Talcott Parsons is the doctor-patient interaction—classic because it perfectly captures how two culturally defined roles can fit together. It also gives us insight into our culture's thinking about health, sickness, and professional medicine. Both the doctor and the patient are interdependent: one can't play his particular role without the other. For the doctor, the patient is an opportunity to demonstrate expertise and exert control. For the patient, the doctor is a source of social approval for deviance. In some of its effects, visiting a doctor is like visiting the neighbourhood crack dealer. Both can release you from any sense of social obligation. Doctors, given their expertise and professional authority, can release you from all your social responsibilities by declaring you sick. No guilt or shame or punishment is attached to your slacking off once the doctor has the authority to make this declaration.

Of course, it comes at a price. To qualify for this dispensation from your duties, you need to describe and show symptoms that the doctor can place within a recognizable category of sickness. Most important, you need to accept the doctor's judgment, buy and take any medicine prescribed, and agree to follow the doctor's orders until further notice. This may mean giving up work, but it may also mean giving up fun. You may be forbidden to eat Brussels sprouts (yippee!) but also forbidden to drink beer (boo!). The point is that our culture accepts this procedure for excusing deviance; that is why you can bring a doctor's note to your teacher or boss and get out of work without penalty. Still, you may not necessarily want to accept the doctor's judgment and follow her advice, even though you want the right to play sick and gain sympathy. That's why second opinions were invented.

As you can see, this is a rich area for further discussion. One issue we haven't discussed is this: where do roles come from, and how do they change? Here, for your consideration, is one possibility: people fall into patterned ways of acting as a result of (sometimes short-lived) constraints and social pressures. For various reasons, they feel obliged to act in certain ways. These regular patterns are then elevated to ideals or norms. People rationalize them, arguing they are desirable and inevitable ways of acting. To act otherwise is abnormal or immoral, they say. When the situation changes, and groups arise to oppose these ways of acting, gradually our sense of propriety (and normality) changes. A prime example, perhaps, is the shift in thinking about homosexuality that has accompanied the widespread shift in thinking about sex and the need for family reproduction.

What is important here is that all the social relations and social conflicts we will discuss in this book have a scripted aspect. If we ever want to understand why society is so hard to change—for example, why we seem unable to rise to the challenge of climate change—we need to look carefully at these social scripts and their underlying cultural bases.

Dyads, Triads, and Small Groups

Social scripts tell people more or less how they ought to behave. Social forms, by contrast, are not prescriptive but descriptive. Social forms emerge without the intention—and often even without the aware-ness—of people in the social situation. In his 1908 essay "On Indi-viduality and Social Forms," Georg Simmel defines sociology as comprising two elements, which are only distinguishable analytically. One element is content, the purpose or motive of an action or inter-action. The other is form, the mode of interaction among individuals through which the specific content achieves social reality.

Fashion is a good example of this distinction, since it speaks to both content and form at the same time. Fashionable dress allows people to display themselves in a way that (they feel) displays their individual-ity; yet fashion, by nature, is social. The group as a whole determines what is in fashion or out of fashion. Individuals cannot, themselves, make fashion—they can only select from it and attempt to personalize it. In other words, fashionable clothing is the social form into which we pour our individual desires for adornment and self-presentation.

Consider another example of social forms that involves two situa-tions. In one situation, two friends are deciding what movie to see on Saturday night. In the other situation, three friends are deciding what movie to see on Saturday night. The situations are similar. Indeed the motivations are identical—to see a movie with friends. However, the two interactions are likely to differ because dyads (two-person groups) rarely work the same as triads (three-person groups). Speaking broadly, two-person groups or multiples of two tend to reach agreement easily or else fall into a hard-to-resolve conflict. These binary groups, as in all things, are oppositional: on/off, black/white, good/bad, yin/yang, and so on. That's why Marx's theory of dialectical materialism—a binary theory about two main classes, the bourgeoisie (or capitalist class) and the proletariat (or working class)—is a theory of conflict.

By contrast, odd-numbered groups (of three, five, or seven people, for example) may have a hard time reaching agreement, but they do not usually fall into hard-to-resolve conflicts either. Odd-numbered groups are characterized by compromise and shifting alliances. In any group of three, for example, one person is likely to serve as peacemaker or intermediary between the other two. No such intermediary is available in a dyad (though in principle intermediaries or brokers could appear in binary groups larger than two). The point here is that any decision process, and indeed virtually any interaction process, is different in a group of three than it is in a group of two, even when these groups have the same goal.

Or consider a third example of social form closely associated with Georg Simmel: the stranger. Simmel, who was interested in cities, was naturally interested in the activities of strangers, given the relatively high number of people living in cities who are unknown to each other (something that is rare in settled rural areas). Simmel recognized that even though there is no prescriptive role or social script for strangers, people who don't know each other do still face socially structured opportunities and constraints, even stereotypes. Strangers are typically marginal to any community. Their marginality prevents them from gaining full acceptance or holding roles that are central to the functioning of the community. Strangers are unlikely to be elected mayor, for example. At the same time, their marginality gives them an opportunity to serve the community usefully in shadowy or even shady ways—as merchants or moneylenders, drug dealers or go-betweens, for example.

From the perspective of ordinary citizens, strangers lead secret lives, outside the communal spotlight, so it is often felt, for example, that they can be trusted with secrets. They will not likely gossip about your business to your friends, since they do not know your friends, and vice versa.

The idea of social forms is fundamental to sociological thinking, since it opposes what has been called the "voluntarist" position. Voluntarism, a social psychological approach, argues that our social behaviour is a clear reflection of our goals, values, and intentions, and that our identities shape our interactions. On the contrary, sociologists believe that our social behaviours may have little to do with our true goals, values, and intentions. People do what they have to do to avoid punishments and receive rewards, within a given social milieu. Further, their interactions shape their identities, not vice versa.

For example, people who find themselves marginal to, or estranged from, the community will find themselves being treated like strangers, then behaving like strangers, then feeling like strangers, then thinking they are indeed strangers. And people who find themselves caught in a conflict between two friends or relatives are likely to become peace-makers, brokers, and intermediaries—roles they never sought to play. In short, we develop our social purposes or motives after being thrust into our social roles.

The strongest and most interesting claim of this sort was made by American sociologist Robert Bales, who in the 1950s studied training groups (known as T-groups) at Harvard University. These groups of undergraduates were recruited to meet once a week over the course of a year and discuss designated topics or solve problems together while being watched through a one-way mirror. Behind the mirror, research-ers recorded all the words and actions of the participants, using a spe-cially designed measure that permitted the interaction process analysis. In this way, Bales was able to advance and test interesting hypotheses about group processes and the ways people used words and actions to express themselves in groups.

Bales's study revealed that each of his groups produced or created three social forms: a task leader, an emotional leader, and a joker. The task leader helped the group organize itself to solve the problem that had been posed; he or she helped to set goals and organize the work. The emotional leader helped the group cope with frustration and con-flict, so that strong feelings did not deflect the group from its task. In effect, the emotional leader was the peacemaker. Finally, the joker was—as the name suggests—the person who helped release tensions in the group by joking and fooling around. This seemingly slack time-waster was as important as any of the other group members; without the periodic tension release of joking, the group might not have performed successfully.

What is the implication? Groups, to survive, need some of their members to perform special kinds of tasks—as task leader, emotional leader, joker, or otherwise. Eventually, in every group, different people step forward to fill these roles, or the group breaks up. This happens without conscious planning or even a conscious awareness of group needs, and no one knows why. This, then, is a small version of the structural-functionalist model of social systems that was associated with sociologist Talcott Parsons and his students, including Robert Bales. The structural-functionalists argued that all social systems—all groups, communities, organizations, societies, and empires—have these systemic, self-maintaining features that enable them to survive, to move forward, and to achieve their goals.

In time, sociologists came to question this model. They noted that this view of social systems does a poor job explaining (or predicting) conflict, change, and deviance. Some felt the model did not adequately explain relationships within groups, describe individual actions, or explain why members behave as they do. Many rejected the approach entirely, while some continued to embrace certain aspects.

Today, most sociologists would still agree that groups have their own logic and follow certain typical self-maintaining patterns. Most would understand that the awkward functionalist language for group behaviour is simply shorthand. For example, when functionalists say, "A group satisfies system requirements to ensure its survival," they typically mean two simple and fairly obvious things. First, they mean that people often invest themselves emotionally, socially, and financially in the groups to which they belong, so they willingly take actions to protect the group; in other words, they protect their investment. Second, functionalists also mean that people with a particularly large stake in the group, who receive particular benefits (e.g., authority and esteem) from group membership, will do their best to keep the group alive.

However, despite the benefits that may flow from group membership, some groups are better at surviving than others. That is a sociologically interesting fact. Take a simple example: all family sociologists would agree that families that are cohesive (i.e., emotionally tight-knit) and adaptable (i.e., flexible) are best able to deal with stressful conditions: unemployment, war, chronic illness, and so on. Families without a history of cohesion and adaptability are likely to break down under these circumstances. For example, a change in circumstance can end in divorce, pathological behaviours (e.g., addictions) or mental disorders can develop, or there may even be a descent into physical violence. Perhaps this is because well-functioning families have at least one person who is a task leader, another who is an emotional leader, and someone who is a joker.

This is not to argue that other family dynamics are unimportant. Families can break down because they lack flexibility and cohesion. However, they can also break down because their most powerful members are unfair, neglectful, or abusive. This, in turn, may reflect certain cultural tendencies—for example, patriarchal tendencies—that favour men over women and adults over children. That said, it is worth noting that these pieces fit together. We can hypothesize that, at least in modern societies, patriarchal families will lack flexibility and cohesion, and therefore will deal poorly with stressful circumstances. The interesting question, then, is under what social or cultural conditions are patriarchal families able to survive at all? This, however, is a question for a different book.

With these ideas about social forms in mind, we can venture a few general observations. First, all small or primary groups have similar characteristics and patterns, whatever their purpose or goal. For example, they are all based on intense, face-to-face interaction, and the members tend to identify with one another. Often, in such groups the emotional boundaries between members are blurred. People identify closely with the group and with one another, and find it hard to leave or betray the group.

Second, in every such group, certain structural changes will significantly affect how the group operates. For example, the demographic factors we discussed in the last chapter will all affect small groups (even more dramatically than they affect entire societies, in fact).

Imagine a family of, say, two parents and two children. Now, double the size of that family to two parents and six children and see what happens. Increase the rate at which parents or children enter and leave the family and see what happens. Change the mix in the family: for example, substitute a stepfather for the biological father, a stepmother for the biological mother, or stepsiblings for the biological siblings and see what happens. Families and other small groups are extremely resilient, but they can also be vulnerable and volatile. That's why divorce rates and rates of domestic violence are so high. Many families and other small groups don't survive because they cannot adjust to changing demographic and other social and environmental forces.

People may be able to realize their hopes and wishes through small group interaction, or they may find these hopes and wishes stymied by other people and by the "needs" of the group as a whole. Desires can be frustrated and disappointed even in small groups—even where people enjoy the closest, most intimate and well-intentioned relations. The same happens even more often in larger groups.

Teams, Bands, and Gangs

Teams, bands, and gangs (I suggest the abbreviation TBG) are three types of larger groups. They are sometimes considered secondary groups because, unlike families, they do not always command our primary social allegiance. By contrast, families—given their small size and emotional intimacy—are always considered primary groups. However, many people consider the teams, bands, and gangs they belong to almost like surrogate families. So we may prefer to locate these groups somewhere between primary groups (for example, families or close friends) and secondary groups (for example, school classes or work offices).

What is interesting, once again, is that social forms dictate similarities between the groups, despite the different goals of participants. A basketball team has different goals from a marching band, which in turn has different goals from a motorcycle gang. However, in many of their social processes, TBGs are very similar, and they are all very different from much smaller groups (e.g., families), larger groups (e.g., college classes), and formal organizations, to be discussed shortly.

First, unlike families, people are not born into TBGs; rather, joining them is a matter of choice. Second, they typically join TBGs because they want to be members, not merely as the means to another end (i.e., more than a wish to earn a course credit or paycheque). In every case, people join because they want to identify with, and be identified with, the team, band, or gang. Accordingly, each TBG has a defined membership—a clear idea of who belongs and who does not. It also has a clear set of goals and main activities. And given the definition of these goals and activities, the TBG has a leadership structure, one or more leaders and lieutenants, whose job it is to set specific goals, mobilize resources to achieve these goals, and motivate the members to participate, according to set rules and directives. In these respects, TBGs are like families, with the leaders acting as parents.

Unlike small groups, TBGs have a rudimentary political structure (i.e., leaders and followers), a rudimentary legal system (i.e., set procedures to resolve conflicts), a rudimentary economy (e.g., a treasury and assets), and a rudimentary culture (i.e., a shared historical memory of great events, heroes, and villains). The group members may even have pet names for one another, long-lived jokes or rivalries, mascots, and cultural artifacts—trophies and prizes, or team colours, for example.

Bands, like teams and gangs, operate according to certain unwritten rules. Band members do not openly criticize one another. If they have concerns about another member's performance, they direct these concerns to the leader; then the leader deals with the problem if deemed appropriate. Members may also quietly suggest improvements or grumble discreetly to another band member. Often, jokes are used to express irritation or frustration. Even the leader may express criticisms in a gentle or roundabout way, suggesting there is a general problem in the band, or in a particular section of the band, but without pointing a finger of blame at the particular offender.

If criticisms *are* to be aimed at particular band members, as is more usual in professional, high-level TBGs, they must be aimed in ways that everyone views as fair and constructive. Leaders also have to be even-handed in their delivery of praise and blame. It does not sit well if they play favourites or pick on the same people all the time. The reasons are obvious. For a band (or team, or gang) to perform well, everyone has to pull together. Each must do his or her required job and be able to rely on others to do the same. There must be co-operation, confidence, and good feeling among all the members. This spirit of co-operation and collegiality is hard to build and preserve if criticism is doled out harshly, unfairly, or unequally.

Now, these comments apply generally to bands, teams, and gangs, but clearly there is much variance within different TBGs. For example, some TBG leaders are more inclined than others to control their members, whether because they want the group to achieve their stated goals ("Winning is everything!") or because they have personal needs for control and domination, as some leaders do. In these cases, harsh criticism is far more common. Leaders may even pit group members against one another in rivalry, in an attempt to motivate certain efforts. Or they may use punishments (ridicule, shame, threats) more than rewards to motivate their members. Sometimes these methods work, and sometimes they backfire. When they backfire, people leave the group, overthrow the abusive leader and the lieutenants, or just give up.

Within bands, and probably within gangs and teams, we also see subdivisions of loyalty and friendship among the members. Sometimes sections of the band engage in friendly rivalries with each other or joke at each other's expense. Here's a joke I heard from a vocalist that reflects some common prejudices among musicians:

> The horn section of a jazz combo was on the way to a gig and were killed in a tragic car accident. When they arrived in heaven, God personally greeted them at the front gate and asked each of them what they did on earth. The first person said: "I was a tenor sax player and I made people happy with my wonderful music." The second person said: "I was a trombone player and I taught people the love of music." The third person said: "I was a trumpet player and I believe you are sitting in my chair."

In sports teams, there may be comparable distinctions between those who play offence and those who play defence; between those who are starting pitchers and those who are closers; between guards and running backs or quarterbacks; between high scorers and enforcers; and between "stars" and average players.

All teams, bands, and gangs must address problems of leadership, recruitment, communication, and control. Most particularly, the basics of group communication and co-operation that we commonly associate with "teamwork" must be mastered: for example, building relationships, solving problems, managing conflict, and giving and receiving feedback. And they have to ensure that the right people are doing the right jobs, in the right ways.

In other words, even in groups as small as teams, bands, and gangs, we find important divisions of labour, associated with differences of personality and social identity. All of these members have to work together to achieve the group goal, but they often carry out different tasks under the general supervision of a leader. It matters little whether the group's purpose is to sound like The Rolling Stones, win a football championship, or control the sale of drugs in downtown Vancouver. In every case, forming and maintaining a group demands leadership and followership: recruitment, training, motivation, reward, and so on.

Of course, it does make *some* difference whether the group is operating within or outside of the law. This fact is amply illustrated in research by sociologist Bonnie Erickson on secret societies. Secret societies—small underground groups dedicated to spying or terrorism, for example—have a paramount concern with secrecy, because if they are found out, they may be thrown in jail or killed. For this reason, groups exercise even greater care in recruiting, training, motivating, and rewarding their members than do ordinary teams, bands, and gangs. They develop procedures to ensure security. One such procedure is to separate the group into small cells, so that if one cell is discovered it cannot reveal the identity or activities of other cells. Another technique is to recruit their members from among friends and relatives. Close kinship and friendship ties among the group members increase the likelihood that members will be loyal to their group.

In short, social forms and not personal intentions determine how a group will operate, regardless of the activity. (We will see later on how this becomes a problem with formal organizations, where we find a tendency for groups to forget their original goals entirely and function mainly to keep the organization alive and successful.)

Cliques, Networks, and Small Worlds

The social network is another form that is of increasing interest to sociologists. Imagine twenty people all connected, either directly or indirectly, to one another. By direct connections, we mean links of kinship, friendship, and acquaintance among all twenty people. Within this set of twenty people, there can be 190 different paired connections—mathematically expressed as [(20 x 19) / 2 = 190]. Clearly this comprises many interesting relationships and combinations of relationships to study.

Indirect connections also are of interest. In fact, some sociologists such as Mark Granovetter argue that weakly tied networks, based largely on indirect links, may be even more useful than strongly tied or completely connected networks. Information, social support, and other valuable resources flow through incompletely connected, or weakly tied, networks. Other things flow as well, like rumours, diseases, innovations, and job information. All these spread geographically through (indirectly linked) networks of weak ties, because weakly tied networks have a vast outreach. They connect large numbers of weakly tied people (for example, acquaintances) at a few removes; this of course can be distinguished from tightly connected networks, which circulate the same information or resources repeatedly through the same set of people (for example, close friends).

In a sense, social networks are only as strong as the pairwise (or two-way) connections—called dyadic relationships—that comprise them. In stable dyadic relationships, based on social exchange, people give each other things they want and need. So long as these relationships satisfy their needs, people remain in these relationships. People usually act in their own best interests, at least when they are aware of these interests. They are rational and sensible, and they preserve social relationships that are useful to them. So people enter, leave, and stay in the larger social networks in which their valued dyadic relations are embedded. Over time, as people enter and leave relationships, networks change in their size and composition. This in turn affects the resources flowing to other members of the network.

Increasingly, people are setting up virtual networks of relationships in cyberspace, as well as real ones. In recent years, Internet-based social networking services such as LinkedIn, Friendster, and Facebook have rapidly increased in popularity. These services collect information from an individual's profile and list of social contacts to create a display of his or her personal social network. This display publicizes how the contacts within the network are interconnected. These online services are often provided free to users, although individuals must disclose personal information to register and use the networking sites. These sites are built on the premise that individuals may be merely a few links removed from a desirable business or social partner and not even know it.

An interesting feature of social networks is their "small world" property. In social networks, everyone—or almost everyone—is indirectly tied to everyone else at a few removes (what has been labelled six degrees of separation). Besides, people within the network differ in their number of linkages and some people are "sociometric stars" or "connectors": online personalities particularly important in linking everyone together indirectly. As a result, a disproportionate share of information and influence flows through these people.

Other people are known as "brokers" or "entrepreneurs," meaning that they are invested with the ability to link two more-or-less separate networks, so that each can benefit from the other. Sometimes they even represent members of one network to members of another. In this sense, then, leadership means integrating society at the top through linkages between leaders, brokers, or entrepreneurs. In practice this is far easier than achieving integration at the bottom, by interweaving the members of all social networks.

This role of leaders is especially important because many, if not most, of us are intensely connected together in cliques, very important nodes in social networks. Sociologically, we would define a "clique" as a group of tightly interconnected people—a friendship circle whose members are all connected to one another, and to the outside world, in similar ways. Usually, clique members feel strong positive sentiments or liking for one another and contempt for outsiders. They spend more time with one another than with non-clique members, share their knowledge with one another, and think and behave similarly. They try to ignore or exclude outsiders—people not like themselves and not friends of their friends.

In short, cliques are groups characterized by friendship, likeness, interaction, exclusion, and the flow of valuable resources: information, support, and opinions (among others). In these respects, cliques are mini-communities, like mini-states. Like states, they amass power and resources. They receive, censor, and direct information flow. Cliques gather and redirect information. They also produce information, distort it, and send information out as gossip and rumour. Cliques, like other organizations, create and concentrate information flow. Because they produce and control the flow of information effectively, cliques are stable structures. They survive largely through what psychologist Irving Janis called "groupthink."

For purposes of comparison, TBGs may or may not be cliques. Cliques are, above all, committed to policing group boundaries through inclusion and exclusion; they do this by increasing cohesion among insiders and distancing the group from outsiders. That is their task, their raison d'être. Teams, bands, and gangs also include insiders and exclude outsiders, but they have more practical, less symbolic reasons for existing: to win games, play gigs, and make money, respectively.

Cliques have no evident reason for their existence, given that they have no practical goals. But although they are seemingly without goals, cliques nevertheless do have an unstated "mission" or purpose: to raise the status of clique members at the expense of non-members. Though lacking an organizational chart or stated division of labour, school cliques (for example) have a clear hierarchy of influence and popularity, with the leader on top surrounded by his or her favourites. In this sense, then, a clique is a group of people working together and coordinated by communication and leadership to achieve a common goal or goals.

Cliques form in every area of life, even within bureaucracies and other formal organizations. But cliques are probably most familiar to us from our childhood school experience. In school settings, cliques typically have a well-defined membership. Clique members are typically similar to one another in background and behaviour. Members often have rituals that exclude outsiders and integrate insiders. There is also a leader who is the most popular member and who dominates the other members. Usually it is the leader who defines the group boundaries, invents group rituals, and chooses the membership.

Cliques are not only organizations: they are communities and miniature societies. In cliques, children first learn the rules and expectations of society outside their family home. Through games and play with clique members, children internalize the beliefs, values, and attitudes of their group. By these means, children also form judgments about themselves. For example, they learn what it means to be "attractive" and "popular," to be chosen or passed over. Children's activities, their friendships, and their feelings about themselves are tied up with their involvement in the cliques that organize their social landscape.

Though often supportive, cliques can also offer excellent examples of structured cruelty; this can be observed everywhere, including cyberspace. Online bullying carried out by clique members is a new phenomenon and potentially just as damaging as the bullying that occurs face-to-face. With "e-bullying," youths can constantly harass their victims over the Internet, through instant text messaging on cellphones and postings on bulletin boards and on their blogs. Thanks to technology, which makes more pervasive and unrelenting forms of bullying possible, victims are always within reach.

Cliques form when people meet others like themselves, in the midst of others unlike themselves. The social structuring of activity itself—for example, grading of activities such as education, entertainment, or work by age—increases the likelihood that people will meet others like themselves. Also, since class or ethnicity often separates neighbourhoods, and since children usually attend neighbourhood schools, they are likely to meet other children of the same class and ethnic background. The more homogeneous the people they meet, the more children will form relationships with others who are similar. It is in the first instance that this structuring of acquaintances leads to cliques.

Then in an environment marked by ethnic, racial, and class similarity, children will form cliques around common interests or abilities; cliques often coalesce around interests such as athletic ability, musical tastes, or preferences in fashion and personal lifestyle.

The cohesion of a clique is based mainly on loyalty to the leader and loyalty to the group. This loyalty, in turn, is based as much on exclusion as it is on inclusion. First, group members hive themselves off from non-members. Lack of contact with outsiders allows members to believe that outsiders are different and less socially desirable than themselves. Also, clique members use gossip to reinforce their ignorance of outsiders and keep social distance from them. They also use gossip to ridicule and spread often distasteful rumours about outsiders. Finally, they may pick on or harass outsiders. Doing so instills fear, forcing outsiders to accept an inferior status and discouraging them from rallying together to challenge the power hierarchy.

Cliques control their members by defining the behaviours that are proper and acceptable. Leaders are skilled in exercising control. They often do so by building up the clique members and then cutting them down. One technique is to draw new members into an elite inner circle, allow them to enjoy brief popularity, then humble them by turning the group against them. Leaders also take advantage of quarrels to divide and conquer the membership. They degrade and make fun of those who are lower in the hierarchy or outside the group. All of these tactics allow leaders to build up their own power and authority. Such rites of degradation also foster clique solidarity by clarifying the norms for acceptance and rejection.

Cliques and the rituals of inclusion and exclusion on which they rely are more than mere children's games. They are small-scale models of how organizations state, teach, and enforce rules; as such, they provide a lesson in social control. Cliques remind us that every inclusive action is, at the same time, an exclusive action. Organizations like cliques can have shared goals that are unstated but real, norms that are unwritten but compelling, hierarchies that are undocumented but powerful, divisions of labour that are effective but unplanned.

Formal Organizations and Bureaucracies

Formal organizations are large secondary groups with a collective goal or purpose. An organization can be a giant multinational corporation, such as Microsoft, or a small corner variety store. It can be a political party or a government, a church, a school, a sports club, or a search party. We can define a formal organization as a deliberately planned social group in which people, resources, and technologies are consciously coordinated through formalized roles, statuses, and relationships to achieve a division of labour intended to gain a specific set of objectives. Typically, a formal organization will have an overarching set of goals framed by its leaders and more or less accepted by its members. However, we cannot assume that these are the only goals of the membership. Workers, professionals, and managers will have their own occupational goals as well.

Despite the endless variety of organizational forms and the millions of specific examples, every organization is a group of people working together and coordinated by communication and leadership to achieve a common goal or goals. Organizations are formal if they are deliberately planned and organized. Within formal organizations, communication and leadership are provided through consciously developed and formalized statuses and roles. Often formal organizations have multiple goals, and they usually have a long lifespan.

The Roman Catholic Church is a formal organization that has lasted nearly two thousand years.

In comparison with the teams, bands, and gangs, and cliques that we discussed in the last section, formal organizations tend to be larger, longer lived, and better funded. This is because formal organizations normally have access to far greater resources and more complex technologies than spontaneous organizations. Certain kinds of formal organizations—particularly corporations—even have their assets specially protected under law.

The main form of the large, powerful, and long-lived formal organization in the twentieth century is the bureaucracy. For most of us, the word "bureaucracy" carries negative connotations. But to sociologists, a bureaucracy is merely a particular type of formal organization that thrives in both the public and the private sectors, in capitalist and socialist societies alike. The fact that bureaucracy is the main organizational form taken by competitive corporations shows that it can be very efficient.

Max Weber first analyzed the particular features of the bureaucratic form of organization. In his study of the major organizations of his day, he identified seven essential characteristics of bureaucracy: a division of labour, a hierarchy of positions, a formal system of rules, a reliance on written documents, a separation of the person from the office, hiring and promotion based on technical merit, and the protection of careers. Weber's idea of bureaucracy has proven to be a useful model for the study of this complex form of organization. It calls our attention to central features of bureaucracy. But it is a simplification, an idealization, like physicists' concepts of absolute zero or a perfect vacuum. In the real world, bureaucracies have flaws, and sociologists have spent much time discussing these flaws. Consider a few of them.

Ideally, every member of a bureaucratic organization is knowingly enmeshed in a network of reporting relationships. In graphic form, a bureaucracy is a pyramidal or Christmas-tree-shaped structure that repeatedly branches out as you go down the hierarchy. At the bottom of the hierarchy there are a great many people whose job it is to carry out orders from above and report work-related information up the tree to their superiors. And at the top are a few people whose job it is to issue orders to their subordinates, process information received from below, and maintain linkages between the organization and its (political, economic, and social) environment. Also at the top, information is shared between the heads of planning, manufacturing, shipping, public relations, and other sectors of the organization.

In practice, however, organizations do not work this way, as sociologists since Weber have pointed out. Alongside the ideal or formal structure—which prescribes how a bureaucracy ought to work—there is an informal structure that controls how it actually does work.

In theory, a failure to report information up the hierarchy would never occur. In practice, it occurs all the time. Workplaces are "politically contested terrains" and controlling the flow of information from below is a means of changing the balance of power between superiors and subordinates. And, as the French sociologist Michel Crozier showed, bureaucracies work differently in different societies. This is because different cultures have different ideas about inequality, obedience, openness, and secrecy. For example, people raised in France or Russia will be much more alert to the inequality of bureaucratic relations and the power of information control to equalize relations than workers raised in the United States. French and Russian workers behave differently, and as a result bureaucracies work differently in these countries.

Bureaucracies also work differently for men and women. Some research suggests that, when playing a managerial role, women are more likely to adopt a collaborative, relational approach drawn from qualities used in family relations; men, by contrast, are more likely to stress purely economic considerations. Women's managerial styles stress the establishment of good employer-employee relations and the sharing of information and power. This may reflect, to some degree, the types of industries and positions in which women most frequently achieve managerial rank—so further research on this topic is needed. Certainly, sociologist and management consultant Rosabeth Kanter asserts that men and women behave the same ways in organizations, and what matters is whether they are in positions that afford them status, resources, and opportunities for advancement based on merit.

In practice, workers everywhere make friends and acquaintances. As a result, they casually share work information. Much of the information that flows within an organization is shared orally, rather than in writing, to introduce civility and negotiation between work teams. Workers will often use information purposely to help one another. Sometimes they may even leak information for personal gain or to subvert their boss or the organization as a whole.

Thus within organizations based ideally on strangers relating to other strangers following written rules, we find workers forming what amount to secret organizations or subcommunities that obey their own rules. Political actors below the top level cannot employ routine channels or resources to negotiate in the idealized manner. "Politics from below" includes all the actions that defy, oppose, or sidestep the rules or roles of the organization. The basis of this informal organization is trust, which relies on friendship, acquaintance, and gossip about third parties that strengthens existing ties. In the end, the same materials that build cliques build the informal, often hidden, infrastructure of bureaucracies.

In the past thirty years, most of the world's manufacturing has moved to low-wage countries and is carried out in settings considerably less flexible and with less educated workers than had once been the case. It's cheaper to manufacture cars in Mexico not because of flexible or educated workers but because it's . . . well . . . cheap! But in North America, organizations need ever more flexibility from workers, which is possible only if those workers receive continuing education and training and take part in planning. Yet worker motivation, recruitment, and training all pose problems for bureaucracies. The motivational problem is greatest in organizations where professional expertise and judgment are most required, as in universities, law firms, and technology-development firms. Here we find the greatest attention given to matters of organizational culture and career development. It is only by giving these workers great autonomy and rewards for strong identification with the firm that the most able workers can be induced to join, stay, and carry out their duties in conformity with organizational goals. Some organizational cultures are more effective than others in creating a high level of worker commitment and high rates of employee retention, and societies vary in their use of one or another organizational culture.

Bureaucracies are thought to be rational in the ways they make and carry out plans. By making impersonal decisions and rewarding excellence, they are more able to pursue long-term organizational goals with huge amounts of wealth and power. However, the sheer size of large bureaucracies and their long-term outlook introduce certain types of irrationality that, in the end, may undermine the organization. A concern with the mere survival of the organization may undermine shorter-term concerns with the quality of decisions, products, and services the organization is providing to its customers. The much-hated "red tape"—or administrative delay—common in bureaucracies persists not because of inadequate technology or personnel, but because it serves positive (as well as negative) functions for the organization.

The bureaucratic characteristic of relying on the rules as written can create another problem. As a bureaucracy grows and more rules are added, the system becomes increasingly complex. This can lead to a situation where no one person knows all the rules, and different offices act independent of each other, creating rules that conflict with one another. As well, *rule by offices* undermines personal responsibility for decisions the organization may take. No member of the bureaucracy is asked, or obliged, to take responsibility for collective decisions. As a result, so-called collective decisions—typically taken by the top executives—are liable to be foolish, harmful, or even criminal. Environmental theorist Thomas ("Tad") Homer-Dixon posited in a recent book that technological society had become too complex for people to understand and manage effectively. Perhaps this is an exoneration of misbehaviour, though overly generous (in my view).

Corporate and government entities are unique in that their deviant behaviour may be caused by systemic patterns in their organizations, rather than only by individual misbehaviour. However, once deviant behaviour has taken place, top managers are well positioned to evade responsibility. Managers may often refuse responsibility by hiding behind organizational structures or by adopting the view that they were merely following orders. The deviant behaviour of big business and big government occurs because of limited information, the establishment of norms and rewards that encourage deviant outcomes, or the implementation of actions by organizational elites.

Such deviance, which is rarely prosecuted or punished, is usually introduced by managerial elites and subsequently institutionalized into organizational culture. It often continues unchecked until it is challenged from inside or outside the organization. Organizations themselves are rarely penalized for deviant behaviour: perhaps the most pertinent example in modern times is the recent meltdown of the American economy and the role of major banks in this process. *The Challenger Launch Decision*, written by sociologist Diane Vaughan, is often cited in this area when discussing botched or perverse decision-making.

Inequality Is Bad for People

Cutting across social scripts and social forms is the issue of inequality. The available evidence suggests that social inequality—whether as income inequality, status inequality, racial inequality, gender inequality, or otherwise—is bad for people and bad for societies. In particular, social inequality increases the likelihood of law-breaking and of poor health. The first is discussed most effectively by Robert K. Merton, the second by Richard Wilkinson.

The effects of inequality on law breaking and conformity are best discussed in a classic (1938) theoretical paper by sociologist Robert K. Merton. This paper, titled "Social Structure and Anomie," is perhaps the best-known, most often cited paper in sociology and has, no doubt, influenced the work of hundreds if not thousands of studies of crime and deviance.

Merton's underlying idea is that anomie—a gap or discrepancy between what people are taught to want ("cultural goals," especially money and material goods) and what they are able to get legitimately ("institutionalized means")—leads people to devise "adaptations." These so-called adaptations or non-conforming strategies include what Merton calls retreatism (a rejection of conventional goals and means), rebellion (a substitution of unconventional goals and means), ritualism (a rejection of conventional goals but continued behavioural conformity), and innovation (a rejection of conventional means but continued adherence to conventional goals). For Merton, much of what we classify as criminal behaviour can be usefully viewed as innovative adaptation, and much of what we consider addiction or mental illness can be usefully viewed as retreatism.

The thrust of Merton's argument is that these adaptations are functional (in other words, necessary) for the survival of social inequality in general, and capitalism in particular. In that sense, they are normal and unavoidable. If people could not adapt to anomie in the ways they do, they would (conceivably) launch a direct frontal assault on social inequality to remedy the condition of anomie. Instead, they make individual, piecemeal efforts to cope with the problem, whether through crime, addictions, or other means of withdrawing from reality. In short, crime and addiction are inevitable outcomes of inequality and allow inequality to continue.

The effects of inequality on health are readily observed in the area of income inequality, which is known to influence a variety of health outcomes, including homicide rates, violent crime rates, the frequency of low–birth weight children, the incidence of sedentary behaviour, and rates of smoking. For example, the famous Whitehall Studies in the UK demonstrated clearly that status inequalities are harmful to health, even under generally favourable economic conditions. The classic writing on this topic is by British researcher Richard Wilkinson. His work on the social determinants of health helps to explain why societies with more equal distribution of incomes have better health outcomes than ones in which the gap between richest and poorest parts of society are greater.

The question is this: how and why does social inequality contribute to poor health and to social problems such as crime, depression, and addiction? Researchers have identified two ways that inequality causes poor health: by reducing social cohesion and by increasing personal stress. First, inequality breaks down social cohesion. It fragments social networks and increases hostility between social subgroups. Social integration and social networks are vital for good health. When functioning at their best, they moderate stress, reduce risky behaviours, provide help in times of need, and offer emotional and spiritual support. At the macro level, social inequality influences the availability and access of health care information to members of a society. People with higher levels of social involvement are healthier and live longer, and communities with more social integration have better health and mortality records.

A breakdown in social cohesion, then, leads to worsened health and higher mortality. It also leads to higher levels of crime and violence. This, in turn, can have harmful effects on health status. It can happen directly, through exposure to drugs and physical injury for example, and indirectly, through community disruption, lower property values, higher unemployment, and lower-quality health care services.

Second, inequality creates dangerous stresses, again both directly and indirectly. According to a theory of "allostatic load," health declines under stressful conditions through the overuse of natural bodily resources. The continued experience of high-level stress results in physiological and psychological harm by raising levels of the stress hormone cortisol. Cortisol is the body's major response agent to chronic stress. Our bodies release cortisol in "fight-or-flight" situations; the hormone prepares the individual for vigilance and long-term action.

However, cortisol also raises blood pressure, disrupts circadian rhythms (sleep patterns), and suppresses the immune system. In the short term, these are useful bodily reactions. They were also evolutionarily important, preparing the body for sudden increased levels of action. However, the bodily responses to raised cortisol levels, if repeated often, are likely to do more harm than good. They lead to problems such as heart ailment (resulting from continued high blood pressure and cholesterol levels) and increased receptiveness to various diseases (resulting from a suppressed immune system and sleep deprivation). Experiencing social inequality over long periods can damage your health, harming those most at the bottom of the hierarchy. As a result, social inequality and the stress it creates affects people's life chances—their health and longevity.

As we have seen, social structures—particularly social scripts and social forms—are similar to the natural environment in that they provide a backdrop to our social relations. Our group relations are shaped by the demands and characteristics of those groups that, as we have seen, have system "needs" of their own. Pressures for loyalty and conformity, for example, influence group members to relate to other people in ways that are useful to the group or organization.

This is made even more complicated by the fact that, in large organizations, people are often nested within smaller structures—in roles, cliques, and small groups for example. People in these organizations are always under pressure to satisfy the varying cross-pressures of their different roles and relationships, all at the same time.

However, as we will see, people's relations are further complicated by the social inequalities that shape and constrain their roles and group memberships. These social inequalities, resulting from gender, age, social class, race or ethnicity, and region or nationality, work separately and in combination to push individuals apart. They create feelings of distance and distrust that prevent people from communicating openly and effectively. In the next five chapters, we will explore the effects of these inequalities: how they evolved, why they persist, how people adjust to them—and how they often undermine people's best efforts to co-operate.

Three

Women and Men

One of the oldest and most powerful social scripts in Western culture involves two characters: a knight in shining armour and a damsel in distress. For centuries, this has remained the archetypal gender script in our society, and even today it continues to direct men to be masculine (active and forceful) and women to be feminine (passive or indirect). People who violate the gender script (men who are too gentle or women who are too aggressive, for example) risk ridicule and rejection.

Yet this gender script is older even than Western culture itself. Of course, a certain amount of research has shown that male and female brains are wired somewhat differently. Perhaps that explains why sex—the distinction between male and female—is a universal and ancient basis of social differentiation. We know of no human society now or in the past that does not divide work and status along the lines of sex. Likely this has some basis in biology and the fact that women alone can bear and nurse offspring. Women are also, on average, physically smaller and weaker than men, and therefore less suited for combat and hunting. Child-bearing also makes women vulnerable and dependent for extended periods. These biological realities have likely led to the widespread social roles of men functioning as protectors/breadwinners and women as procreators/caregivers.

This simple distinction varies from one society to another. History and anthropology show us that women can also be breadwinners and protectors; men, though they cannot be procreators, can be caregivers. What's more, in societies with low fertility, this male-female distinction is much less important, since in these societies women spend relatively little time in reproduction and much of their lives breadwinning.

Societies differ in the extent and ways they dramatize this sex-based difference, that is, in the ways they enact gender roles and gender differences. Some societies enlarge these differences, while others diminish them. In other words, there is much variation in the degree to which sex differences *seem* large or small, important or unimportant. There is also much variation in how societies rationalize their enactment of these differences. Some invoke religious edicts (Biblical commandments, for example), others secular principles like the moral commitment to equality; still other societies rely on scientific or pseudo-scientific theories (for instance, ideas about evolutionary selection) to justify differences in how men and women are treated.

Strange to say, given that half of all humans are women and the other half men, the study of gender relations had almost no presence in sociology before the mid-twentieth century. Before 1900, there was little exploration of gender by any of the major European sociologists. The two main exceptions were philosopher John Stuart Mill, who was passionately concerned about the issue, as were his friend Harriet Martineau (mentioned below) and Friedrich Engels, intellectual partner of Karl Marx. Engels's book *The Origin of the Family, Private Property, and the State* (1884) made an imaginative attack on the problem of patriarchy, relating it to class relations, but many would say the work had little subsequent impact. Finally, the French utopian thinker Charles Fourier had ideas for reorganizing love and sexuality in new, free communities he called phalansteries.

In England, Mary Wollstonecraft in the late eighteenth century and Harriet Martineau in the nineteenth century gained fame, if not notoriety, by drawing attention to the economic and political problems women faced and the need for gender equality. In these efforts, they were helped by influential male admirers: Wollstonecraft by her husband William Godwin, an English utopian thinker, and Martineau by prominent philosopher John Stuart Mill. However, these were the exceptions. Though many notable women novelists emerged in nineteenth-century England (starting with Jane Austen), before 1900 most women lacked the time, income, independence, and/or "a room of their own" (as Virginia Woolf famously argued). Women were not admitted to university until the late nineteenth century; before the twentieth century, few women were university educated, and before mid-century they rarely taught in universities. No surprise that until relatively recently, women have enjoyed little social standing and virtually no institutional support for any intellectual ambition.

But of course women have always had intellectual ability, a passion for learning, and occasionally the good fortune to receive tutoring at home. In the late nineteenth and early twentieth centuries, women became more visible as thinkers about social matters, especially about poverty. This was obvious among the Fabians in England, where Beatrice Webb worked alongside her husband, Sidney Webb, and in the United States, where church-promoted and social service–related research delved into problems in the growing cities, led by women like Jane Addams. Perhaps more important, the growing feminist movement continued to press for gender equality and related social concerns (for example, abstinence). It's worth noting that the early feminist movement was mainly concerned with women's suffrage; the right to vote was achieved in Canada, the US, and Britain in the early decades of the twentieth century.

Tellingly, until the early 1970s, no sociologist seemed to notice that housework was work, not just a casual outpouring of family affection. It was only then that English sociologist Ann Oakley published her seminal book on the sociology of housework, which drew needed attention to domestic inequality and its relation to other forms of gender inequality. (I will say more about this later.) The arrival of a full-fledged sociology of gender relations coincided with, and was promoted by, the large-scale entry of women into higher education throughout the West. It took women's contributions, and the third wave of the women's movement, to bring gender inequality and gender relations to full sociological attention.

The failure by major male sociologists, from Marx, Weber, and Durkheim onward, to contribute to gender issues tells us something interesting about the connection between social structure (especially the social distribution of power) and the propagation of knowledge. Evidently only the powerful get noticed, studied, and discussed. Therefore, to put gender issues on the list of research topics, women needed access to power. Once powerful, the next step was to draw attention to topics that concerned them directly and that had been neglected by male scholars.

In fact, then, we can see that the subject matter of sociology itself is a measure of a society's equality, openness, self-awareness, and social concern. Changes in sociology reflect changes in the distribution of power. These changes are achieved largely through changes in the intellectual class and the institutionalization of knowledge, peer review, research funding, and journal publication. The "discovery" of gender relations as a field of study was a necessary (though not big enough) step toward addressing some of the problems we will now consider.

Opportunities for Co-operation across the Line

COUPLES AS CO-OPERATIVE VENTURES: SPOUSES

One of the key facts about male-female relations is that most people mate across gender lines: they select partners of the opposite sex. This mating, often based in our society on sexual attraction, is perhaps the strongest and most widespread basis for male-female bonding across the lines. For most people, it is preceded by dating, a process by which men and women learn about one another. In fact, one of the defining aspects of human development is the movement from same-sex play groups (at early childhood ages) to sexually indiscriminate play groups (at later childhood ages and early adolescence) to paired (opposite sex) play in the form of dating in late adolescence and early adulthood.

Most of what many of us learn about the opposite sex occurs while dating and mating, and later during marriage. In these respects mating and marriage are great experiments in cross-gender living. (And increasingly, they are also interesting experiments in same-sex intimate living.) They provide ample opportunities for learning about the different goals, attitudes, and inclinations of the opposite sex in an environment motivated by love and a search for pleasure—strong inducements indeed. After marriage, these inducements are reinforced by wishes to share a long-term investment in children, a household, and other material and psychological properties (for example, a shared social life).

Of course, most of us learn about the opposite sex well before we start dating. We do so by learning to co-operate with family members of the opposite sex through conflict or co-operation between brothers and sisters, mothers and sons, fathers and daughters. These cross-sex forms of interaction are often emotionally charged in ways that may be different from same-sex interactions (for example, between brothers or between fathers and sons). To some degree, this may be because most cultures expect same-sex family members to pass along gender-specific knowledge to one another. An example of this is the expectation that fathers will socialize sons, and older brothers will socialize younger brothers, by introducing them to the "secrets"—pleasures or demands—of manhood. Equally there is an expectation for mothers to socialize daughters and older sisters to socialize younger sisters in the skills, rules, and etiquette of womanhood.

It is likely that these early experiences with cross-sex relations play an important part in moulding our ideas about gender, and perhaps even in how we mate and who we select as mates. The way our parents interact also shapes our early thinking about what normal cross-gender relations might look like and what role we ought to strive to perform when we ourselves mate.

From early childhood onward and through the school years, many children are members of peer groups and cliques that influence their understanding of, and interaction with, people of the opposite sex.

Though many peer groups and cliques are same-sex, all male or all female, many are not.

Peer groups include both actual and notional groups, also known as reference groups, from whom we acquire ideas about proper behaviour. These groups may be large and loose or small and compact; what is important is that all peer groups provide access to peer culture and ideas about age- and sex-appropriate norms of behaviour. For example, this culture will usually include norms about how to behave toward people of the opposite sex, especially where sexual attraction exists. Both peer groups and cliques teach young people about a great many things, of which cross-sex relations is only one example. The desire for social acceptance at this age is so strong that young people are highly motivated to learn and follow the dictated rules.

Perhaps one of the strongest messages communicated by peer groups and supported by families involves sexual conduct. Sexuality, and responses to sexuality, are almost always gendered. Sexual beliefs and practices, and deviations from them, are rooted in beliefs about men and women, and by extension the social roles that many believe men and women *should* occupy. It is this arbitrary set of distinctions that results in what we call a "double standard."

The most common form of sexual deviance, in our own and other societies, involves violating this so-called double standard: the rule that women are supposed to behave differently from men, often where sexual matters are concerned. Specifically, men are supposed to want sex intensely, to be the sexual hunters, while women are supposed to be passive, almost asexual—the hunted sex-objects of men, their sexual prey.

Paradoxically, this long-lived double standard is at odds with another valued tradition: romantic love. Anyone who doubts how passionately our society values romantic love need only turn on the TV or consult the movie listings at the local multiplex. Yet romantic love can serve as a basis for sex only in societies that allow both males and females the freedom to give (or withhold) sexual love freely. If you want romantic intimacy between men and women, you have to start with gender equality, or something close to it. Feminist philosopher Simone de Beauvoir came close to saying this when she declared, "The word love has by no means the same sense for both sexes, and this is one cause of the serious misunderstandings that divide them." On this theme, in her classic work *The Second Sex* (1953), she wrote,

> On the day when it will be possible for woman to love not in her weakness but in strength, not to escape herself but to find herself, not to abase herself but to assert herself—on that day love will become for her, as for man, a source of life. (361)

While it is impossible to estimate how common violations of the double standard may be, it seems certain that this form of rule breaking is becoming more common. Such deviance is central to the establishment of gender equality and romantic sexuality. Yet despite these theoretical advances, even today there are limited ideological avenues available for women to develop positive identities that include being sexually assertive. Many are stigmatized or ridiculed if they are too honest about their sexual needs, while males are praised for the same thing. Sexually assertive women still struggle to create and maintain a space for sexual freedom. Many lack support systems to help keep this positive perspective.

Despite liberalizing changes in the past fifty years, the double standard remains. Sexual liberation—a sure result of access to secure birth control and the economic independence of women—continues to spread. Gradually, the extent of the double standard in the sexual behaviour of men and women is decreasing for younger generations, and the age of sexual initiation is decreasing as well. More people are having more sex, with more people, at younger ages.

Research continues to show that sexual freedom is related to other kinds of human freedom. For example, cross-cultural analyses also find that the absence of a double standard toward sex outside marriage—premarital and extramarital sex—is correlated with other variables that signal freedom and liberty. Where women are as sexually free as men, husbands are prevented from physically disciplining their wives, women are considered equal to men, women are as likely as men to take leadership roles in family and business, and a high value is placed on female life. The disappearing double standard in sex suggests the growth of broader gender equality.

ADULT EXPERIENCES OF GENDERING

In later youth and adulthood, most people witness and perform gender-play in workplaces. They learn what it means to be a boss or a subordinate and what it means to be a colleague. Here, they learn workplace etiquette: the unwritten rules of behaviour across gender lines. These roles include a male boss with a female subordinate, a female boss with a male subordinate, a male colleague with a female colleague, and so on. There is a large literature and much folk wisdom about the opportunities and dangers associated with office romance and workplace mating. There is also a large literature about workplace harassment. (More on this to come.)

What is important here is that, in the workplace more than in the home, school, or playground, gender is strongly and visibly involved in the distribution of authority, status, income, and power. We are at least as much aware of gendered inequality in the workplace as we are at home. And because the inequality is not usually associated with love (nor is it imagined to be unique to our own experience), it is far more likely to give rise to the sharing of grievances and public protest. At the same time, cross-sex relations in the workplace expose us to adults of the opposite sex in ways that allow us to co-operate, compete, and assess our own skills and merits in comparative terms. We learn that people can be competent, ambitious, meritorious, lazy, double-dealing, or backstabbing whether they are male or female. This discovery is an important basis for future cross-sex alliances.

Through the mass media, we also gain vicarious or second-hand experience with people of the opposite sex. By seeing cross-sex relations modelled, we see how men and women are supposed to act toward one another and what supposedly happens when they do not do so. Of course, the mass media are mainly a source of entertainment and fantasy, not properly a guide to the real world. But because many people learn more about the world vicariously through the mass media than through their own experiences, these fantasies can have important effects on our real behaviour and expectations.

Forces Pushing People Apart

EVIDENCE OF CONFLICT

Despite all that we have said about the opportunities and forces leading to cross-sex co-operation, a great divide exists between men and women in our society. In this section we explore the nature and extent of that divide. Much of it is marked by conflict, but the conflict can take various forms; some forms are more visible than others.

This conflict is obvious in all the domains mentioned above where opportunities exist for cross-sex co-operation. For example, we are well aware of high rates of relationship dissolution (for example, divorce) between intimate partners. These rates of dissolution are especially high in dating relationships, where an estimated 60 percent of couples break up at least once, often reuniting to ultimately break up again. They are somewhat lower for couples who cohabit, but these rates (admittedly tricky to calculate with consistent accuracy) are nonetheless higher than one might like. Among married couples rates of legal divorce are lower still, but far more marriages fail today than a century or even fifty years ago. Indeed, since the liberalization of divorce laws in the late 1960s, the chances of divorce have risen to somewhere around 35 to 40 percent. These rates vary demographically, of course. Richer, more educated people are less likely to divorce than average, especially if they marry late. So are more religious people. Nonetheless, the evidence provided by marital dissolution argues that mating, attraction, romance, and love are no guarantee of long-term continuing cooperation and attachment across the sexes. Divorces are often followed by new efforts to bond across the sexes, but these efforts also carry high risks of failure.

We know that families are fertile grounds for conflict between parents and children, as well as between siblings. Not all of this conflict is based on gender differences; in fact, it is impossible to say how much may be. However, what is clear is that families provide no more guarantee of stable bonding across sexes—between parents and children, or between siblings—than it does of bonding between husbands and wives.

Peer groups are seemingly more gender-blind today than they once were. For example, many young people date in groups, allowing them to enjoy the benefits and pleasures of opposite sex interaction while protected by the nearness of same-sex friends. That said, we continue to see—in cliques, teams, fraternities, and otherwise—ample evidence of same-sex mobilization. We see the same in gendered entertainment (e.g., "chick flicks" like *Sex and the City*, which celebrate shopping, lunching, and gossiping as common forms of female bonding). We also see this in what has been called, mainly in the male context, homosociality: young men slapping each other with towels and loudly drinking beer together, for example. Young people, though perhaps less inclined to stereotyping than their parents, have not lost sight of culturally defined differences between men and women.

In workplaces, some of the more blatant forms of sex discrimination have, for the most part, been outlawed and expelled. Antidiscrimination legislation makes it illegal for bosses to promote men over more competent women or to pay women less than men for the same work. Suspicions of a continuing "glass ceiling" at work remain, however, especially in some careers. Moreover, in some circumstances, a wage gap persists between men and women, types of work remain different and segregated, and child care poses a far greater concern for many working women than for their husbands or male colleagues.

As for the mass media and popular culture, the changes that have occurred—and those changes that have not occurred—are obvious in various ways. There have always been jokes about the opposite sex and about marriage. Such jokes, especially by male comedians about their wives and mothers-in-law, were for a long time a staple of the professional humour industry. Today, we can still view male comedians on television making these jokes, although often the tables are turned: both male and female comedians, as well as situation comedies, are likely to depict women (especially wives and daughters) as savvy and competent, while men are dreamers and goofs.

Likewise, the mass media continue to objectify women; that is, to portray them as sex objects on display and seemingly for purchase. This is evident in advertising and pornography, at televised sporting events, and in other entertainments aimed at young male viewers. There has been some decline in the depiction of women as brainless beauties: some women depicted in the mass media visibly have brains, and others are visibly not beautiful. Yet such traditional stereotypes of masculinity and femininity have not died out. Women's advertisements for mates still stress their beauty and youth; men's advertisements still stress their ambition and earning power. In other words, men and women still signal to each other in the same time-honoured ways.

Segregation

One sign of an ongoing conflict between men and women is the evidence of continued segregation or social distance between them.

Despite blurring, there continues to be a (mainly) women's world and a (mainly) men's world, and this distinction corresponds largely to a distinction between the private and public spheres of life. It is easy to overstate the extent of this separation, so what follows below is intended as a caricature, or simplified "ideal-type," simply to make the point. In fact, the gendered separation is much less marked today than it was a generation ago.

Public life, especially in the top echelons, is mainly inhabited by men. This includes, but is not limited to, the world of paid full-time jobs. Though women are increasingly entering paid work, men are more likely than women to work full-time, and they are more likely than women to hold executive positions. The most obvious example of gendering in the for-pay sector, however, is in politics. Here, men are far more likely than women to hold high political office, whether elected or appointed. Indeed, the proportion of women in a parliament or legislature is a good indicator of the general level of social equality in a society. This is especially true at the highest levels—in cabinet positions, or as presidents and prime ministers. A recent book by political scientist Sylvia Bashevkin, *Women, Power, Politics* (2009), has shown all too little change over time in this respect.

Religious positions represent an interesting example of gendering. On the one hand, they appear to be pastoral, and in that sense, encompass caregiving positions that ought to admit and recruit women. On the other hand, in many denominations, high religious positions—priests, bishops, archbishops, cardinals, and popes in the Roman Catholic Church, for example—are socially powerful and almost entirely restricted to men. Like political positions, such religious positions show the degree of gender segregation in a society. The most gender-segregated societies have the fewest women in important religious positions.

A continuing problem with such segregation is the minority group status that women often meet when they enter occupations that were previously restricted to men. This issue is nicely explored in a study by the American sociologist Rosabeth Kanter. Kanter argues that the barriers women meet in large corporations are a result of numerical minority, not sex. Kanter's classic work, *Men and Women of the Corporation* (1977), challenges many assumptions about the traditional system of merit and reward within organizations. Contrary to the common belief that women's opportunities are limited because they act differently from men (for example, that they are too "feminine"), her study shows that *because* women have fewer promotional opportunities, they act "like women." When men and women enjoy equal opportunity, both sexes act the same way. Weak, unproductive managerial behaviour, then, results from holding weak, unproductive positions. People who suffer from blocked opportunity, powerlessness, and tokenism, regardless of sex, tend to act in similar ways; for example, they may display less ambition.

Women in organizations like the one Kanter studied are severely disadvantaged. The secretaries, however ambitious and talented they may be, are tied patrimonially to their male bosses. Their fortunes rise and fall directly with those of the boss, regardless of the women's own efforts. The wives of organizational executives, also often ambitious and talented, are also tied to their spouses' fortunes. Their fates rise and fall with those of the men to whom they are connected. Both secretaries and wives are powerless, yet tied to the fates of the men whose careers they serve. And because of this powerlessness, they behave in "typical" female fashion: they are subservient, devious, yet seemingly unambitious. Such apparently typical female performances support the male view that women, by nature, are not good executive material.

In Kanter's view, a woman's sense of self reflects her real opportunities. Change her opportunities and you change her identity and ambition. In this respect, the unequal organization of society, by disadvantaging women, makes them docile and unambitious.

Kanter also hypothesizes that group members who are in a numerical minority will feel restricted in what they can do. Kanter's "tokenism theory" predicts that members of a social group who find themselves in situations dominated by members of another group will suffer various adverse effects, including increased psychological stress. The more outnumbered the token individual, the more pressure he or she will experience. Conversely, as minority and majority social types within a group reach equal numbers, isolation between the two groups will lessen. Interaction and communication within the organization, and across group boundaries, will increase. However, merely adding a few "token women" to a group or organization will not necessarily result in a significant increase in available choices and newfound freedom to flourish.

Clearly, it is no easier to change a woman's life by urging her to raise her consciousness than it is by urging her boss to raise his consciousness and restructure the organization. Large organizations exist in an organizational environment, nested within an economy. External relations with other firms in the industry (or the economy at large) may hinder their ability to change. More often than not, organizations copy one another and remain locked in patterns set outside their borders. As well, large organizations have an internal environment that resists change, despite the best wishes of one or more bosses. They contain islands of vested interest, small domains with their own culture and power structure. Those in control will resist change. Movement and communication across traditional lines of authority (ideal when new groups are to be introduced) is difficult in hierarchical organizations with long lines of authority.

Kanter's tokenism theory can be applied to any organizational setting that contains different "kinds" of people, whether men and women, racialized workers and whites, anglophones and francophones, immigrants and native-borns, and so on. We can apply the general principle that tokenism prevents us from seeing how people could potentially adapt and grow into their roles in a wide variety of situations. Kanter's work is fertile and valuable, even beyond the study of gender.

PREJUDICE AND DISCRIMINATION

Prejudice and discrimination are often harder to nail down than other forms of gendering. Prejudice is a state of mind and is investigated chiefly by psychologists in laboratories or by using interview techniques. It may result in discrimination, but here a problem arises. Not all prejudice is acted upon: it may not express itself in any external behaviour, except possibly in private conversation. It therefore does not always give rise to actions that harm or exclude people on hostile grounds.

Moreover, not everything that appears to be discrimination is proof of prejudice. The decision that, say, firefighters must be of a certain height or weight may have been made for reasons related to the assumed requirements of firefighting. These reasons, sensible or not, may not have had in mind the exclusion of any particular groups. Yet at the same time they may have resulted in the exclusion of women or groups whose height distribution is lower than the average Caucasian male (Asians, say). So while this decision may be discriminatory in its effect, it is not necessarily so in its original intent. It does not prove the existence of prejudice against women per se. Even so, many believe that such structural discrimination, whether it is motivated by prejudice or not, must be eliminated because it is unfair and harmful in its overall social sequences. This argument has led to greater recruitment of women into firefighting, the police, and the military, to name a few examples.

There is continued vigilance on the issue of gender inequality, as well as discrimination, in respect to what is called "employment equity." Here, an effort is made to ensure that women and men will have an equal opportunity to enter and advance in occupations for which they hold the requisite skills and credentials.

But for all these good intentions, this initiative has been hindered by several difficulties. Take one example. Ample evidence shows that women and men often choose different careers and occupations. Much research is still underway to determine why this is, to what extent are these choices a result of differences in genetic inclination versus learned preferences versus sensed social impediments to following certain courses of training and employment. Given our ongoing ignorance on this matter, many continue to argue that we must assume the worst: that gendered differences are due to socially structured unfairness, to prejudice and discrimination.

This, then, argues in favour of "equal pay for work of equal value." Even when men and women do different work, the reasoning goes, they should be paid the same if they are doing roughly equivalent work. Of course the difficulty here lies in discovering when and whether two jobs are of "equal value." In a society like ours, the "value of a job" is largely determined by the marketplace. If the marketplace has determined different pay levels—for example, for doctors and nurses—then how can this be questioned?

In many other instances, the value of a job is determined by labour-management agreement. Assuming labour and management can figure out a way to reach an agreement on the equality of, say, a mainly female office job and a mainly male equipment-servicing job, how do we establish the equal value of jobs that are not unionized? Who is to do this, and how is it to be done fairly: that is, how can it be done in a way that everyone can agree is fair? And how is this equity to be enforced without creating an unmanageable bureaucracy? Efforts have been made to address these problems, but they remain far from solved.

There is little doubt that most Canadians would say that they are all for fairness and against gender prejudice and discrimination. But we are far from achieving this fairness. Although in principle few would express negative feelings toward the opposite sex, in many circumstances we still see what appear to be discriminatory conditions.

SUSPICION, UNCERTAINTY, AND DISTRUST

Often as sociologists, we study circumstances that seem obvious; yet we have trouble finding the suitable measures or indicators. It stands to reason, for example, that in the realm of gender relations, given all the unsolved problems, there should be much suspicion, uncertainty, and distrust.

The reasons for this supposition are simple: this is an area of social life that has been changing rapidly for the past fifty years. To a large degree, women have achieved equality with men (for example, in the realm of education). However in many other areas, equality with men appears to be a long way off. One example is within the domestic sphere. Here, sociologists continue to find ongoing inequality in the division of domestic labour. Similarly, in many careers, and especially in religion and politics, women are still far from equal. It would be no surprise, then, if they harboured feelings of frustration, irritation, uncertainty, distrust, and suspicion about men.

For their part, Canadian men have seen a rapid decline in their relative power—in families, workplaces, politics, and elsewhere. Nowhere is this clearer than in schools, the main place where young men and women compete with one another for grades, approval, and eventually scholarships. In our society, men are no longer the unassailable authorities on everything from science to morality, work to politics. With this rapid and continuing decline in men's traditional authority, we should expect to see a backlash. At the least, we would expect men to be nursing feelings of frustration, irritation, uncertainty, distrust, and suspicion about women.

One place we see signs of this is in the separate cultures of men and women. The jokes men make about women, and women make about men, reveal anxieties and irritations. Though I have seen no systematic study of this, it seems likely that a high proportion of gender-based jokes (compared to, say, gender-neutral jokes or class-based jokes) should point to a high level of concern, and also of suspicion, uncertainty, and distrust.

Another place we see signs of this are in advice columns and online chat rooms, where people seek guidance about etiquette, social propriety, and risk-taking. Under what circumstances should a young woman have sex on a first date, for example? This question is now open for public debate as it was not, perhaps, fifty years ago. The answers one might give to this question—and even raising such questions—provide a measure of relations between men and women. The easier cross-sex relations become, the less likely they will be discussed and the more likely people will make confident individual decisions. Currently, many men and women are afraid to do so, given their distrust of the opposite sex.

Everywhere in the West, people are more hesitant to marry and bear children. They understand the costs and risks of these important decisions, and the dangers associated with making the "wrong" decision— for example, marrying the wrong person or producing children at the wrong time.

This decline in marriage and child-bearing is only partly the result of suspicion and uncertainty. (On this, sociologists will learn more as we investigate whether same-sex relationships lead to marriage with a higher frequency than opposite-sex relationships.) It is also a result, and perhaps mainly a result, of prolonged education and longer periods of financial dependency, for example. It has to do with the availability of education and jobs to women, and not wanting to compromise these opportunities with the demands of procreation. The decline in marriage reflects the widening range of choices: you can marry if you want, but you don't have to; you can also cohabit, break up, divorce, remarry, and so on.

In short, the economic calculus surrounding marriage has changed. Yet women continue to bear the heaviest responsibilities associated with child care, so they have to choose wisely and well. The reasons

for this are clear in the work of the British pioneer mentioned earlier, Ann Oakley. Her landmark book, *The Sociology of Housework*
(1974), was the first to consider housework as work (since men rarely
did housework, they failed to consider it an important topic). And
given the unpaid status of housework, male sociologists and economists had ignored its contribution to the economy.

Oakley's research is based on a small sample of working-class and
middle-class homemakers. Social class, in her sample, makes little
difference: both middle-class and working-class women report similar (negative) attitudes about housework and a similar (high degree
of) identification with their role. For both middle-class and working-
class women, housework is unpleasant. But in spite of this dislike,
the role of homemaker is central to the identity of many informants;
their social identities are intimately bound up with it. Most women
report a dissatisfying monotony, isolation, and low social status of
homemaking, especially compared (sometimes) with prior higher-
status occupations.

Oakley concludes that women are both disempowered and imprisoned by their beliefs about the proper role of women, and especially of
mothers, in a modern society. Despite their unhappiness, they feel obliged
to play a fundamentally alienating and frustrating role. They are socialized by a patriarchal gender ideology into accepting servitude in marriage
and motherhood. Housework is the visible symbol of this submission.

Oakley has strong views on this topic. Here are a few of her more
pointed observations about marriage as a gendered institution:

- Society has a tremendous stake in insisting on a woman's
  natural fitness for the career of mother: the alternatives are
  all too expensive.
- Families are nothing other than the idolatry of duty.
- Housework is work directly opposed to the possibility of
  human self-actualization.

- If love means that one person absorbs the other, then no real relationship exists anymore. Love evaporates; there is nothing left to love. The integrity of self is gone.
- There are always women who will take men on their own terms. If I were a man, I wouldn't bother to change while there are women like that around.

In a 1977 review of the book, Judith Hammond claimed that Oakley "narrowed and distorted the picture of housewifery into that of a thankless joyless task." Perhaps. However, Oakley has openly and forthrightly called our attention to the neglected topic of housework. We are now more aware of its relation to gender inequality and to the need for sensitive qualitative methods to explore this problem.

ABUSE AND VIOLENCE

By far the most telling evidence of continued conflict and dissension between the sexes is the ample evidence of woman abuse by men. This abuse, which occurs in various forms—physical, mental, sexual, and financial—takes place in every form of cross-sex relationship: dating, cohabitation, marriage, separation, and after divorce. Even total strangers attack, molest, and sexually assault women. Men use guns, knives, fists, and other weapons in attacks.

By contrast, women seldom abuse men in any of these ways and rarely do so as severely as men. If anything, they are more likely to resort to mild physical abuse, verbal abuse, or emotional abuse. And their motives are usually different. Men are far more likely to murder their wives than women are to murder their husbands. Men typically resort to murdering their wives (or lovers, or ex-wives) in order to secure and preserve control, to deny these women liberty or intimate relations with other men. By contrast, women typically murder their spouses only in self-defence or to free themselves from continued control and abuse.

This is not to argue that men are devils and women saints. It is, however, to point out that intimate relations between men and women remain a battleground. Abuse and violence are commonplace, and we are still finding out just how common they really are. We don't have a long history of reliable statistics—perhaps, little more than twenty years' worth—so we don't know (for example) whether recent increases in reported violence prove increases in violence or increases in reporting.

Dangers of abuse and violence are greater in some societies and communities than in others. According to cross-national comparative research by sociologist Rosemary Gartner, typically the risks of femicide—the murder of women—are greatest in societies that are, or have been, deeply religious and patriarchal (that is, male dominant). It seems likely that the transition from stable male dominance to gender equality unleashes male violence, given the uncertainty associated with status loss. In Canada, the same dynamics lead to greater risks of abuse and violence in some ethnocultural communities than in others. With assimilation and education, along with continued vigilance and law enforcement, these group differences disappear.

Of course, it may be that men in patriarchal societies are the most abusive of all, and that they beat their wives and children regularly. This is suggested by recent research on publicly reported suicide attempts in Afghanistan; there, many women have set fire to themselves in effort to call attention to their unacceptably vulnerable status.

The point here is that because of the continuing inequality between men and women in many families, communities, groups, and societies, and because of the dramatic social changes in the recent past, some women run daily risks of violence and abuse. Of course, violence between men—intra-sex violence—is (probably) more common than inter-sex violence (between men and women). However, in our society, there is far more inter-sex violence and abuse than there is violence that is interracial or inter-regional or inter-religious or inter-ethnic or inter-class. This marks out gender as an especially important topic when we try to discover how people can live together.

Undesirable Outcomes

As we have seen, people's lives are strongly gendered in our own society and in others. This fact shows itself in various undesirable outcomes associated with all inequality, conflict, and violence.

UNHAPPINESS, DEPRESSION, AND ANXIETY

Researchers have found a widespread tendency to unhappiness, depression, and anxiety among women. Since measures of depression (in particular) are well standardized in socio-medical research, it is possible to argue confidently that other things being equal women are far more likely to be depressed than men.

Of course, this finding is more complex than it seems at first. All things are never "equal," though researchers make every statistical effort to take all the relevant variables into account. Beyond that, the meaning of the finding remains elusive. Are women in some way more physiologically or hormonally prone to depression? That is, would they still be more depressed than men even in Heaven, even in the Garden of Eden, even if they were leading perfect, stress-free lives? We don't know.

On the other hand, we do know that women and men lead different and unequal lives, with women (still) below men, on average. So it may be that women are more depressed because they lead more depressing lives. If men led the lives that women lead, they might be just as (or more) depressed than women. For example, if men experienced the same prejudice, discrimination, underpayment, objectification, exclusion, and abuse—perhaps then they would be equally depressed.

We cannot run the social experiment that would answer this question. That said, we have yet to see proof that women are becoming less depressed as their lives equalize with men's, although there is some suggestive evidence. For example, even women who are time-crunched (in demanding careers they love, with responsibilities to families they love) tend to be happier than women without careers and time-crunch. So although there are some apparent obstacles like the career woman's double day of work and home responsibilities, this does not necessarily result in depression if the woman has chosen and continues to choose this life.

We do know, however, that men and women are socialized differently: women are taught to internalize their problems in the form of anxiety and depression, and men to externalize them in the form of outward aggression or violence.

As well, people are happiest and least depressed about lives that they have chosen freely and can freely leave if their desires change. For various reasons, women still have less choice in these matters than men do. This in large part is because women continue to bear children and assume the main responsibilities for raising them. If they divorce, women typically take on the role of custodial parent, and they suffer a severe decline in income and living standards. If we leave children out of the picture, and imagine comparing a highly educated woman to a highly educated man, it seems likely both will have a lot of choice and, as a result, a lot of happiness with little depression.

POOR PHYSICAL HEALTH

Minds are located in bodies; nowadays we believe that there is less separation between mind and body than early philosophers did. This means, among other things, that mental distress—unhappiness, depression, and anxiety—will often cause, mirror, or result from physical distress. Though mental and physical health are analytically separate, they are closely interconnected.

This fact makes itself evident in diseases that are partly psychosomatic; for instance, some diseases have physical signs and strong links to underlying mental conditions. An example is irritable bowel syndrome. Another would be intestinal ulcers or even the common cold. Far more complex is the problem of pain. We know far too little about the reasons people experience pain. Sometimes there is no clear physical cause for pain, and sometimes the extent of pain suffered is not correlated with what is expected for a given ailment. Often the experience and expression of pain varies between men and women and among different ethnic or cultural groups.

We do know that people's experience of a physical illness is often intensified by their sense that they are failing to fulfill their socially mandated roles. For example, research on chronic back pain shows women are likely to feel guilty and distressed by their inability to fulfill their domestic and parental duties. Equally, men disabled by severe back pain are likely to feel guilty and distressed by their inability to earn a steady income and perform their sexual duties.

CRIMES

The most interesting single fact about crime is that it is heavily gendered. Men, and especially young men, are far more likely than anyone else to commit crimes. For that matter, they are far more likely than anyone else to take dangerous risks: to drink to excess, drive wildly, or demand unsafe sex, for example. They are also far more likely to pick a fight, according to published assault statistics.

What makes this interesting is that men are far more likely than women to behave like many of the people sociologist Robert Merton described in his theory of "adaptations to anomie," discussed earlier. In particular, men are more likely to externalize frustration, behaving like so-called innovators: people who seek new and usually unacceptable, antisocial ways of gaining our culture's success goals. They are also more likely to take on the role of "rebel," who (according to Merton) rejects both the culture's goals and accepted means for gaining them. Women, by contrast, are more likely to choose other non-criminal "adaptations" like ritualism and retreatism. That is, they are less likely to directly break society's rules and more likely to internalize their disappointment and frustration. "Ritualists" are zombie-like in their continued adherence to rules and activities that no longer have any meaning for them personally. "Retreatists" are people who, one way or another, drop out of life as hermits, drug or alcohol addicts, or home-less people, for example.

It will be interesting to see, as child-bearing continues to decline and women have increasing access to education and better jobs—in effect, taking on roles traditionally occupied by men—whether women also take on male styles of "adapting" to anomic, becoming more criminal and more masculine in their criminality. A surge in murders by women will be the last and strongest indicator that we have arrived at gender equality in our society.

ADDICTIONS

We might expect women to have far higher rates of drug and alcohol abuse than men, since as we have seen, they are far less likely than men to "act out" and far more likely to internalize their distress. Certainly, the evidence supports this expectation with clear signs of gendered dif-ferences in depression and suicidal thinking.

Yet much of the research on addictions, especially on drug and alco-hol abuse, shows that women are much less likely than men to self-medicate with these substances. They are also much less likely than men to go out drinking with same-sex friends, drink until drunk, and act drunkenly in public places. What's more, they are less likely to be diagnosed by doctors as having a substance abuse problem.

A recent analysis of American data (the 1997–2004 National Ambulatory Medical Care Survey) collected during visits to the doctor for other reasons found a substance abuse diagnosis was recorded in 0.9 percent of general and family practice visits, 0.8 percent of internal medicine visits, and 5.1 percent of psychiatry visits. Statistical analysis revealed, other things being equal, that women were less likely than men to be given a substance abuse diagnosis.

However, researchers Jim E. Banta and Susanne Montgomery go on to conclude that more research is needed on the diagnosis of drug and alcohol abuse issues. For one thing, female addicts suffer more social stigmatization than male addicts, so they take more effort to hide their addiction. Doctors may also be less likely or willing to recognize signs of substance abuse in women patients. As well, alcohol and other drugs work differently on men and women. Women develop long-term (physical) complications of alcohol dependence more rapidly than alcoholic men. Women also have a higher mortality rate from alcoholism than men, even if they drink less to achieve this.

Finally, it seems likely that substance abuse is more gendered for some groups than it is for others. It may be useful to think about the externalizing/internalizing difference between men and women as a difference in blaming. Other things being equal, men tend to blame others for their misfortunes while women tend to blame themselves; so under adversity men produce more aggression while women experience more guilt and shame. But in some groups women are less likely to blame themselves for misfortune; they are more likely to (justly) blame others. It's worth noting that in some groups, women may be relatively more successful than men, and therefore less inclined to humble themselves or feel guilt and shame at all.

These factors may account for the 2006 findings by Sarah Rosenfield, Julie Phillips, and Helene White that African-American adolescent women are much less likely than white adolescent women to internalize their problems. In short, gender differences are complex; they interact with race, class, culture, and personal psychology in ways too numerous to treat lightly, though we are still speculating about the reasons.

The biggest difference between men and women, sociologically speaking, is the imbalance in power within families and in society more generally. This includes, most importantly, economic power.

Women with children often stay with their husbands—they can't afford to leave—even under miserable, abusive conditions. Single-parent, female-led families are likely to live in poverty. Society has always been this way. True, more women work outside the home now. But for most working-class women, outside work just means increased burdens. The husband/father has historically been "the boss," and still is, often because he enjoys the larger income and does not have custody of (and responsibility for) the children. Middle-class, better-educated women have more choices, of course. Most of them choose to have one or two children, and if possible, to have a career as well, perhaps with the help of a nanny. They are the best able of all women to live independently, if need be.

Pat and Hugh Armstrong may have struck the right note when they coined the term "double ghetto" to describe the condition of ordinary Canadian women today. The title of their 1978 book implies that modern Canadian women lead captive, isolated lives. What's more, it suggests that women live not in a single ghetto but in two ghettos at once. Often the work women do is socially invisible, making it all the harder for people to recognize the segregation of women's work. At work they occupy a women's ghetto, often of "pink collar jobs." In offices, factories, and shops, they face job segregation at low rates of pay. The second ghetto is unpaid, low-status work at home. Here they are metaphorically locked into domestic servitude.

Why are women forced to occupy separated, largely invisible workspaces both at home and in the paid-work sector, and what, if anything, is the connection between these two kinds of segregation? The sociologist's job is to answer those questions, and we will consider them further in the next chapter.

FOUR

Age Groups

Age usually interests old people the most. That's no surprise—they've aged the most. In recent decades, our society as a whole has aged rapidly, a fact that not only holds important implications for the nature and structure of society, but which has created a surge of interest in the study of aging and age groups. At the same time, interest in the study of young people has also intensified, at least in part because of their increasingly important role as consumers.

The study of age groups has had a fluctuating history in sociology. An early twentieth-century sociologist, Karl Mannheim, wrote an important article entitled "The Problem of Generations" (1928) on the importance of generations and generational differences in society. Mannheim argued that generation is a social location—like gender—that has the same potential to affect people's consciousness as social class. In his words, "individuals . . . who share the same year of birth, are endowed, to that extent, with a common location in the historical dimension of the social process" (*Essays on the Sociology of Knowledge*, 105).

Members of each generation, beginning around the age of seventeen, experience society differently from older generations. Their consciousness begins to shift visibly, as they come to rely less on the appropriated memories that they have learned from their parents' generation, to memories they acquired themselves, through first-hand experience. These first-hand memories are much more powerful. Of course, not all members of a generation have the same experiences or interpret their experiences in the same way. They form subgroups that Mannheim calls "generation units." These generation units might, for example, be differentiated by gender or class.

Nonetheless, they share certain common features—a common generational consciousness that comes to include beliefs, experiences, songs, and a variety of cultural heroes and villains that become the "basis of continuing practice." Or, in other words, they become the generation's own cultural storehouse, out of which they cobble a distinctive language and way of thinking. This often gives rise to youthful activism, as generational consciousness comes to challenge childhood socialization and young people challenge the authority of their parents and teachers. Sometimes, as a result, generation units may even mobilize as a political force for social change.

Not surprisingly, in the 1960s interest in age as a sociological issue revived with the rise of youth protest movements in the US and Canada, Western Europe, and Latin America. Israeli sociologist S.N. Eisenstadt and US sociologist S.M. Lipset wrote a series of important books about youth protest. For a time, an interest in youth culture increased; it continues today but has quieted significantly.

Far more important has been the rise of interest in gerontology—that is, in older age groups and, generally, in the aging of Western societies. Ironically, this interest does not derive from the increasing importance of older people in our societies; in general, older people have become *less* important. Advanced age is no longer valued as it once was when older people were rare and regarded as fonts of wisdom. On the contrary, aging today is of interest because it poses new problems in families, workplaces, and health care systems. Put simply, older people are (often) economically dependent, and there are more of them now (both in absolute terms and as a percentage of the total population) than ever before, thus begging the question: how can we support so many of them? Even as the number of youthful dependants (infants and children) has fallen, the number of aged dependants has exploded. Complicating matters, aged dependants are more expensive to maintain than the young, and they now live longer than in the past.

The reasons for this have been understood for decades, and indeed this crisis of aging could have been foreseen. For forty or fifty years, European economists have been asking how it would be possible in the future to fund public old-age pension schemes, given that payments to retirees largely depend on the contributions of current workers. This is a problem in view of the continuing decline in the number of younger workers and increase in the number of retirees. Why are there ever fewer young workers and ever more elders? Demographers have long understood the answer to this question. The average age of a population increases for two main reasons. First (and least important), a population ages because, even in less developed societies, people live longer—thanks to better nutrition and public health measures. Life expectancy increases for everyone, from the wealthy to the most vulnerable members of society—the aged, the sick or disabled, the very young, and the poor. These increases are more dramatic in more developed societies than in less developed ones, and among rich people in those societies.

Far more important in this age transition is the worldwide shift to lower fertility. The average age of a population goes up when fewer babies are born; so, as worldwide fertility has fallen from levels of six, seven, or eight babies per mother in many populations a century ago to two or three babies per mother today, all populations have grown older. Today, most Western industrial populations are reproducing at below replacement levels. This means that fewer babies are being born than are needed to replace their parents. In turn, the result is that the populations of these societies are gradually shrinking. Were it not for immigration from less-developed, often higher-fertility countries, these societies could look forward to complete extinction within foreseeable centuries. This is certainly the case in Canada, where current fertility rates among native-born people are well below replacement levels. (It is only immigration, and the relatively high fertility of new Canadians, that keeps our population growing.)

This decline in fertility and gradual aging, masked by high rates of immigration, has been taking place in North America for nearly two hundred years, and certainly has been in full swing for over a century. Our seemingly sudden awareness of population aging and the rapidly growing number of old people should shock us out of complacency. It affirms that most of us, most of the time, pay attention only to our own lives and the immediate present. This is another reason why social science is needed: to call attention to the bigger picture and larger, inevitable trends. The big picture is that our society is getting older and there are ever more aged individuals around.

Yet the relations between old people, middle-aged people, and young people remain problematic. Each group occupies its own social and cultural sphere, largely preoccupied with immediate concerns and problems. Old people are often focused on health issues and finding a new purpose in life following retirement from paid work. Middle-aged people are largely concerned with marriage, careers, paying the bills, and providing care for children and aging parents. Young people are largely concerned with finding their personal identity and life goals, enduring an ever-lengthening period of education and economic dependency, and weathering conflict with their parents and peers. No group has a clear sense of what the other group is all about, nor (given its own concerns) a strong motivation to find out. As a result, each group often complains about and resents the other.

Perhaps this has always been the way. Parents have seemingly always complained that their children do not constitute as "good" a generation as they did: they are not as moral, hardworking, serious, respectful, and so on. Jokes abound about parents describing their own sufferings as children—how they had to walk many miles through the snow, shoeless, to the nearest unheated schoolhouse, so they could gain the crumbs of knowledge that would eventually feed and clothe their own ungrateful children. This kind of posturing illustrates the general principle that all groups see the world through their own eyes, eyes informed by their own unique histories. They have less ability to see the world through other people's eyes. Moreover, all groups have a tendency to aggrandize themselves and their histories, at the expense of other groups with whom they are in competition. And parents and children have always been in competition for control over the household. In the 1960s, with the baby boomers coming of age, this competition exploded, and as a result, these two groups also came into competition over the political domain.

Sociologists have sometimes pointed out the interesting fact that age groups form alliances based on mutual opposition to a common enemy. Often grandparents and grandchildren can form a stronger bond than parents and children, precisely because they share the middle-aged (parents) as a common enemy. This is not always the case, but it is often so. What it means is that the social and cultural distance between age groups is not linear, a simple function of the number of years separating one group (or individual) from another. It reflects alliances and coalitions that may cross age lines.

The dominant fact remains that as children have become rarer and old people more common, the balance of power in societies has changed. More specifically, the flow of resources between age groups has changed. In most societies throughout human history, social resources—wealth, respect, obedience—flowed upward from the young to the old. The implicit social contract read as follows: young people will serve the old; if and when they survive to be old themselves, the next crop of young will serve them in turn. Today, the social contract reads something a little more like this: parents will serve their children; when they become parents themselves, these children will return the favour. They will pay forward wealth, respect, and obedience to their own children.

Of course, this oversimplifies the demographic changes that have taken place. Some parents are far less willing than others to follow this agenda. Some ethnocultural groups resist the transformation with particular alacrity, remaining "traditional" in their views. But even so, the evidence of this transformation can be seen everywhere. First, it is amply evident that young people are no longer a source of benefits for their elders. Prolonged formal education makes this impossible, not just unlikely. On the other hand, young people are no longer as dependent on their parents, or their extended families, for economic or other benefits. For this and other reasons, young people no longer accept arranged marriages. They tend to marry who they want, whether it benefits the family or not. Likewise, they choose their own jobs and careers as they wish. Families can no longer deliver jobs and careers as they once did, so parents can no longer demand compliance with family wishes.

Second, there is what some have called the "flight from parenthood." The single most important reason for the worldwide reduction in fertility is that parenthood has become a net cost, not a net benefit. It costs too much to raise children and the benefits of parenthood are mainly psychological. There are unlikely to be gains in wealth, respect, or obedience from bearing any children, let alone many children. There are also few economies of scale in child-bearing today: when everyone needs a university education to succeed, it is *not* "cheaper by the dozen." Middle-aged people have good reason to put less time, effort, and money into raising children and more into other psychosocial and economic investments.

Age relations in our society continue to be in flux. These changes are among the most difficult to navigate for new immigrant groups from traditional, high-fertility societies, societies which continue to embrace time-honoured notions of age relations. In a country like Canada, with many recent immigrants from many countries, it is difficult to speak simply about this change—more difficult than it would be in a culturally homogeneous advanced society like, say, Sweden, the Netherlands, or Austria.

One more general point needs to be made about age relations: very few men will ever become women, or vice versa. Almost no dark-skinned people will ever become, or be taken for, light-skinned people. And relatively few people born into very poor families will end their lives being very rich. There is a tendency in societies—even in relatively open, high-mobility societies like our own—for people to stay put, socially. But everyone who is old today was once young, and everyone who is young today will eventually be old if they just keep on breathing. So age relations represent one area of life where people attempt to bridge their differences where they share common experiences, or can expect to do so.

This adds an important dimension to the piquancy and personal relevance of cross-age relations for everyone, at every age.

Opportunities for Co-operation across the Line

As with cross-sex relations, our first experiences with cross-age relations are as children in the family home. We learn about older people by observing our older siblings and cousins, our parents, aunts, and uncles. We learn about "old people" from our grandparents, our great-uncles, and great-aunts. And, as we age, we learn about younger people from younger brothers and sisters.

Most of us have trouble remembering the first time we actively thought about what it meant to be young or old, younger or older. My own first memory, if it is a valid one, is of playing under the old iron stove in my grandmother's kitchen—perhaps reaching under it to retrieve a toy that had rolled there—and bumping my head. I must have been very young to have done this, possibly one or two years old. But that is probably the kind of thing we first learn about age: when you are young, you are small, and when you are small there are advantages and disadvantages. Among the advantages, you can go places that (larger) adults cannot.

Sometimes when you are young those around you are adoring, as were my grandparents. I recall how on Friday nights my grandparents' friends came over to play cards on the dining room table. With my parents out for the evening, I was permitted to witness this social activity and, when sleepy, to pass out on the prickly horsehair couch in the living room. This was my first discovery of many important facts: of the different social lives of old people and young people, the different rules applied by parents and grandparents, and the flow of respect and affection downward, from old to young, for example. As the oldest grandchild, I was an ornament to the family, a source of pride and aspiration, an investment in the family future. This gave me the best possible opportunity to watch "the show."

Yet we also recall that with small size came powerlessness, and this may be the most central fact about infancy, childhood, and youth: the young do not make those rules that demand their obedience. As children, we enter a world that is not of our creation, and that we can scarcely understand. The people in charge are older, bigger, savvier, and often more devious. This understanding is perhaps the most important remaining insight of traditional psychoanalysis and Freudian psychology, an insight emphasized in particular by the American psychoanalyst Alfred Adler. Many if not most of the traumas we experience in childhood, traumas that more often than not shape our personalities and our future lives, occur because we are small and powerless. Because of our size and naïveté, as children we are easily victimized and easily terrorized, even if this happens inadvertently.

This is not to say that children have no influence over their parents and other older people; to suggest otherwise would be clearly false and would also contradict the theory of resource flow described above. Children have enormous influence over their parents, and vice versa. But parents have the benefit of size and power. Children, like other disadvantaged groups, have greater powers of resistance. Without other important obligations (the need to hold a job, clean the house, or pay the mortgage, for example) they have a clear opportunity to employ terrorist tactics, using chaos, noise, and subversion to their advantage. This is the way of all disempowered groups in society: a lack of overt power leads to agency, and often the tactics that spring from this are

effective. These terrorist methods are frequently successful in forcing the larger, savvier parents to make treaties, to give in to children's
wishes in return for temporary peace and tranquility.

As well, parents are terrified by the prospects of parental failure,
blame, and guilt. Besides love for their children, they feel a responsibility to raise them well and prepare them for life. They feel obliged to
ensure their children do well at school, are healthy, make friends, and
stay out of trouble with the law. They don't want to fail at these tasks,
feel like failures, or stand accused of failure. So they make strategic
deals that, while keeping the peace, will raise the likelihood a child
develops as well as the experts say should be expected.

In every household, then, there is the basis for an implicit deal
between parents and young children. To some degree, the same
dynamic applies between grown children and their aged parents. In
addition to love, grown children feel a responsibility to help and care
for their increasingly dependent and infirm parents. Like children,
elderly parents sometimes capitalize on guilt and shame to encourage
greater efforts (for example, more frequent visits and telephone calls).
However, mostly, older parents are less likely to use terror tactics with
their grown children than are young children with their parents. As
dependants, elderly parents are generally more tractable than young
children, for several reasons.

First, elderly parents often enjoy independent lives they don't want
to relinquish. Second, they may have their own resources and neither
need nor expect support, including obedience or money, from their
grown children. (In fact, some elder generations, such as that born and
raised during the Depression, may even be a source of support for their
grown baby boomer children.) Third, and perhaps most important,
unlike young children elderly parents have already experienced what
it means to be a middle-aged parent, squeezed by young children at
one end and aging parents at the other. As a result, they may be more
capable of empathy and self-restraint than children, who have (so far)
experienced almost nothing.

Other opportunities for cross-age co-operation are encountered at school and, later, in the workplace. At school, children are introduced to other children older and younger than themselves. They experience bullying, for example, both as victim and perpetrator, often across age lines. More important, the age distinction is associated (once again) with authority: teachers are old, pupils are young. Old people give out the homework and dole out the rewards and punishments. Young people must do the homework, gain the rewards, and avoid the punishments.

Workplaces exhibit something of the same dynamic as schools. In most workplaces, seniority and rank are closely connected; this means that age and rank (and also authority and power) are closely related. In turn, younger workers often have to take orders and punishments from older ones, with the assumption implicit that when they are more senior they will dole out their own orders and punishments to new and younger workers. Of course, the match between age and rank is less exact in workplaces than it is in families, or even in schools. In workplaces, some people fall behind, failing to advance with seniority for various reasons (incompetence, discrimination, or the enmity of superiors, for example). More important, some classes of worker are younger at every stage than other classes of worker. For example, an organization may have a relatively stable and therefore old secretarial or administrative staff but a professional (e.g., engineering or legal) staff that constantly turns over. As a result, relatively young engineers or lawyers will often be interacting with older secretaries and administrators.

This of course poses a classic problem in social organization: the problem of respect for age (and presumed experience) versus respect for expertise. How should the respectful young lawyer or engineer relate to the supposedly less powerful, but older, more experienced and savvy secretary or administrator? It is a well-known fact that people do well to cultivate subordinates with inside information, even if they hold positions of nominally low authority in the organization. People who foolishly ignore this rule of thumb often find themselves organizationally blindsided by misinformation or false information, rumours or gossip, their careers derailed or at least slowed down by a failure to take this age- and authority-related struggle into account.

The most interesting example of this problem is found in a classic book by Francis Ianni entitled *A Family Business*, an ethnographic study of an American crime family. In organized crime, success means millions of dollars in revenue and failure can mean death, so members of "the family" are keenly aware of organizational problems related to authority and succession. For example, should they take advice from nephew Donny, the bright young whippersnapper with an economics degree from MIT but little experience or standing in the family? Or should they listen to Uncle Vito, the high-ranking capo, not too bright but a tough, responsible, and reliable leader in times past? True, it's Vito's "time" to rule, but clearly Donny has more up-to-date ideas about marketing, competition, and legitimate business. What to do? Follow age or not?

Forces Pushing People Apart

EVIDENCE OF CONFLICT: INTRODUCTION

Whether we talk about families, schools, organizations, or total societies, there are ample opportunities for co-operation across age lines and, in fact, deep needs for such co-operation. But at the same time there are also difficulties in securing co-operation, some of which we have already considered; others are discussed below.

The place to start is by noting that age relations, like cross-sex relations, present a mixed, messy, and rapidly changing picture. We saw that the age structure of Western societies has been changing for well over a century. This orderly movement toward more old people and fewer young has been interrupted in only two ways. First, the baby boom (roughly between 1947 and 1967) unleashed a surge of child-bearing which had previously been held in check by the Great

Depression and World War II. There is some evidence that during the baby boom many people who were flush with prosperity returned briefly to higher fertility norms—that is, choosing to have larger families. This is what Thomas Malthus warned about in 1800: people will sometimes consume their material bounty by producing more children, with the result that they remain at or near the same level of material well-being, despite opportunities for improvement.

Second, gradual movement toward an aging and aged society has been slowed and masked by high rates of immigration. Large numbers of young men and women of child-bearing ages, and young families, have entered the country. What's more, many of these are groups of people with higher fertility norms; for a range of cultural and religious reasons, these groups continue to hold higher-than-replacement child-bearing desires. They largely put into practice these desires when economic opportunities permit, just as Malthus predicted.

On balance, then, it seems that the effects of immigration have masked or temporarily offset the long-term effects of aging. We have remained a younger society, but only for a time. Now, with the rapid assimilation of immigrants and clear evidence that many will face restricted economic opportunities, there has been a "Baby Bust." The proportion of old people is rising rapidly in many parts of the country, especially in regions with the lowest rates of foreign immigration and highest rates of youthful out-migration: for example, in small towns and rural areas, especially in the Maritimes, Manitoba, and Saskatchewan. Conversely, other areas continue to draw high numbers of young people. The frontier areas of northern Alberta, the Yukon, and the Northwest Territories enjoy both relatively high rates of (Aboriginal) fertility and high rates of youthful immigration for resource-related jobs, for example.

In short, while the picture of age relations is mixed and messy, we are able to discern the general outlines of change. We can also see similar changes in other countries that have previously passed through a comparable age transition, and passed through it more completely than Canada has: think of regions such as Northern and Western Europe, where there are long histories of fertility decline and low immigration. Looking closely at demographic change in these countries also helps to prepare us for the problems ahead.

Segregation or Distance

People of different age groups often have their own age-specific activities. When I was a toddler foraging under the stove for lost toys, my grandparents played cards for a penny a point. We could not have exchanged roles, nor did we want to. The question of sociological interest is not whether people of different ages typically have different activities. Rather, it is how the differentiation of social activities and cultural norms by age is becoming stronger or weaker, more or less institutionalized, more or less competitive in our society. Here, the evidence is mixed.

Let's take a running leap into the evidence by going back to the Middle Ages with French historian Philippe Ariès. Using a variety of historical materials that include paintings, literature, diaries, and other sources, Ariès argues that "childhood" as we understand it is a cultural invention. It does not exist naturally: it was invented in late Medieval Europe and perfected in industrial times. It had the effect of segregating children from adults; no longer were young people, say under age ten, to be viewed as proto-adults with "adult-like" tasks to perform in the home and workplace. Now they were to be viewed as somewhat different kinds of beings, with pre-adult developmental needs to fulfill before they could enter adult life.

Over the course of the modern era, children became segregated from adult society for ever-longer periods of formal education. Today formal education can take as long as fifteen to twenty-five years, and we may not have seen the end of this increase. Yet, five hundred years ago, only the very wealthy could afford the luxury of educating their children. Everyone else continued to treat their offspring as proto-adults, with important economic or domestic roles in the family. With the rise of mandatory public education in the nineteenth century, all families were forced to give up their children for at least some part of their youth to this developmental, educational task. Since then, as the paid workforce has required ever more literate and better-educated workers, formal education has increased in length and complexity. In effect this has extended the period of "cultural childhood": or, to look at it in different terms, the period of non-adulthood—and some version of social marginality and economic dependence—has become increasingly longer.

In the late nineteenth and early twentieth centuries, a new cultural label was devised to cover this new life stage: adolescence. One might argue that the stage itself (like childhood before it) was also invented, though it does correspond with certain important, visible changes that distinguish young children from older ones: notably, hormonal changes (including menstruation for girls and increased sexual attraction for both sexes) and the emergence of secondary sexual characteristics (e.g., breasts on girls, facial hair on boys). Some believed that adolescence also brought with it a greater emotional volatility than was normally witnessed in young children. Such volatility may have been a secondary result of rapid physical growth, hormonal change, new sexual interest, issues of sexual embarrassment and confusion, and prolonged economic dependency.

The point here is that childhood and adolescence became clearly segregated from adulthood when permitted by economic growth and required by formal education. The same can likely be said about the segregation of old people from the middle-aged. In societies where people lived shorter lives on average, few had to cope with life much beyond the age of sixty. Those who survived and were healthy continued to participate fully in family and economic life, especially in rural areas characterized by extended family formations. Those who were infirm sat by the fire and watched. It was only in the nineteenth century, with industrialization, urbanization, and unionization, that the current practices of paid "retirement" came into effect. People over sixty or sixty-five were encouraged and helped to retire from paid work, to start a new phase of life. As their financial status improved, their desires to lead a life full of leisure and live among other same-aged retired people were actualized.

However, this ability of older people to lead separate, different, ful-filling lives—away from family members and young people, sometimes even in gated communities or hotels restricted to seniors—was predi-cated on a high level of economic prosperity. Any society, family, or individual had to be able to afford such unpaid seclusion and relative luxury for elders.

Today, as we pass into a new period of economic recession, global competition, and large-scale aging, it may no longer be possible to afford retirement and lengthy dependence at the upper end of the age scale. So the segregation of healthy old people from the rest of society may not persist, because it is not socially useful except insofar as retire-ment vacates jobs needed by younger people. That said, the segregation of healthy young people from the rest of society is bound to persist, because higher education adds to the "economic capital," long-term productivity, and competitiveness of society.

PREJUDICE AND DISCRIMINATION

"Ageism" is a word invented to connect with the more familiar con-cepts of sexism and racism, and signifies a conflict between age groups in our society. Ageism describes the existence of prejudice or discrimin-ation, chiefly against seniors, but by implication against any members of society on the basis of their age.

It should already be evident why prejudice and discrimination might follow age lines. Historically, age (like sex) has been an important criterion for doling out social advantages and disadvantages. Even in today's workplace it is seniority (i.e., length of time in the organization, or "organizational age") that counts for a great deal in decision-making with regards to promotions and rewards, rather than merit. When people experience disadvantages, or fear disadvantages, they often resort to prejudice and discrimination as a means of balancing the scale, as a kind of moral equivalence.

The result of this is that we do see some evidence of ageism in our society. The most obvious and consequential is job discrimination based on age, a reluctance of many employers to hire older workers, instead choosing younger ones. Some of this discrimination is based on prejudice: for example, an untested and unproven belief that older workers are naturally or necessarily less flexible and adaptable than younger workers or that they possess fewer, less relevant skills (especially in relation to technology). Some such discrimination is based on issues of cost: the employer may think that the older worker, especially if he or she has held a "better job" in the past, will not be willing to accept low pay and limited authority. Equally, an employer may imagine that older workers will cost more in lost days of sickness, or that the investment in training will be lost more quickly since the older worker may soon retire. Or employers may believe that younger workers with the prospect of long career advancement ahead in return for present compliance may be more obedient and loyal than older workers.

These are all little more than unfounded prejudices; although they sound sensible and may contain a grain of truth, there is little evidence to support them. What's more, counter-arguments could be offered in every instance. For example, since they are more socially vulnerable, older workers may prove to be more loyal and grateful than younger ones, and therefore, more compliant.

At the other end of the age continuum, we encounter other prejudices and other kinds of discrimination. Young people in our society also experience many social disadvantages because of prejudice. For example, many well-informed young people are kept from voting in elections while many poorly informed older people are permitted to vote. This is partly based on the presumption that old people must be better informed than younger people, perhaps because of their longer experience in society. This might be called the "breathing test" for eligibility: if you have continued breathing for long enough, you are equipped to vote. Or it might be justified by another logic. Older people, however ill-informed, deserve the right to vote because they have paid taxes or participated in society, "paid their dues" so to speak, for long enough.

Similar age-related disabilities apply to young people in a variety of domains: these include legal rights related to ownership, alcohol consumption, and driving. In every instance, a one-size-fits-all age rule applies, regardless of actual measurable competence. If we rule out blind prejudice as the basis for this age-discrimination, we can only conclude that society is unwilling to spend the money needed to devise and apply merit-related testing to people of all ages.

Suspicion and Distrust

"Dirty old man": no accusation a young person might hurl is likely to be as irritating as this one to men over, say, sixty-five (perhaps even over forty) who spent much of their youth pursuing sex with young women. This fact, among many, neatly captures the state of culturally institutionalized suspicion and distrust between age groups.

According to the baby boomers (although most likely recognized even earlier), "sex, drugs, and rock and roll" are the *rightful* preoccupation of young people. When the baby boomers were young themselves, they suggested that perhaps sex, drugs, and rock and roll were the *unique* domain of young people. And there is no denying that youth is often devoted to the pursuit of sensual pleasure to a degree that will never be repeated in other stages of life, for a range of reasons. First, young people are at the peak of their physical energy and sexual powers. What they may lack in experience they make up for in enthusiasm. Second and more important, compared to middle-aged people, young people have more spare time and fewer significant obligations that might stand in the way of sexual pursuits: no spouse or children, no full-time job or career, no mortgage to pay.

This leads to the institutionalized supposition that sexual interest is reserved for young people and that older people with sexual interests are "dirty"—that is, impure, abnormal, perverse, and laughable. More generally, old people are often viewed by young people as less potent (physically, psychologically, or sexually) than they; also, less hip, cool, and "together." This of course is in partial payment for the supposition promoted by parents that young people are less stable, rational, or insightful.

In short, different age groups produce and promote ideas about other age groups that are intentionally hurtful as part of a universal battle for respect and authority. This is, of course, what Karl Mannheim told us in 1928, and it may be especially evident in high schools, where teachers are vilified as representatives of the older generation. Perhaps school boards should provide danger pay to high school teachers.

However, suspicion and distrust between age groups is not only a result of warfare between them. It is also based on genuine generational differences that make it difficult for people of different ages to understand each other. Consider only two examples (likely you can think of many others). First, most people over forty would view with puzzlement the current tendency of young people to use the terms "ho," "slut," "skank," and "bitch" as terms of mere description or even endearment, without any intended disapproval. A generation ago, these terms were rarely used and, if ever, were covered with shame.

Then, at the other end of the age continuum, there is my ninety-five-year-old father and his movie reviews. Most Sundays when we get together, we discuss movies we have recently seen. In general, my father disapproves of current movies, with people forever jumping into bed at the drop of a hat. "There's too much sex and not enough of anything else," he says. "Why don't they make good movies anymore, movies with a social message like *12 Angry Men*?" Or consider his comment on the Woody Allen film *Vicky Cristina Barcelona*. Dad disapproved of the leading male character who was, he said, a "bad family man, married but having affairs and paying no attention to his wife."

This comment falls some distance from what Woody Allen might have been trying to say in his film. (In fact, from one standpoint, it precisely misses Woody's point that, to be fully alive, we humans must follow love and sex wherever they lead us.) But as a man who grew up in the 1910s and 1920s, survived the Depression, and spent his life providing for his wife, children, and other family members, my father does not take this matter lightly. For him, "bad family man" versus "good family man" is a central human issue not to be turned into a joke. Teenagers might not get that; neither, in fact, might Woody Allen.

ABUSE AND VIOLENCE

In recent years, just as we have become more aware of domestic violence against women, we have also become more aware of domestic violence against children as well as elders. In general, any vulnerable individual or group is at risk of violence and abuse, regardless of whether the abuse is physical, verbal, emotional, or sexual. What is especially pernicious about domestic violence against young people *and* old people is that it takes place within the family, a setting that is supposedly committed to love and protection. Child abuse and elder abuse are not only dangerous and hurtful, they are deeply hypocritical.

What sense can we make of such abuse and violence? What is it about? It seems evident that children are most at risk of violence in the same households where women (wives and mothers) are at risk. From this angle, child abuse is part of the package of domestic abuse associated with patriarchal values: the notion that an all-powerful father has the right to punish family members at any time and in any way he deems appropriate. This generalization likely covers many cases, but it does not cover them all. First, mothers are often the family disciplinarians, the source of at least some child abuse. This inconvenient fact is not covered by the theory of patriarchy. Patriarchy or not, it is evident that people who experienced violence and abuse as children are more likely to dole it out as adults.

Second, the patriarchal theory does not explain elder abuse, whether carried out by the husband or wife and administered to an elderly male or female. Here, one possible explanation is that grown children (or grandchildren) abuse their elders as a repayment for the abuse they suffered in their own childhood. As some people say, what goes around comes around. No doubt many grown children harbour continued animosity toward their parents, owing to abuse, neglect, and other hurt they suffered at the parental hand as children. The stewardship of these now-infirm parents provides an opportunity for payback.

A third, more general explanation has to do with caregiver burden. A voluminous literature shows that caring for children or other vulnerable and infirm dependants can be terribly taxing. It can give rise to depression and illness in the caregiver, among other problems. Conceivably, some of the abuse and violence levelled against dependent children and elders is a result of burnout. In this way it can be seen as an irrational, excessive, and entirely unproductive response to unmanageable demands. To say this is not to free the abuser from blame; it is to look for solutions. Most likely, if we as a society have any real desire to help families, we are going to have to help them with their caregiving; this would address the problem of abuse and violence suffered by many vulnerable groups.

In the end, cross-generational violence is a complicated issue about which we know far too little. Clearly it is related to the distribution of power and powerlessness in our society and within families. The way relative powerlessness—regardless if deriving from age, gender, class, or otherwise—translates into abuse requires more research. It is not just sociologists who are grappling with this problem but also social policy–makers.

Undesirable Outcomes

UNHAPPINESS, DEPRESSION, AND ANXIETY

One of the great paradoxes about aging is that although old people are likely to develop depression for mainly biochemical reasons, generally they are happier than young and middle-aged people. If asked, they are more likely than teenagers to say they are satisfied with life.

One might ask what old people have to be so happy about. Or to put the question differently, how can they possibly be happy, given the evidence of prejudice, ridicule, abuse, and loss of social import- ance that we have been discussing? Likewise, what are young people so miserable about? How can they be so unhappy, given their physical health and all the sexual, educational, and career opportunities that await them? The answer is so simple as to be (almost) overlooked: how happy you are is a function of where you set your expectations. With sufficiently low expectations, you can be happy with almost anything. And a long life gives people plenty of time, and ample experience, in lowering their expectations.

Perhaps equally important, seniors today as a group are far more economically secure than seniors in the past. If they compare their own lives with those of their parents and grandparents, they are likely to feel happy, even blessed.

The result of this is that unhappiness, anxiety, and depression may not be good indicators of an age-relations problem for old people. However, unhappiness, anxiety, depression, and even suicide may reflect the many pressures young people face in our society. These prob- lems are related to the difficulty of transitioning from dependence to independence, childhood to adulthood. These are not primarily problems of ageism or age-related mistreatment by parents and other elders. They do, however, reflect the difficulties young people face in meeting the huge pressures on them to succeed and to make their parents proud.

POOR PHYSICAL HEALTH

Poor physical health may provide a better indicator of faulty age relations. Just as young and old family members suffer risks of domestic violence, they also suffer risks of domestic neglect, including poor nutrition, poor supervision, poor preventive health care, and poor compliance with medical advice. These forms of health negligence often translate into poor health for young and old family members, though they may also affect other members of the family who are old enough to know better.

Accidents are another source of poor health. Some families are much more accident-prone than others. This usually results from a lack of parental supervision, which in turn may reflect too many competing demands on the parents' time—a common problem particularly in single-parent families. Faulty supervision may also reflect other problems, such as parental addiction or depression. Finally, higher risks of accidents may reflect residence in a particular dangerous household, neighbourhood, or community; this tends to reflect income and class disadvantages.

So like unhappiness and depression, poor physical health is a poor indicator of faulty age-relations, or ageism. These may play a part in producing poor health, but so do many other important factors.

ADDICTIONS AND CRIME

Many people in our society are concerned about addictions, particularly addictions to nicotine, drugs, and alcohol. (Other addictions, for example, to gambling, shopping, eating, or sex, are less common and more poorly understood.) It seems likely that young people are the main users of illicit drugs; middle-aged people are the main users of alcohol; and old people don't use as much of either, relying instead on prescription drugs for an enhancement of well-being. Does the illegal use, or excessive use, of nicotine, recreational drugs, or alcohol reflect an age-related problem?

Much research on young people suggests that early initiation into (and continued use of) cigarettes, drugs, or alcohol typically reflects developmental problems at home, at school, with friends, or otherwise. True, there are also neighbourhood subcultural norms that regulate the use of these substances by adolescents. Usually, drug use by adolescents reflects a combination of peer norms (including opportunities and pressures) and parental failings.

Since the literature on this topic is so similar to the literature on youth crime and delinquency, it makes sense to discuss both together. One of the best understood facts about delinquency is that few of the young people who commit delinquent acts graduate to adult criminality. Likewise, few of the young people who experiment with nicotine, alcohol, and recreational drugs graduate to adult drug addiction. From this we learn that an important transition takes place between youth and adulthood that turns most people away from addiction and crime, whatever tendencies they may have experienced to that point.

A theory propounded by sociologist and criminologist Jackson Toby is that tendencies toward crime and addiction weaken as people develop a "stake in conformity." This happens as they develop and pursue educational and occupational plans, form strong love relationships, and otherwise develop a sense of purpose in their lives. A more general version of this social control theory asserts that we are all inclined to break the rules (whether these are criminal laws or rules about drug use), but we are less likely to break these rules if we give ourselves over to social control. Typically, this social control involves direct relations with significant others. However, it can also mean internalized values based on relations with significant others.

The crimes and misdemeanours of young people, including their abuse of drugs, may indeed be a response to conflicts with parents, teachers, and other adults in authority: a form of acting out or youthful protest. It is also a way young people ingratiate themselves into their peer group, demonstrating rebelliousness and, therefore, worthiness of respect and love.

People today lead longer, more varied and complex lives. There is also reason to think that people lead more idiosyncratic lives from one another today—that there is hardly a normative pattern for the life course anymore. Indeed, with the overall increase in life expectancy, there is almost enough time now for people to lead several lives, with several careers, perhaps even multiple mates and families. Nonetheless, we are still grappling with aging and age-relations. We see decreasing certainty about age-grading and age-related markers: what it means to be twenty or forty or sixty or eighty, for example, or what is proper for a person to do, or not do, at a given age. With advances in assisted fertility, some are now discussing the wisdom and propriety of pregnancy for post-menopausal women and assisted or adoptive parenthood for people over sixty. At the other end of the age continuum, we are wondering when it is time for a child to become financially independent for the last time. How much education is enough? When is child-bearing undertaken at too young an age? When is marriage too soon? And so on.

Though uncertainties remain, and age-categories and boundaries have become blurred, there remains a widespread tendency to link wisdom and authority with age and enthusiasm, and innocence with youth. So long as these folk beliefs persist, age groups will oppose and combat one another, laying claim to merit and legitimacy on these vastly different grounds. And that means the debate will not easily be resolved, if ever. Perhaps all we can realistically hope is that the conflict can be managed and softened.

FIVE

Race and Ethnic Groups

All people look different from one another, but some look more different from the local "average" than others.

These visible differences are a result of our long evolutionary history, and they confer one great advantage: they are an important aid to distinguish among ourselves. Unlike the mass-produced suburban homes that almost invite us to enter and mingle with total strangers, our unique faces discourage indiscriminate interaction. Thanks to these differences, every day we safely navigate our way back to familiars, relying mainly on our eyes (and to some extent our ears and noses).

This happy outcome is largely the result of localized, ingrown gene pools that over many millennia produced what we call racial variations: noticeable differences in skin tone, hair texture, and facial features. But human beings are a migratory species, and given our tendency to move around in recent centuries, we are able to find every racial feature in almost every part of the world. And increasingly we find mixtures of people with different racial features. This has led some people to hope that intermixing will lead to the decline of our species' long and shameful history of racism.

There has been a similar evolution of "ethnic" relations. Unlike races or racial groupings, ethnic groups often have no distinctive visible features. It may be impossible, for example, to distinguish among people whose ancestors originated around the Mediterranean Sea, people of Spanish or Italian or Greek descent, just by looking. Yet we are readily able to distinguish them on other grounds. Among other possible differences, there are a variety of languages and religions. Different groups carry different bodies of national knowledge (about important events, heroes, and wars, for example), and feel an allegiance to different nations, communities, and peoples. Ethnic sentiments are relatively specific: alas, people rarely feel a common allegiance to the human race. But they may feel a cross-national or cross-ethnic religious allegiance, for example, to other Jews, Christians, or Muslims. They may even feel an allegiance to local subgroups: to Sunni or Shiite Arab subgroups, for example, or to Ashkenazic or Sephardic branches of the Israeli population.

That said, these remain—at least from the outside—identifiable ethnic groups. And from the inside they are what historian Benedict Anderson usefully called "imagined communities": groups of people who belong together because they feel they belong together, owing to a shared history and seemingly common fate.

The survival of such imagined communities depends to a degree on the behaviour of outsiders (the same is true, of course, of racially defined communities). Ethnic identification tends to thrive and maintain itself when people are socially isolated and especially when they are (or feel) endangered by outsiders. So to the degree that members of different ethnic ancestries have gone forward as international immigrants to all the countries of the world, ethnic identities have been weakened. Others note that daily news events show such a prospect remains far distant.

The extensive success of the human diaspora has led some groups (such as Jewish people) to fear for the disappearance of their small group through high rates of intermarriage with people of other ancestral groups, as well as low levels of both reproduction and of cultural identification (an example of this would be falling attendance at synagogues and Jewish schools). Other ethnic groups in Canada and elsewhere may be facing a similar fate: think of ongoing anxieties about Ukrainian-, Greek-, or French-Canadian cultures. These may all go the way of Dutch-, Icelandic-, and Australian-Canadian communities, swallowed into the great mass of non-ethnic consumerism that characterizes modern Canadian life.

The study of racial and ethnic relations has a long history in sociology; certainly longer than the study of gender or age groups. First were the studies of religion that made reference to the historic role of religious hatreds throughout much of world history. Many eighteenth- and nineteenth-century proto-sociologists, starting perhaps with Voltaire, noted the role of religion in establishing "imagined communities" and promoting prejudices and wars against one another. Karl Marx was possibly the first sociologist to observe that employers often deployed racist sentiments and fears, for example against Irish Catholic immigrants in England, to split the working class and set workers against one another. In the late nineteenth and early twentieth centuries, Max Weber studied the important role of religion in promoting or dampening the "spirit of capitalism" in various ethnocultural communities: in Calvinist Protestant Northern Europe (where capitalism arose) versus in Roman Catholic Southern Europe, ancient Hindu India, ancient Confucian China, and ancient Hebrew Israel (where it did not).

The specific study of racial and ethnic groups, with less reference to religion, had to await the development of American sociology in the early twentieth century. In that nation of immigrants, ethnic differences were of great interest and social importance. A long string of important studies, starting in 1920 with William Isaac Thomas and Florian Znaniecki's *The Polish Peasant in Europe and America*, traced the difficult course of immigration and assimilation by newcomers to America, and most particularly, to urban America (e.g., Chicago). Thomas and Znaniecki noted especially the radical effects of assimilation on family life, including changed gender relations and age relations. Likewise, the study of race relations was central to the development of American sociology, given that racial oppression and conflict—rooted in a history of slavery—were part of the American cultural psyche. Early works both by sociologists like W.E.B. Du Bois (an African American), as well as by Caucasian sociologists, including Gunnar Myrdal, Swedish author of *An American Dilemma* (1944), plumbed the features and consequences of racism for American society.

In Canada the systematic study of ethnic relations began with a book by the visiting American sociologist Everett Hughes. His book *French Canada in Transition* (1943) clearly pointed out the fault lines in Anglo–French-Canadian relations, fractures that continue to beset Canadian society today. Other community studies followed, but the most important Canadian study directly related ethnicity to social class—John Porter's classic work *The Vertical Mosaic* (1965). More clearly than any American work on ethnicity and race before or since, this book asked how and why ethnicity is related to a group's position in the economic structure. How does ethnicity relate to wealth, power, prestige, and disadvantage? This was an important shift away from anthropological or social psychological perspectives, favoured by US scholarship, to an approach grounded in political economy, on which Porter had carried out graduate work at the London School of Economics.

We cannot understand race and ethnic relations in Canada today unless we understand a little of the history behind these relations. From the sixteenth to the twentieth centuries—and some might say well into the twenty-first century—powerful nations have claimed moral and cultural superiority over others. This alleged superiority has been an excuse or justification for conquest, colonization, or economic and other exploitation. Some would say the same pattern is observable in Iraq today, where Americans, motivated by a need for self-display, oil, and a political foothold in the Middle East, justify their actions by implying that Islam is morally and culturally inferior, evidenced by its alleged support of international terrorism. (Happily, this seems to be changing under the influence of Barack Obama.) However, similar strategies have been used by every other imperial power—British, French, Belgian, Spanish, and Portuguese, to name a few—to justify their own self-interested actions.

This logic of moral and cultural superiority has often been under-written by at least one of the following rationales. First, Christianity, as the supposed "true faith," justified the conquest of all unbelievers. From the Crusades onward, imperialistic Christian rulers claimed that it was the right, if not the duty, of Christians everywhere to defeat the heathens (or "white man's burden") and convert them to Christianity. Second, cultural parochialism and a commitment to nation-building, in addition to advantages in technology, weaponry, and other material achievements, allowed European countries to overwhelm less powerful, "less advanced" civilizations in European national interests. Finally, and perhaps most importantly, an (incorrect) version of Darwinism maintained that imperial successes proved the natural superiority of Western European societies and cultures.

These beliefs were carried to every part of the world as part of the colonial enterprise. Even colonized people sometimes came to believe in these "natural" distinctions, leading to people of comparatively light skin within an overall darker-skinned group enjoying higher status and more power in many former colonies (think here, for example, of Haiti and Colombia). Similar dynamics continue in the mating patterns of American black people today; we will see below how some commenta-tors have seen this as evidence of learned self-hatred.

Relations between all groups in North America have been influ-enced by these beliefs. In Canada, for example, there has been a ten-dency to portray white Anglo-Saxon Protestants ("WASPs") as being at some level superior to white francophone Catholics, white allo-phone Northern Europeans (for example, German immigrants), white allophone Eastern Europeans (for example, Ukrainian immigrants), and white allophone Southern Europeans (usually Catholics, par-ticularly Italian immigrants). All of these, in turn, were preferred to non-Caucasian peoples: Asians such as East Indian or Chinese groups, Africans or West Indians, and Latin Americans. Within this hierarchy, Jewish and Aboriginal groups have traditionally held a peculiar, often undulating, position.

Interestingly, qualities associated with northern hardiness influenced Canadian immigration policies. According to some nineteenth-century thinkers, only immigrants from colder climates would be able to thrive in Canada's cold winters. Whether this opinion was a mask for prejudice against the supposedly soft and lascivious Southern European Catholics (not to mention non-Christian foreigners), like the Spanish, French, and Italian "papists" so disliked by Englishmen for so many centuries, cannot be easily determined.

The history of Canadian immigration recruitment and immigration policy has long reflected a range of cultural prejudices. It has only been in the last thirty-odd years, with education, historical awareness, and the decline of so-called WASP cultural control, that we have seen a more inclusive immigration policy in Canada. It has taken a long time for this country to come to terms with the distorted thinking of earlier centuries. (Some would say we have not yet fully completed the task.)

Opportunities for Co-operation across the Line

How do we get to know, meet, and work with people of different ethnocultural and racial backgrounds? Here understanding the complexity of family dynamics provides little insight. Though the numbers of intercultural and interracial marriages are increasing, they are still relatively rare; few children are growing up in ethnically and especially racially mixed families today. Likely the numbers of children doing so will be much greater in twenty or thirty years, especially in large multi-ethnic cities like Toronto, Montreal, and Vancouver.

As a result, schools, universities, neighbourhoods, and workplaces provide the most important opportunities for encounter and co-operation across ethnic and racial lines. And though some workplaces may be socially homogeneous, the vast majority of large ones comprise people of many ethnic and racial backgrounds. The same is true—even more so—of schools, universities, and neighbourhoods in large cities.

A large urban university like my own, the University of Toronto, has huge numbers of ethnic and racial "minorities"; in fact, here Asian and other one-time minorities may soon make up a majority of the student body. This is in part the result of large-scale immigration to Toronto, as well as high rates of attendance at the local universities and colleges. It is also the result of large numbers of foreign students coming from Asia specifically to study here. At this and other large universities, students inevitably meet people of diverse backgrounds.

The picture is somewhat different for elementary and secondary schools in large cities. Most students attend schools in their own neighbourhood, and most neighbourhoods display a concentration of certain ethnic or racial groups. Such ethnic concentration, or segregation, is less marked in Canadian cities than in American cities, where, for instance, black, white, and Hispanic neighbourhoods are usually distinct. But some evidence of this kind of concentration exists in Canada, too. In Toronto, largely for economic and linguistic reasons, recent Portuguese immigrants live near other recent Portuguese immigrants, recent Vietnamese immigrants live near other recent Vietnamese immigrants, and recent South American immigrants live near other recent South American immigrants. As these groups become more assimilated culturally and economically, they tend to move to more prosperous and often more culturally mixed areas, frequently beyond the city core.

What this means is that in a given neighbourhood a child will mainly meet other members of his or her own ethnocultural group; the mix will be far less varied than at, say, a large urban university. Likely this cultural homogeneity is even more marked at schools and neighbourhoods in smaller, less ethnically mixed towns and cities: in, say, Charlottetown, Lunenberg, Trois-Rivières, North Bay, Saskatoon, Red Deer, or Kelowna.

"Recruitment" into neighbourhoods, schools, and organizations is also affected by education and social class. John Porter argued that ethnocultural groups came to Canada to fill particular niches in the occupational and economic structure. Then, however, owing to limited opportunities for higher education and upward mobility, they were often unable to escape these niches. Ukrainian immigrants came to farm the rural west while Italian immigrants came to build urban Ontario and Quebec. By 1965, when *The Vertical Mosaic* was published, these groups were still stuck in their respective locations—geographically, occupationally, and socially. Porter argued that only with the expansion of higher education would ethnic patterns of segregation break down, both in the general population and in the elite.

Since 1965, higher education has mushroomed. This is in part a result of Porter's urging, but mainly because of the baby boom and Canada's need for more human capital. Improved higher education has led to increased geographic, occupational, and social mobility. Moreover, research consistently shows there is no longer a correlation between *ethnicity* and occupation or income. What the research does show, however, is that there is a correlation between *race* and occupation or income, a topic not discussed by Porter. As with ethnicity, the influence of race is largely mediated by education. That is, minorities with more education get further and faster ahead than those with less education. Highly educated racial minorities—like Chinese and Southeast Asian groups—do very well in Canada today, while less well-educated groups—Aboriginal and Caribbean, for example—do poorly.

Clearly, formal education plays a large part in bringing together people of different ethnic and cultural groups. It creates opportunities for co-operation and mixing that are often otherwise largely absent. At the upper end of the social scale, it mixes different "kinds" of people in prosperous neighbourhoods and prosperous neighbourhood schools.

This is not to deny the existence of discrimination, even against relatively well-educated minorities. Evidence continues to show that non-white minorities often pay a price for their race in the form of lower income returns to education and experience. In other words, non-Caucasian immigrants, especially recent immigrants, are likely to earn less compared to equivalent Caucasians than their education and experience would justify. That said, these effects on immigrant minorities are relatively short-lived; they wash out after about five years in the country. And among all income earners, Chinese immigrants and their children do extraordinarily well in Canadian society. Racism is not a problem for all racial minorities.

Two other factors need to be taken into account as influences on the experience of racial and ethnic minorities in Canada: these are social networks and ethnic communities. First, sociological research has shown repeatedly that many job opportunities depend on membership in networks of friendship and acquaintanceship. Employers, other things being equal, prefer to hire friends, or friends of friends, acquaintances, or acquaintances of acquaintances. Friendships, in turn, are often racially or ethnically homogeneous.

The reasons for this "network effect" on hiring should be evident: employers are likely to get more and better information about friends and acquaintances than they can get about job applicants who are total strangers. (The same is true when seen from the opposite end: job applicants are more likely to get good information about the job from friends and acquaintances than from total strangers.) And, to some degree, both the employer and employee feel more secure with people who they know through an interpersonal network. Employees and employers who are connected socially are more likely to behave appropriately in the workplace, to avoid disrupting other relationships.

So until people of diverse ethnocultural and racial communities gain membership in the same social networks, employment opportunities will probably remain limited. The jobs available to them will most likely be concentrated within ethnic enclaves. As long as ethnic and racial minorities limit their friendships and acquaintanceships to members of their own group, they will suffer limited job opportunities. This may look like discrimination, but it has less to do with prejudice than it does with prudence.

On the other hand, there is an ample literature in Canada indicating that communities with much "institutional completeness" (as sociologist Raymond Breton has called it) will do better in every respect than communities without. The term institutional completeness describes the presence in an ethnocultural community of a wide range of resources and services, including churches, schools, newspapers, shops, and professionals. These institutions allow community members to obtain most necessities from others "just like them." This institutional completeness can be viewed as a form of group self-segregation; it can also be viewed as a form of group mobilization. Groups that have been the most institutionally complete—French-speaking Quebecois, Jewish communities, Chinese neighbourhoods—have been the most successful in Canadian society. They have advanced not only as groups, but their members have also advanced well as individuals, compared to members of groups that are less complete (for example, West Indians and Aboriginals).

This suggests that the strategy of mobilizing as a self-segregated group may work as well as—or in some cases, even better than—the strategy of individual networking. More research needs to be done on this question to understand the conditions under which one strategy works better than another.

Forces Pushing People Apart

EVIDENCE OF CONFLICT: INTRODUCTION

A clear sign of conflict in race and ethnic relations today is political correctness. It seems impossible to discuss openly the criminal violence, and in particular gang violence, of Jamaican youth in Toronto, or the Aboriginal over-representation in prisons, the mistreatment of Aboriginal women, and the seemingly frequent misuse of public funds on Native reserves. As well, it feels difficult to talk about the increasingly evident ethnocultural variations in school performance and school dropout rates, which implicate not only West Indians and Aboriginals but also many Caucasian groups, such as Portuguese immigrants.

Beyond this, there is the seeming impossibility of talking openly and safely about the disputes between Islam and Western society; about the conflict between Israel and the Arab world, particularly with the Palestinians; and about the treatment of women in many Islamic societies. On one university campus after another, demonstrations have turned ugly when people put forward their views on these complex matters. This fear of open (but civil) speech prevents the discussion of concrete solutions to problems, or even of preliminary frameworks for addressing them. And it makes it impossible to discuss whether anti-Israeli sentiments are a veiled form of anti-Semitism, a veiled form of anti-Americanism, or whether, as claimed, they are merely shouts of concern about the plight of Palestinians sequestered in the Gaza Strip.

Some of the more extreme commentators allege that all apparent misbehaviours by disadvantaged groups are due to racial profiling: an institutionalized pattern of watching the disadvantaged more closely and harassing them with impunity. We will discuss this again later; suffice to say, there are those who view racial profiling as central to understanding crime rates and those who don't. At best, people have agreed to disagree.

Another manifestation of this problem is the tendency to point an accusing finger at people who want to discuss race differences, for example, in crime or educational attainment. In other words, there is a tendency to "racialize" the discourse. The implication is that race doesn't really exist and doesn't really have any effect on social life; this is clearly not the case. To say otherwise is to inject false notions and prejudices, or to blame the victims. To be sure, in one sense the critique is valid—"race" exists only if we think it does. But one can have no doubt that differences exist between ethnocultural groups and, as sociologists, we need to study these differences more closely.

SEGREGATION OR DISTANCE

I will argue in later parts of this book that personal familiarity is a minimal requirement for overcoming conflict and distrust. By gaining familiarity, we usually understand and even make allowances for people we know, even when they belong to groups we say we don't like. This is an old and well-tested finding about anti-Semitism and racial prejudice generally: that prejudiced people are often willing to grant "special status" to a favoured member of an otherwise despised or disliked group. An example of this might be a trusted Jewish accountant or loyal black servant. Familiarity doesn't necessarily guarantee intergroup trust and friendship, but it does make a new level of interaction at least thinkable. Perhaps in order to overcome prejudice and fear, we need a good deal of familiarity with many members of different ethnic groups.

Yet as I noted earlier, many groups segregate themselves for a number of reasons: these include economic and linguistic disadvantage, a fear of strangers as potential sources of discrimination, or a sensed need for institutional completeness and group supports. These factors all work against open mixing and against outsiders gaining familiarity with different groups. But segregation, whatever its causes, is a significant problem that impedes interaction, communication, and understanding across group boundaries. It is not merely a psychological problem: it is what sociologists call a "structural problem," in the sense that, once set in motion, it continues to operate outside the will or control of any particular individual. The longer such group segregation operates, the more effort and courage it will take for any given individual to break through it. It is often difficult to date or to marry "outside" the group. To risk this kind of boundary-crossing is to risk criticism, exclusion, and even stigmatization by parents, relatives, and friends.

That said, we see this boundary-crossing much more often now than in the past. During much of the twentieth century, inter-religious, inter-ethnic, and interracial marriage was unusual. In some US states, interracial marriage was even illegal. Today, throughout North America, mating across religious, ethnic, and racial lines is increasingly common, especially in large, heterogeneous urban centres and among better-educated people. From this standpoint, a place like the University of Toronto, with its multi-ethnic, multicultural population, is a laboratory for the remaking of human history. Here we see the blending of groups through friendship, dating, mating, and marriage.

Along with this comes the social psychological process of decreased "social distance." Social distance is a concept devised by the psychologist Emory Bogardus in the early twentieth century to measure the extent of intergroup segregation and, conversely, the willingness of group members to mix with other groups. Today, most ethnocultural groups are far less "distant" from one another psychologically than they were eighty years ago. In other words, today most people are far more willing to cross group lines: to live in the same neighbourhood with members of another ethnocultural group, work in the same workplaces, become close friends, accept one another as neighbours, and even accept one another as family members through marriage. Of course, some ethnocultural and racial groups are still more standoffish than others. And too, some groups are still more often rejected, as neighbours, friends, or relatives, than others. The specifics are less interesting or surprising than the generality that overall we are becoming more open to variety and more accepting of difference.

Perhaps the most interesting and enduring finding by Bogardus is that social distance is like a ladder. As you move up the ladder of acceptance, you open yourself to all the options below you. Take a specific example. If you are willing to have a close friend who is, say, Turkish, you will likely be willing to live in a neighbourhood that contains Turks or to work alongside Turks. Or further up the ladder: if you are willing to marry a Turk, you are likely willing to have a best friend who is Turkish, to live among Turks, go to work with Turks, admit Turks to the country, and so on down the ladder of social distance.

And what this means to me is that, at the University of Toronto, where so many people from different ethnocultural and racial backgrounds are dating and mating, young people are solving the entire problem of social distance all at once. They are starting at the very top of the social-distance ladder and buying into everything lower down, and this is one of the best reasons I can think of to support ethnic and racial intermarriage.

PREJUDICE AND DISCRIMINATION

There are various interesting reasons why people feel prejudice and discriminate against others. Some are more sociological, others more psychological. They all have some support and all seem credible, to some degree.

The best single reason is that discrimination confers an economic or social advantage on the discriminating group. For a boss to decide that he will not hire anyone who is not (say) Irish, like himself, significantly reduces the complexity of the hiring process by reducing the number of possible candidates. It also confers an advantage on anyone who is like oneself. This makes discrimination a form of self-love and a sign of ignorance about people unlike oneself. Perhaps it can be seen as a veiled form of nepotism, even narcissism, as sometimes seen in a desire to hire only friends and relatives. And if every boss who is Irish agrees to hire only other people who are Irish, this captures the entire local job-market for Irish applicants; it becomes a way of protecting and advancing one's ethnocultural group at the expense of all other groups. It becomes a form of ethnic self-protection or self-advancement.

However, this example is really more about discrimination than it is about prejudice. When discrimination is (or seems) economically rational, we do not need to import the concept of prejudice, which is essentially a form of irrationality (that is, either ignorance or error). Some discrimination is indeed based on prejudice, and here we have to return to the troubled concept of "racial profiling." The common criticism of racial profiling is that the police will tend to pull over black drivers merely because they are black—or DWB ("driving while black"). It is a form of harassment against blacks, especially blacks who look prosperous and "uppity" and are driving nice cars.

One interpretation is that the police force is staffed by bigots who hate black people and enjoy giving them a hard time by goading them into stepping out of line so they can be arrested or beaten. Perhaps this explanation applies at some times and some places. If so, we are looking at blind, irrational prejudice as the basis for racial profiling.

Another interpretation is that the police force is staffed by people who have studied the statistics on, say, drug possession or illegal weapons possession. Suppose the statistics say that although one out of every twenty vehicle inspections will yield a positive result, this yield is twice as high when the vehicle's driver is black. If this is a statistical reality then, all else being equal, the police officer whose job is to search suspicious vehicles will do well to concentrate on those with black drivers. If his goal is a maximize success, that approach makes sense. Once again, we do not need to import the concept of prejudice to understand this behaviour.

A third and much less obvious theory about prejudice and discrimination was proposed by psychologist Gordon Allport in the 1940s. Adapting a variation of Freudian thought, Allport argued that ethnic and racial minorities become a kind of blank screen onto which we project our fears and fantasies. We all have fears, from time to time, about being cheated or deceived, so we may focus those fears on an ethnocultural group that is identifiably different from ourselves; if we are given to feeling cheated, we may blame them for cheating us. Stereotypes of "the Jew" have often played this role. As a general rule, any group that has historically served as a minority merchant class or moneylender has been envied, hated, and feared. Depending on the society, this role has been filled by Arabs, Turks, Armenians, East Indians, Chinese, Koreans, and also Scots.

All men have fears from time to time of being beaten up, made to look timid, impotent, and insufficiently masculine. (Even Freud remembered his childhood embarrassment at seeing his father's hat knocked off by an anti-Semite.) So according to the Allport theory, we need at least one ethnocultural group that can be viewed as stupid, loutish brutes: all brawn and no brain, with excess sexual energy. They are people who endanger us with physical violence. Here, the stereotype of "the black man" can fill this role. (According to this theory, the same role could be filled by any group that has been historically limited to heavy physical labour, slavery, or at least servile peasantry.) This fantasy group corresponds to Freud's *id*: raw physical and sexual energy, uncontrolled by reason. The first fantasy group corresponds to Freud's *ego*: pure self-seeking reason, uncontrolled by morality.

So long as we carry around these unarticulated, submerged fears and beliefs, we run the risk of maintaining social distance, hiding our prejudice, and justifying acts of unthinking discrimination.

Suspicion and Distrust

There is a lot to be said for the non-sociological theory of prejudice proposed by Allport. It certainly helps us understand why certain groups are vilified more often than others, and why they are vilified in certain ways rather than others. (In these hostile fantasies, Jews are not usually characterized like blacks, and vice versa.) However, the theory is just a little too tidy, too limited, and not quite sociological enough. Granted we all fear being cheated, and we all fear being made to look ridiculous. But these are not the only fears we harbour, so we need a theory that covers a wider range of hurts and humiliations. And we need to better understand the mechanisms that engage these fears, a theory that in effect sets them in motion.

As usual, humour is a great place to unearth preoccupations and fears. We can find out a lot by looking at the jokes made by different groups. Here are three Russian jokes about different ethnic groups:

(1) A Ukrainian is asked: "Can you eat an entire pound of apples?"
     "Yes, I can."
     "Can you eat two pounds of apples?"
     "I can."
     "And five pounds?"
     "I can."
     "Can you eat 100 pounds?!"
     "What I cannot eat, I will nibble!"

(2) In the zoo, two girls are discussing a gorilla with a huge penis: "*That's* what a real man must have!" A Georgian passerby sarcastically remarks, "You are badly mistaken. *This* is what a real man must have!" and produces a thick wallet.

(3) A rich Chukcha buys a truck and brings it to his tribe to show them the "technological miracle." People crowd around it. The old chief appears on the scene. He examines it from all sides and then looks underneath and sees the exhaust pipe. "A male one, however," he points out.

Who are these people in the jokes, and what do they connote to Russians? The Ukrainian in the first joke, evidently, connotes to urban Russians the "generic peasant": sly, greedy, and a little foolish. Sometimes he will beat the city person in a bet, sometimes not. But he is crafty. He knows what he knows, and he keeps his own counsel. The Ukrainian peasant can never be taken for granted. Interestingly, when I read out this joke in class one day, a student who self-identified as Ukrainian said her own group tells this joke about Poles.

The Georgian depicted in the second joke is some combination of "Jew" and "black" in Allport's theory. In Russia, Georgians are viewed like Armenians, as shrewd dealers. But this Georgian also has sex on his mind: he hopes to get some booty by flashing his bling. He intends to talk those two girls into bed. Finally, the rich Chukcha in the third joke is a northern frontier Aboriginal: somewhat behind the times, but nevertheless eager (and holding enough cash) to catch up. The old chief doesn't quite know how to evaluate the truck so he uses old, inappropriate methods. Still, he is observant and cannot be dismissed.

What seems likely is that we make jokes about people that we fear, and we fear those with whom we are, at some level, in competition. A very troubled or vulnerable population like present-day Russia is, therefore, likely to have a lot of jokes and a lot of different ethnic scapegoats or objects of ridicule. Given this, the sociologist wants to know not what is said about a particular group, but why the joking group feels vulnerable and endangered. Under what conditions does competition produce fear? And under what conditions does familiarity assuage fear?

Abuse and Violence

In some parts of the world, inter-ethnic and interracial strife is signified by extreme violence. Consider the mass murder of Kosovo Muslims under the Serbian (Orthodox) leadership of Slobodan Milošević in the 1990s, or the genocidal warfare witnessed in Rwanda where one tribe, the Hutus, tried to wipe out the Tutsis in 1994. While they did not succeed, they may have killed as many as 800,000 in one short, explosive period. Currently, the mass murder of hundreds of thousands continues in Darfur in western Sudan, loosely based on regional and ethnic differences.

A history of violent relations between groups is likely to engender fear in one or both groups. In Rwanda's neighbouring country Burundi, Tutsis had wiped out an estimated 100,000 Hutus in 1972. Similar intergroup strife between Sunni and Shiite Arabs has characterized the history of Iraq. Typically, the group that has been historically victimized fears further victimization. Recently in the United States, for example, many blacks feared Obama would be assassinated if he ran for president. And in turn the group that previously perpetrated the violence may fear payback. Many Southern whites feared the consequences of electing a black president, though this fear may have been unwarranted.

Today, violence and abuse (in general, race-related hate crimes) are rare in North America. However, some scholars have theorized that the continued practice of capital punishment in the United States is a holdover from slavery and lynching. The US states that today make the most use of capital punishment are the same states that held slaves and practiced lynching in the nineteenth century. Violence against black people in the US has certainly not ended; it has arguably taken a more legitimized, legal form. At the same time, violent crime and gang violence in American cities is largely perpetrated by black youth, usually against other blacks. How is this to be explained by a theory about race relations? Why aren't black people killing white people? Why are they killing other blacks? Here, we realize the deep importance of collecting all the relevant information about criminals and their victims, despite the risk of "racialization."

Arguably, blacks are killing other blacks because they are in most frequent contact with other blacks. Typically the most violence is committed against those with whom we are in frequent, even intimate, contact: partners, family members, friends, acquaintances. Others might say that black people committing violence against other black people (as opposed to Caucasians) signifies black self-hate and an absence of political consciousness. There may be something to both explanations. Only one thing is certain: violent acts by white people against black people are no longer common, nor are violent acts by black people against white. This probably speaks to the continued segregation of racial groups in the US. By and large in North America today, people act violently against others of the same racial group.

POOR PHYSICAL HEALTH

The same can be said about physical health. There is little if any un-ambiguous evidence that race and ethnicity have any direct effect on physical health. Job discrimination, race, and ethnicity may have a dir-ect effect on income, and income in turn influences physical health. It may also be true that, through residential segregation, race and ethni-city may have an effect on physical health (and safety). People who live in rotting, poorly maintained housing in dangerous, poorly serviced neighbourhoods—and whose children attend poorly equipped, unsafe schools—will undoubtedly suffer worse health problems.

However, these health problems are all class-related. They are to be solved by addressing class problems in the society, not race problems. So, for example, if we know that First Nations peoples, who typically endure lower incomes and worse housing in segregated, poorly ser-viced neighbourhoods, suffer worse health than other Canadians, the policy implication is simple. Provide better medical care, better job training, better housing, and better schools. Don't spend time and money fighting racism and building racial self-esteem. Perhaps these matters will take care of themselves when people can afford to live in a decent neighbourhood, send their children to decent schools, and enjoy a comfortable, secure lifestyle.

And since class, not race, is the problem (a view that John Porter would have endorsed), we will look more closely at these matters in the next chapter. Equally, we need to turn our attention to class politics, not identity politics.

Undesirable Outcomes

UNHAPPINESS, DEPRESSION, AND ANXIETY

What are the human costs of racism and inter-ethnic conflict or distrust? In the early and mid-twentieth century, many argued that racism and discrimination had cultivated self-hatred, or at least low self-esteem, among those who belonged to minority groups. Supposedly, this resulted in psychiatric problems and self-loathing, illustrated by violence, drug addiction, and the rejection of dark-skinned mates, among other things. The model for this kind of argument was the classic book *The Wretched of the Earth* (1961), in which psychiatrist Frantz Fanon described events that he had witnessed in Algeria, a former French colony. For Fanon and many other mid-twentieth-century revolutionaries, including black Muslims like Malcolm X, violent protest was needed to regain a sense of worth and agency by those who had been oppressed. (Religion and political mobilization were also important.)

That said, there is little reliable evidence that racial or ethnic inequality today continues to bring unhappiness, depression, or anxiety once we control for social class. Poverty and economic failure—more common among certain ethnic groups than others—clearly do contribute to unhappiness, depression, and anxiety. But if we compare similarly poor or similarly rich people, the effect of race and ethnicity appears to wash out. Rich black people seem just as happy as rich white people, even if they are less numerous. And poor white people seem just as unhappy as poor black people. What seems to make a difference is wealth versus poverty—though of course, feeling like the member of a community is also important.

Evidently even America, with its long, violent history of slavery, is willing to elect a black person as president, so long as the candidate in question holds a law degree from Harvard. Social and cultural capital matters in American politics and, to a lesser degree, in Canadian politics. (One cannot fail to notice the similar intellectual profile, and manner, of Barack Obama and Michael Ignatieff, the Liberal contender for Canadian prime minister.) The problem is that few Americans from humble origins, black people or otherwise, are able to amass the necessary social and cultural capital. Many say that the election of Obama has raised the stature of America in foreign eyes, effectively forgiving centuries of slavery and decades of isolationism; similarly, it has been said that it has given black people optimism and a new sense of worth. This may be true, but many black people also viewed Bill Clinton as one of their own, largely because he was not the scion of hereditary wealth, like George Bush.

In short, the evidence is clear that—compared to other countries with a recent history of racism—even in Canada race still makes a difference to people's sense of well-being, except when it correlates with wealth and poverty. It appears that being poor is more damaging than being non-white.

ADDICTIONS AND CRIME

It makes sense to study addictions and crimes together in a discussion of racial and ethnic inequalities. The reason for this is that groups with high rates of crime and delinquency also have high rates of addiction. Sometimes the crimes and delinquencies for which minorities are arrested are related to public drunkenness, drug possession, or drug selling. Often, their crimes of violence, especially domestic violence, are committed while under the influence of drugs or alcohol. And many property crimes are ultimately in the service of acquiring money to feed an addiction.

The other reason for treating these together is because, in a classic analysis of deviance, sociologist Robert Merton saw crime and addiction as merely different "adaptations" to the same problem of "anomie" in modern American society, as we mentioned in an earlier chapter. The definition of anomie here is a "gap" or discontinuity between the cultural goals one was taught to seek, in particular material success, and the socially accepted means one was taught to use. In short, disadvantaged peoples—for example, American black people or Canadian Aboriginals—were likely to find themselves without access to the socially or institutionally acceptable means of pursuing wealth and success. Put simply, they lacked the educational credentials, the social contacts, and the cultural capital.

Faced with the impossibility of gaining wealth in the acceptable way, according to Merton, some chose to retreat into drugs and alcohol (or into depression and suicide). They gave up the impossible quest and deadened their desires. Merton called this adaptation retreatism. Others chose instead a process Merton called innovation—to adopt and perfect socially unacceptable, even illegal means of pursuing wealth and success, becoming delinquents, criminals, and gangsters. Often, these criminal groups fell to fighting one another: Russian gangsters against Vietnamese gangsters, and so on.

Merton's theory does not provide a tidy explanation of why some disadvantaged racial or ethnic minorities adapt by retreating, as many Aboriginal people have done, while other minorities adapt by innovating, as in the case of many American black people. Presumably, the answer is that some groups, owing to their geographic and social locations, are more likely to develop the skills and find the opportunities to become successful "innovators." And, as sociologist Daniel Bell argued in his 1960 essay on the "queer ladder of social mobility" in American society, virtually every disadvantaged urban ethnic minority has, at one time or another, used crime to advance to success. (The same groups have also used sports and entertainment as means to success. All three—crime, sports, and entertainment—require relatively little capital, much personal effort, and contacts "in the business.")

Though racism and ethnic exclusion are weaker today than they once were, they persist in many communities. As a result, we continue to see conflicts arising between ethnic groups. Often they are rooted in conflicts raging thousands of miles away; for example, the conflicts in Canada between Arabs and Jews reflect continued animosity over the Israeli-Palestinian conflict on the other side of the world. Other ethnic and sectarian conflicts are imported into Canada by recent immigrants—for example, by Sikhs, Tibetans, and Tamils.

That said, the main cause and main dynamic of inter-ethnic or interracial conflict in Canada today seem to be based on class or income. It is not that groups hate or fear one another for irrational reasons; it is that they are often locked into, or feel locked into, economic competition against one another. The least successful, or most impoverished, become the most demoralized and the most likely to fall into addiction and crime. The symbols of racial and ethnic difference, today so visible in multicultural celebrations, are ultimately signifiers of recent immigration and/or economic accomplishment.

With this in mind, let's turn now to discussing classes—social groups defined specifically in terms of their access to wealth and economic power.

Classes and Workplaces

The study of classes and class conflict is perhaps the oldest, most central topic in sociology. The only topic that comes close to the importance of class as a "founding concern" of sociology is the question of order: what holds people together in societies?

The first question, about class, is associated with the work of one sociological founder, Karl Marx; the second question, about order, is associated with the work of another sociological founder, Émile Durkheim. By this point, it is probably clear that this book is mainly about the second question. The present chapter is about how social order is affected by class conflict. The connection between these two—social order and social class—is central to this entire book.

Some people think of classes as income groups and as reflections of how much people earn. This definition makes class easy to measure but doesn't fully capture the significance of the concept, which in the end is related to power and status as well as earnings. Other people think of class in terms of wealth, both earned and inherited, whether in the form of cash, property, stocks, or otherwise. While closer than income to the potential for acquiring power, this notion is still only weakly related to what sociologists finally have in mind.

"Classes" in sociological thinking are groups of people who share a common economic condition, interest, or—as Marx described it—relationship to the means of production (that is, to technology and capital). In Marx's logic there are two main classes: the people who own the means of production and the people who work for those who own the means of production. This binary—have and have not—is fundamental to all social relations and all class conflict, since these two classes are forever locked in conflict.

The relationship of people to the "means of production" is critical to this way of thinking. This dividing line separates those who must sell their work, their time, or labour power to earn wages so they can survive from those who buy this work and gain profits from the goods and services that workers produce. The profit gained by the second group depends mainly on the price of the manufactured product minus the cost of labour. As a result, profit-making depends on keeping prices high and wages (and other costs of production) low. But high prices, low wages, and poor working conditions are not good for workers; so workers struggle—through unions, co-operatives, legislation, and other means—to improve their wages, working conditions, job security, and the prices they have to pay for food, shelter, and health care.

People in the same relation to the means of production ought to have an interest in banding together: the workers to protect their wages and working conditions, the employers to protect their profit and control. But for this to happen, people in the same class must develop an awareness of their common interest, commit themselves to working together for common goals, and come to see their individual well-being as connected to the collective well-being of the class. This development of class awareness and class consciousness is, however, harder than it sounds. Many factors interfere with it.

A prime example of this would be employers taking steps to prevent the formation of unions or discussions of worker concerns. Legislators sympathetic to the interests of owners may make laws that give employers more power or workers less power in the event of a conflict. The police or military may be used to break strikes. Workers themselves may be reluctant to share a common cause with people of different racial or ethnic groups. Or the unions and workers' representatives may not agree on how best to promote workers' interests. The workers may suffer from what is sometimes called false consciousness: a willingness to believe ideologies that promote individualistic solutions to problems or to blame the poor and unemployed for their problems. Workers may also be so alienated from politics and from one another that they cannot put their faith and trust in the collective enterprise of unionization and class conflict.

Workplaces, where the classes meet, are "contested terrains," in the words of economist Richard Edwards. Here workers and bosses struggle for control, devising first one strategy and then another to overcome their opponent.

Of course, this portrayal is far too simple for today's class structure. First, it is no longer necessary to own a business in order to control the means of production. Second, today the working class is international, a result of global ownership and economic competition. This introduces an even larger difficulty into the mass mobilization of workers.

Consider the first point: the importance today of management rather than ownership in class conflict. The economic downturn into which we plunged in 2008 was due not to the misbehaviour of *owners* but to the misbehaviour of *managers* of the means of production. It was a result of mismanagement on the part of directors, executive officers, financiers, speculators, and bankers. Bernie Madoff, who is said to have embezzled $50 billion in a Ponzi scheme (destroying many banks, charities, and personal fortunes), was a speculator, not a manufacturer or factory owner. He had no link whatever to workers, products, or services. As well, recall how billions of dollars worth of junk mortgages were sold and traded until someone noticed that they were worthless; these mortgages had no connection with manufacturing or the creation of new property or valuable services.

In late capitalism, then, it is the class of people in control of capital—real and imaginary—who control the fates of workers, investors, pensioners, and all their dependants. These are not the easy-to-define bourgeois factory owners who Marx characterized as the class enemy of workers (or proletariat, as he called them). They are much farther from ownership and the shop floor than Marx ever imagined.

Related to this is the rise of new classes that neither own the means of production nor sell their labour to capitalists. This includes professors of sociology, doctors, civil servants, judges, elected officials, and other employees of organizations outside the for-profit sector (for example, nurses in hospitals or social workers who work for cities). Typically, all of these people have knowledge or other special skills. They exercise authority without possessing or even controlling wealth. Sometimes the power of these non-capitalists—these cabinet ministers, senior civil servants, and high court judges—is even equal to that of capitalists. In an information society like ours, knowledge and expertise are also important inputs into wealth production and statecraft, so they gain social importance: they carry status, prestige, and even power.

What's more, not all power or authority is exploitive in the sense that Marx meant. Some of it contributes to social well-being. In a modern society, the occupations associated with judging, legislating, governing, managing, and assigning resources are all valuable. If they are done poorly or improperly, people suffer and resources are wasted. Consider a recent example of this: the effect of US President George W. Bush on the country he was elected to govern. In eight short years, his mismanagement turned an economic surplus into a deficit; plunged his nation into an expensive, unwinnable, and unnecessary war; allowed the destruction of a major US city; undermined civil liberties; and set the stage for a global economic meltdown through a failure to regulate the finance industry.

In addition, not all wealth is achieved through exploitation. Whether they are morally deserved or not, the high salaries paid to sports champions and movie stars reflect the operation of a free market. If more people choose movies starring Meryl Streep than Jennifer Aniston, then Meryl Streep will command a higher salary. If Phil Mickelson wins more golf tournaments than his closest competitors, he will be paid more to endorse Acme golf balls. What's more, the market-driven earnings of these sports and movie stars are easier to understand and justify than the huge bonuses received by executive officers of failing banks and automobile companies.

Some sociologists have even argued that the inequalities in a modern democratic society are chiefly based on the agreement about the value of different jobs and social roles. The functional theory of stratification (1945), credited to Kingsley Davis and Wilbert Moore, maintains that most people in most industrial societies agree about the relative social value of particular roles. They agree, for example, that a doctor, judge, professor, or scientist is worth more to society than, say, an unskilled labourer, door-to-door salesman, or news vendor. Therefore people are willing to see the first group receive higher salaries (also more respect and authority) than the second group. We can replace news vendors more easily than we can replace doctors, so we "agree" to reward the doctors more to ensure a continued flow of recruits into training for these highly valued roles.

Some research supports this argument. It has shown that popular ratings of different occupations—their prestige and social value—tend to be stable over time and vary little from one industrial society to another. (Of course, non-industrial societies with different value systems, like societies that put a high premium on warfare or religion, will rank jobs differently.) This means that inequalities of wealth, authority, and respect are to some degree based on shared values.

However, this functional theory fails to consider several facts. First, it cannot explain why the differential between top-paid and bottom-paid workers is wide or narrow—why, for example, the differential between lower-salaried groups and higher-salaried within major American manufacturing companies was roughly ten times in 1980 (in other words, upper management earned some ten times more than workers), but nearly thirty times more in 2008. Nor does it explain why the range of salaries is much wider in one capitalist society, like the US, than it is in another like Germany, France, or Japan. Nor why some people get high salaries regardless of whether they confer a social benefit—here again, consider movie stars, sports stars, professional criminals, auto executives, and bank executives. In fact, sometimes the public knows very little about the amount these people are paid or the reasons for this payment.

All we can say for certain is that not all inequality in modern Canada or the US is due to exploitation in the form that Marx imagined. Some of it is a result of unregulated market forces, like inadequate laws governing the finance industry. Some is a result of the tax structure, which enables more or less wealth to be redistributed from poor to rich, or rich to poor. In turn, this redistribution is a result of the connection between the state and the ruling class, and the extent to which rich, powerful people can rely on elected politicians to serve their interests.

Opportunities for Co-operation across the Line

What opportunities do people have to meet and co-operate across class lines? The short answer is not many.

Family members, including the members of extended families, usually belong to the same social class. Of course, there may be relatively poor branches of a rich and powerful family, but these branches are unlikely to have much to do with one another. Usually families preserve and transfer wealth from one generation to another. In fact, family inheritance is the main mechanism for ensuring class stability—this is the reason why there is a stable upper (or rich) class and a stable lower (or poor) class in society.

Nor do neighbourhoods and public schools offer much opportunity for people to meet and co-operate across class lines. Most neighbourhoods and neighbourhood schools are class-segregated, in the sense that they bring together people with similar social backgrounds. Rich people buy homes in expensive parts of the city and even then may send their children to costly private schools. Poor people are unable to do the same; they live in poorer parts of the city and send their children to neighbourhood schools that have fewer resources.

Colleges and universities offer more opportunity for people to meet and co-operate across class lines. Historically, students from widely varying backgrounds have attended all the major Canadian universities. Still, some Canadian colleges and universities have drawn disproportionately from the higher social classes, and today, increasing numbers of well-off Canadian parents send their children to the Ivy League or other expensive international universities.

As John Porter showed in *The Vertical Mosaic* (1965), there is some opportunity for people to cross class lines at the highest occupational levels. People from humble backgrounds—having performed well at university and risen through the organizational ranks into positions of ever-increasing authority—may acquire the opportunity to work and socialize with people who have inherited their wealth and power. The professions of engineering, management, accounting, and law are especially good ladders of upward mobility. And at the elite levels of society, people in the highest union positions, political positions, and civil service positions are sometimes able to work and socialize with people in the highest economic positions of society; again, this can happen regardless of their class of origin.

That said, social mobility in capitalist societies has its limits. There is little chance of entering the upper class—say, the top 1 percent of income earners or wealth holders—from below. Similarly, there is little chance of escaping the poorest class, say the bottom 1 percent. There is more opportunity to enter the top income decile (that is, the top 10 percent) and more opportunity to escape the bottom income decile, though such movements are still rare. In the middle of the income distribution, among the middle 80 percent of all income earners, there is plenty of intergenerational mobility all the time, a good deal of movement upward and downward in income and occupational prestige.

What makes this movement possible is higher education. In our society, educational credentials are the key to social mobility.

People who are more socially mobile are more likely to gain opportunities to interact with people of higher social classes. In fact, educated people are also more likely to interact with people of *lower* social classes. Research shows that people with more education have larger, more diverse social networks. They know more people by name and can link indirectly with a larger number of people through networks of friendship and acquaintance. This is partly through their exposure to many people in institutions of higher education and through their exposure to many people in their professional and managerial work. But it is also because educated people know many other people who also know many people.

Of course, most people have some indirect access to people of higher (and lower) social classes. This is known as the "small world phenomenon." With the help of "sociometric stars," we can all connect with people of diverse class backgrounds at one or two removes. There are probably only six degrees of separation between you and Conrad Black, Bruce Springsteen, or even Nelson Mandela. But for practical purposes you don't have a connection with these people. In the end, most of our interactions are with people from the same or a similar class background.

Immigration policy has provided considerable (if unintended) opportunity for interaction across class lines by denying many college-educated immigrants the jobs to which their education qualifies them. It is not unusual to ride with a taxi driver who has a university degree from an Asian or African university, or to be served in a store or restaurant by a college graduate from Eastern Europe or Latin America. The non-recognition of foreign credentials means that many immigrants suffer downward mobility, however temporarily, when they come to Canada. In this capacity they are likely to interact with native-born Canadians who have much less education and a lower occupational status. These cross-class interactions are, however, complicated by differences of ethnic origin and birthplace.

Opportunities aside, some evidence suggests that people avoid others of a different social class. Sociologist Peter Archibald put forward a series of hypotheses about this. Drawing on Marx's concept of alienation, Archibald asserts that our alienation from others is characterized by four features: (1) we feel indifference or separation from others; (2) when we approach others, it is for narrow, egoistic purposes; (3) when we interact with others, we feel more controlled than in control; and (4) when we relate to others, it is with feelings of dissatisfaction and even hostility. According to this theory, we feel some fear, inadequacy, and discomfort when we interact with people from a different social class, especially a higher one. We are not certain of the other person's norms, expectations, and likely responses.

For the many reasons we have cited, people usually marry within their own classes. After all, they spend much of their time in places frequented by other people of the same class: schools, churches, clubs, summer camps, colleges, universities, and workplaces. As well, they are likely to share the same interests and values, and to have some of the same friends in common. What's more, evidence shows that people who attend elite schools, universities, camps, and clubs marry other people who also attend elite schools, universities, camps, and clubs. People who attend Ivy League schools marry other people who attend Ivy League schools (or at least their friends or relatives). So even at the top there are important status gradations. This is why anthropologist W. Lloyd Warner has said that well-established communities have a nine-level status order ranging from a "lower-lower" class all the way to an "upper-upper" class.

There is one main force that pulls people together across class lines, and that is the homogenizing cultural force of the mass media. Across class lines, people often watch the same television programs, go to the same movies, and listen to the same popular music. Although this mass culture may not bring people together for interaction, it can ease the interaction if their paths happen to cross. Young people of different classes will at least be able to discuss *The Simpsons* and popular music groups. Among people in higher age groups, a common interest in sports events may perform the same integrative role—though its potential for integrating people may be in decline, given the continuing proliferation of sport and entertainment channels available to viewers.

Forces Pushing People Apart

EVIDENCE OF CONFLICT: INTRODUCTION

During the first half of the twentieth century, it was possible to see armed conflicts between workers and bosses, mediated by police, militia, and hired goons. The famed Winnipeg General Strike and the "March on Ottawa" were events in Canadian labour history that showed just how harsh class conflict could become, even in so moderate a country as Canada.

In other countries, especially countries with a feudal tradition or large peasantry, class conflict has often been extremely marked. In countries without a strong middle class, a strong peasantry, or a self-aware working class, the transition to industrial "modernity" was often violent, as sociologist Barrington Moore has argued. Germany, Italy, and much of Latin America—countries dominated by the military, a hereditary land-owning class, and the church—entered modernity via fascism. (Of course, Germany did have a large middle class as the country entered modernity, but before World War I that class lacked political influence and had "bought in" to the aristocracy's world view.) As industrial development progressed, the wars between owners, workers, and the state were intense. Other countries without a working class, like those with a large indentured peasantry and a small, repressive landowning class (for example, China, Russia, Vietnam, and Cuba) entered modernity through communism. There the conflict between an owning and a working class was seemingly avoided by state ownership of the means of production.

But fascism and communism both failed, at least in their original forms. In the last thirty years, almost every country of the world has adopted one or another version of capitalism, whether they came to it through private ownership or state ownership, an open market, or a tightly regulated economy. Still, as Marx predicted, the transition to capitalism has been far from smooth. In every instance, economic change in the twentieth century was accompanied by class conflict and occasionally by armed violence between classes (whether between the workers and owners or between the peasants and landowners). Today class conflict, now globalized, is largely submerged by national competition as jobs migrate from high-wage, often unionized societies to low-wage, non-unionized societies.

Ronald Inglehart, an American political scientist, has shown that in many parts of the world, class conflict has seemingly disappeared. Few young and middle-aged people hold what he calls "materialist" values that necessitate conflict over the means of production. For example, relatively few people in North America put higher wages, job security, or more economic equality near the top of their social concerns. Instead they express more concern about cross-class issues like the environment, peace, or terrorism. Related to this, in many countries, is the fact that class politics—the institutionalized version of class conflict—has been replaced by identity politics. People express more concerns about addressing racism, sexism, ageism, or religious discrimination than about achieving economic equality or reducing poverty.

Inglehart says that this has occurred because most voters today grew up in relative postwar plenty, where workers had largely succeeded in reducing class inequality. Many members of the North American baby boom generation, for example, felt that concerns over equality across gender, race, and sexuality took precedence over class issues. Today's worries over economic equality are therefore filtered through these particular concerns. As a result, there is much less concern expressed today than in the past about the economic plight of white working-class men and their families. In general, the economic analysis of social problems has largely given way to concerns about prejudice and discrimination.

Nonetheless, we are beginning to see the pendulum swing back again, as many come to realize it is impossible to understand any issue of inequality without addressing the economic or class dimensions, and the ways they interact with other issues such as racism, sexism, and imperialism. A prime supporter of this view is the American sociologist William Julius Wilson, who continues to argue for an understanding of the links between class inequality, racial inequality, and the urban "culture of poverty."

SEGREGATION OR DISTANCE

Competition from issues of racism and sexism aside, class issues often hold little interest because people are largely segregated from people of other classes. Members of different classes each live in a different *habitus*, the term French sociologist Pierre Bourdieu used to describe the set of dispositions that are shaped by people's social location and help to reproduce social structure. This results from class and status distinction—the means by which we learn to distinguish culturally and socially between one another.

These ideas may sound unusual and even unlikely, given the extent of cultural sharing brought about by the mass media that we mentioned earlier. However, outside the mass culture (typified by network television and Wal-Mart), we see a multitude of class subcultures serviced by specialty or niche institutions: particular television channels, magazines, stores, and clothing brands, for example. Rich people and poor people do not dress the same way. They have different ideas of style and fashion. They furnish their homes differently. They prepare different menus. They vacation in different places. They amass and use different stores of cultural knowledge, sometimes called cultural capital, in their conversation.

We can start anywhere with this: the consumption of sushi among the upper and upper-middle class; their clothing from Abercrombie & Fitch and Brooks Brothers; their knowledge of grand pianos and fine wines; their membership in racquet clubs; their holidays in out-of-the-way places; and their high-tuition private schools. Or we can start with living room furnishings: are there framed photographs on the wall, perhaps a picture of Elvis, a family photograph of a large-eyed little girl, or the Pope on a velvet canvas; a rack of bowling trophies; or back issues of *People* magazine? Or are there original paintings and fine reproductions of modern art; small sculptures on display, perhaps small pieces of folk art from Africa and Latin America; or back issues of *Architectural Digest* on a coffee table? Equally important, is the space crowded with "stuff" or is the room planned to contain lots of empty space and interesting individual objects?

You can read a person's class position and status aspirations—who she claims to be, what group he is hoping to belong to—from these material objects and consumer habits. It is fully possible to view consumer behaviour as the expression of consistent, well-developed tastes that are learned from childhood onward. As market researchers have shown, these tastes are shaped by various factors, among them sex, age, household composition, and region of the country. However, education and income, the main indicators of social class in North America, have a strong effect on forming these tastes.

This is the reason why educational institutions often play a major role in cultivating these tastes. Doing so is what marks the difference between an elite educational institution and a non-elite institution: the elite institution takes its class responsibilities seriously. Consider Princeton University. When I spent a year there in the early 1970s, I discovered a room in the gym entirely devoted to developing the skills needed for polo. I have never seen polo played, except in the movies by wealthy playboys. But Princeton was taking no chances. It was preparing its students to be wealthy playboys, when the occasion arose. And when I spent a year at Yale in the early 1980s, I joined a group of undergraduates who, each week, studied fine wines under the tutelage of a sommelier. Together, we tasted wines, discussed their history and nuances, and capped the course with a field trip to a magnificent wine and spirits store. Clearly, knowledge of fine wine was considered at some level to be part of a Yale education.

The benefits of this? At a minimum, this storehouse of cultural knowledge and experience allows people to name-drop with the best of them, and lay claim to membership in a privileged class that excludes those without comparable advantages. Social status and social interaction, including friendship and marriage, is built on just such distinctions.

PREJUDICE AND DISCRIMINATION

Often we think of discrimination as arising from prejudice, distinction, and exclusion. We imagine that people distinguish between themselves and others—in other words, they exercise prejudice—because of rational self-interest or non-rational fears. And we imagine that discrimination flows from this prejudice. However, where social classes are concerned, this is clearly putting the cart before the horse. The whole point of class distinction is to preserve visible class differences—to ensure that we can tell people "like us" from people "unlike us," so that we organize our social lives around people "like us." Class prejudice, then, is not a by-product of class conflict. It is a tool in class conflict, a means of conducting the conflict.

In this respect, classes are like social cliques. Our purpose in creating cliques, as you know from having survived high school, is to include our friends and reject our enemies; to reward loyalty and punish disloyalty; to heap praise on ourselves and others "like us," and to heap ridicule on people who are different from us. Social classes do the same, but they do it throughout life, and in more complicated, costly ways. Sociologists have been studying these processes for a long time. In addition to Bourdieu's work on "distinction," there are at least two other important statements on the matter.

One is by the early twentieth-century sociologist Georg Simmel, who noted the importance of clothing fashion as a means of expressing both individuality and group membership. Fashion evolves continually, not because people change continually, but for other reasons. Partly it is a result of the fashion industry's need to create new products and new profits. But largely it is a result of the upper class's need to keep redefining what is "in fashion" to exclude those in the lower classes. They, in turn, have adopted the current (or recently past) fashions in hopes of appearing to belong to classes "above their station." (An interesting historical anecdote here is that in the centuries before fashions changed so quickly there were sumptuary laws that banned people from dressing and consuming in ways that were "above their station." We no longer make laws about this: we merely price people out of the competition and deny them the cultural capital to understand fully what is "in.")

In fairness, we should note that fashion is no longer a preserve of only the upper class. Fashion belongs to everyone, and the media are constantly reminding us of the importance of street fashion, with popular celebrities setting the styles. However, these new fashions know they have made it when they are adopted by the wealthy and displayed in fashionable places celebrated in elite publications.

Studying this process, early twentieth-century sociologist Thorstein Veblen made reference to what he called "conspicuous consumption" (also known as "conspicuous waste"). Why, Veblen asked, do the idle rich devote significant resources to learning sports like polo and impossible dances? Why do they spend money on lavish entertainment and travel? And why do they keep changing their tastes so trivially and promiscuously, with never a thought to cost or value? The answer is precisely because they can and others can't. Only by doing these foolish, costly, fickle things can the unspeakably rich "leisure class" separate itself from pretenders and nouveaux riches who can't keep up the pace. The whole point is to create visible bases on which to achieve discrimination, boundary lines that protect class lines and preserve segregation and distance.

SUSPICION AND DISTRUST

We have already noted Archibald's observation that people of different social classes are likely to suspect and distrust one another and, therefore, to maintain distance from one another. For similar reasons, they are likely to hide their true motives and limit the flow of information.

We see these tactics of class warfare everywhere. Especially in the United States, people have perfected a public manner of complete openness and candour that masks access to their real fears and concerns. "Have a nice day (smiley-face)!" A Marxist might say that this gap between appearance and reality in public interaction is a result of alienation from others. A Freudian might say that this gap is a neurotic separation of *superego*, that what we show publicly is what we are supposed to show (from the *id*) about what we are really feeling. But the explanation may be far simpler.

First, our society is a consumerist one. This is promoted by a shallow, superficial, and dishonest "smiley-face" approach to interaction. As C. Wright Mills pointed out in his 1951 work on white-collar jobs, we are all trained to be salesmen. We need to persuade and manipulate others using face-work and emotion-work. That's why God invented the weather and the Maple Leafs: so Canadians would have something superficial to discuss with non-intimate acquaintances.

Second, and equally important, the control of information is a means of struggling for power. Anyone who controls knowledge in an information society like ours controls other people. This is, of course, why the privately owned mass media constantly provide misinformation and slanted information, and withhold information that is inconvenient to the owner's political agenda. (Nowhere is this more obvious or more often discussed than in respect to the Fox News Channel in the US and the Asper media empire in Canada.) However, the same processes operate within large organizations, even government and business organizations.

The first extensive discussion of this fact was by French sociologist Michel Crozier in his book *The Bureaucratic Phenomenon* (1964). Crozier takes off from the theory proposed by sociologist Max Weber that bureaucracies are especially good at storing and spreading information in rational, efficient, and effective ways. (That presumably is why bureaucracies were invented.) But this fact about bureaucracies is not universally true, if true at all. In societies with rigid class or status hierarchies—for example, mid-twentieth-century France and Russia—bureaucracies may not work in these rational, efficient, and effective ways. Instead, they become terrains for fighting class and status warfare. Lower-ranking employees (such as the record-keepers) are able to undermine and manipulate higher-ranking people, supposedly the decision-makers, by withholding or distorting the information they preserve and pass along. Anyone who has watched the famous British sitcom *Yes Minister* knows that this happens in Britain as well.

Such behaviour occurs because people fear, suspect, and distrust people in higher ranks whose self-interest may pose risks to those in lower ranks. And in the same way, people also fear, suspect, and distrust others from lower ranks who may covet their job and salary, and whose self-interest is (therefore) also dangerous.

ABUSE AND VIOLENCE

There is little evidence of cross-class violence in Canadian society, whether by the rich against the poor or the poor against the rich. Most cross-class abuses are psychological or economic, not physical; further, most are sins of omission, not commission. The rich (try to) ignore the poor as much as possible. They try to dismiss evidence of poverty, deprivation, and inequality. We will soon discuss what Richard Sennett and Jonathan Cobb called the "hidden injuries of class."

That said, the dominant form of abuse of rich against poor is psychological. It takes various forms: in the mass media as blaming the victim and in the legislature as under-financing social measures that would protect or help the disadvantaged. For example, in the "social construction" of poverty and welfare in the mass media, we often see people slandered for their personal inadequacy or inadequate prudence. People are poor supposedly because they failed to get enough education, failed to make good choices about occupation or personal lifestyle, or got into trouble with the law.

Here, two aspects are neglected: first, these "choices" were often structured by other class-based factors. Not everyone can readily afford to go to university, for example. And not everyone is lucky enough to have parents who are healthy, supportive, and well informed, a resource rather than a liability to their children. Second, many people who inherit wealth or social contacts make equally poor "choices" about their lives, yet do not have to suffer damaging outcomes because they have family resources to protect them.

Third, and most important, the legislation we make and the taxes we collect and spend as a society provide a framework within which it is either safer or more dangerous to be poor. A society with universal health care and free university tuition, and with public housing for the homeless and secure public places, is a lot safer for poor people than a society without these resources. By contrast, these public resources are relatively less important to rich people, who can generally manage their own health care and educational costs, their own housing and security. Yet some societies—specifically, some commentators and politicians—choose to ignore these facts, justifying tax cuts for the rich and spending on programs that will provide less help for the poor but more political appeal to particular regions.

Take the tar sands development in Alberta. By polluting and destroy-ing the natural environment, the project manages to produce highly expensive fuel—perhaps with more energy going in than coming out. Why is this being supported by the federal government? The answer is because it wins votes in Alberta and it pleases the oil industry, matters of political interest to both major parties. Many would (and do) argue it would be better to suspend the project and invest in developing alter-native energy sources.

The point here is this: politics is about framing public issues and public spending in such a way that it seems rational, even while main-taining defined political and class constituencies at the expense of other constituencies. So the class conflict today is fought out politically in a shadow-world of justifications, ideologies, and half-truths. Even issues that have no immediately obvious relationship to class warfare (like the tar sands) have indirect bearing on it, because of the ways it shapes public taxation and spending.

Undesirable Outcomes

UNHAPPINESS, DEPRESSION, AND ANXIETY

We heard earlier about Sennett and Cobb's influential book, *The Hidden Injuries of Class*. This title aptly captured the fact that although modern class warfare is usually fought without guns, instead drawing on ideologies and legislation, it nonetheless injures the body and spirit.

We know this in several ways, all from the rapidly expanding study of social correlates of health and sickness. First and most important, we know that both poverty and income inequality have significantly harmful effects on people's mental health, influencing levels of hap-piness, depression, and anxiety. It may be true that "money can't buy you love" (or happiness either), but an absence of money can buy you illness, a lower quality of life, and a shortened lifespan. Factors associated with too little money or job security are reliably associated with stress, anxiety, depression, and illness.

This is particularly true for people in extreme poverty and insecurity (for example, think of the urban homeless). True, many people are homeless because of earlier conditions like poor mental or physical health that rendered them jobless, socially isolated, and without money for rent. However, the conditions of poverty and insecurity experienced on the street continue and intensify mental and physical deterioration. This has a range of causes that include exposure to violence, lack of suitable food and shelter, and lack of hygiene and health care.

The same problems are evident, to a lesser degree, among people who are housed but unemployed and on welfare; underemployed; or without a stable, predictable, and sufficient income. The reasons here are not so much violence as anxiety and the physical consequences of anxiety. (Job safety—the risk of injury at work—is important and is related to class position, but it is not what we are discussing here.) Stress and anxiety induced by harsh economic conditions have direct and observable effects on physical and mental health. And employment of certain kinds also has a negative effect on mental and physical health.

POOR PHYSICAL HEALTH

Two key studies have been particularly informative about the link between stress, mental health, and physical health. One, by health researchers Karasek and Theorell, used US and Scandinavian data to show that people with stressful jobs are far more prone to heart disease than people with less stressful jobs. The interesting fact about this correlation is its connection with social inequality.

Karasek and Theorell find that many common jobs like waitressing—which carry little authority, respect, salary, or job security (given the ease with which positions can be filled)—are particularly associated with risks of heart disease. This is because of the lethal combination of high demands with low control. The waitress is at the mercy of different people: her customers with their whims, moods, and schedules, and the kitchen and bar staff who may not co-operate in speeding along the correct orders. Conversely, the best possible job is one that lets the worker set his or her own pace and control the work flow: what is to be done, as well as how and when it is to be done. Such a job, as Marx would have said, almost entirely eliminates the alienation of work. (Complete absence of alienation would also allow the worker to keep all the profits of his or her labour.) By this standard, professional jobs such as professor, physician, or independent lawyer are the healthiest and least alienating.

A large-scale study that arrived at similar conclusions by a different method was the Whitehall Study (this was in fact a series of studies conducted in Britain, which analyzed the health and employment records of British civil servants who work in a block of buildings collectively referred to as "Whitehall"). This large-scale study, using data collected over many decades, showed that a given individual's position in the job hierarchy was a key predictor of health and longevity: the higher the position, the better the health and prospects for a long life. This finding remained strong even after controlling for such likely influences as smoking and other health-related lifestyle patterns. Poverty and job insecurity were not part of the explanation, since all the employees studied earned a regular, adequate wage or better.

What this study revealed is that economic and social inequality, not merely poverty, affects people's health. It likely does so by affecting their stress level—the demands made on them and their ability to control how they deal with demands. The continued high stress that results from difficult demands and limited control undermines the immune system, making the body vulnerable to a wide variety of illnesses. Stated simply, the body cannot adequately cope with insults to the brain and emotions that are due to social subordination. This is, indeed, a hidden injury of social class!

ADDICTIONS

As we know from Merton's theory of anomie, people deal with their social disadvantage (the gap between their opportunities and aspirations) in various ways. Some adopt what Merton called a "bureaucratic personality": they become ritualists, going through the motions of conformity without believing in the stated societal or organizational goals. In effect, they become zombies: people who are metaphorically walking among the living dead.

Others become retreatists, either physically (by isolating themselves from society as hermits in low-pay jobs and low-rent surroundings) or mentally. The mental retreatists often rely on mind-altering drugs. Some rely on prescription drugs for anxiety or depression if they can persuade a doctor to provide them. Others self-medicate with alcohol, which our culture condones and promotes, until it reaches the state of undeniable alcoholism. At that stage, the self-medicator can no longer control his needs for the drug, can no longer do his job, and becomes an embarrassment or even a danger to friends, family, and co-workers. Then society holds him responsible for his fall from "normalcy" and sends him off for therapy.

Many young people, perhaps affected by the example of their parents and older siblings, become anticipatory self-medicators. They become regular users of drugs and alcohol in their teens, before they have even given themselves a chance to fail in life as adults. There are many within the middle classes who are critical of these young drug abusers, claiming they personify the declining standards of our society or the diminished moral quality of young people. These critics hope that, through ridicule and a savage "war on drugs" (which includes high rates of arrest and punishment for such youthful self-medication), they will turn the tide on "immorality." Of course, many factors enter into this youthful addiction, not least adolescent experiences at home with family, at school with peers, and generally within their neighbourhoods.

But clearly it is far easier and less costly to blame the youthful victims than change the unequal society that makes such self-medication attractive to many.

CRIMES

Crime is another common response to social inequality and poverty. Merton termed it a form of "innovation" aimed at solving the socially structured problem of a gap between ends and means. To call it innovation is rather to glorify it: there's not much innovation in breaking into people's houses, stealing their cars, or taking a wallet at knifepoint. Most street crime by the poor is not innovative at all; it is age-old and relies on stealth, threat, or violence. Even the ancient Babylonians could likely have figured out how to rob a milk store.

The real innovators in crime are the corporate criminals: the Bernie Madoffs and other wealthy embezzlers, the so-called financiers and investment bankers. These innovators, aided by friendly or wilfully uninformed politicians, steal billions in ways that the Babylonians could never have imagined. In fact, prior to 2008, many North Americans were not even aware of the possibility of such crimes until their homes, jobs, and life savings disappeared. Criminal innovations, like other innovations, arise out of new opportunities and rely on new technologies, new political opportunities, and new social and cultural formations. The largest criminal innovations are possible in the most unequal, greediest, most gullible, and most risk-friendly cultures, where people are the most willing to believe in taking chances and in the idea that you can get something for nothing. They readily accept that something too good to be true actually is true.

North America, especially the US in the late twentieth century, forgot much of what it had ever known about the importance of hard work, private and public morality, and government regulation—the hard lessons of the Great Depression of the 1930s. It embraced a

Las Vegas–style pursuit of glamour, fame, and instant wealth, and a reliance on chance and inside information. Seemingly, everyone did this. "What happens in Vegas stays in Vegas," says the popular slogan encouraging impropriety and fantasy. It was against this cultural backdrop of fantasy and greed that we were reminded again about the possible range and consequences of criminal innovation. The Wall Street money-managers made the Mafia look penny-ante. Now, that's innovation! It relies on, creates, and maintains class inequality.

Knowing where to end this discussion is almost as hard as knowing where to begin. Many books can be and have been written about class inequality and its effects on physical health, mental health, addiction, and crime. And new books are always needed, because structures and forms of inequality keep changing. They change with new economic conditions, new political formations, new cultural beliefs and social ideologies. They also change with declines in the availability of jobs— for example, with the export of unionized manufacturing jobs to non-unionized countries.

The one thing that is clear and unchanging, where Karl Marx pitched his proverbial tent, is that most people need paid work to survive. They need it to feed, clothe, and shelter themselves and their families. To survive, they have no choice but to sell their labour and their time to others who, for various reasons, are lucky enough to own or control their jobs. So long as this is the case, class inequality will continue, and so will the consequences we have discussed. Only the innovative adaptations will change. There will be new drugs and new crimes.

SEVEN

Regions, Nations, and Empires

The subject of this chapter—regions, nations, and empires—is complicated.

On the surface, these are simply places on a map. But of course there is more than geography at stake, since these are also political, ecological, economic, social, and cultural units.

Every region, nation, or empire is defined by political and legal jurisdiction: who rules it and under what body of laws. The British Empire, for example, was a set of dominions, colonies, and protectorates loosely ruled from London. Within each of these dominions, colonies, and protectorates, people were ruled by a local version of British common law, managed by local judges and magistrates.

Empires have taken a range of different approaches in how they managed their subjects. The Roman Empire famously decided to tax its colonies, but not to meddle in their cultural or religious affairs; this wise decision contributed to a relatively long period of peace and stability. Other empires, including the British, tried to convert the beliefs and practices of many of the people it ruled, favouring the Christian religion.

Nations are mainly political units. In the modern world, most national societies are (political) states and most states are national societies. Where the nation and the state do not coincide—as in Canada, where Quebec sovereignists demand an independent state for their French-speaking "nation"—conflict arises and secession is threatened. Such conflicts and threats are visible throughout the world. In Turkey and Iraq, Kurds would like to create their own state, as would the

Basque region in Spain and Macedonians in Greece. In some parts of the world, including the former USSR, the former Yugoslavia, and the former Czechoslovakia, states have already been fragmented by "national" movements for independence.

"Regions" are often just combinations of political or jurisdictional units. Sometimes political units have banded together to form an alliance against Ontario or Quebec, or against the federal government, as we have seen in the Maritimes or the Prairie provinces. However, regions are not fundamentally political units: they are better understood as geographic, ecological, economic, social, and cultural units.

Some small nations like the country of Andorra in the Pyrenees may include but a single unified ecosystem. But most nations and all empires span more than one geographical zone, comprising shorelines, mountains, prairies, and sometimes even deserts. By contrast, most regions are ecologically homogeneous; their common ecology, and the common lifestyle to which this gives rise, makes them into economic and cultural communities.

In North America, the St. Lawrence watershed is a natural geographical boundary. However, the national political borders transect ecological regions that run mainly from north to south. The Canadian Maritime provinces are similar to (and historically connected to) New England in the US. British Columbia is similar both in terms of climate and geography to the West Coast states of Washington, Oregon, and California. And Alberta is similar to the central mountain states of the US: to Montana, Idaho, Wyoming, and Utah.

Some of the similarities between, say, New Brunswick and Maine, or British Columbia and the state of Washington, are environmental. But we saw in an earlier chapter that environmental factors can lead to cultural differences between regions. And these factors can also result in economic differences. Atlantic coastal locations, for example, share a history of early settlement, commercial fishing, and trans-Atlantic shipping. Mountain regions in North America share a history of resource extraction, lumbering, and cattle grazing. Central plains regions are all agricultural, whether in Canada or the US. Around the Great Lakes, where all the resource supply routes converge, is the continent's industrial heartland: Ontario, Ohio, Indiana, Michigan, Pennsylvania, and New York.

No wonder, then, that research on the attitudes of Canadians and Americans has found little evidence of national differences, with two main exceptions: Quebec francophone attitudes and Southern US ("Dixie") attitudes are distinct. In many domains, no significant differences are detectable between those who live across the border from each other in, say, Ontario and New York, Nova Scotia and New Hampshire, or Alberta and Wyoming.

This was documented in *The Nine Nations of North America* (1981) by journalist Joel Garreau. A later book on the topic by sociologists Ed Grabb and James Curtis, *Regions Apart: The Four Societies of Canada and the United States* (2003), also argued that in many respects Canada and the US are similar, and only Quebec and the Southern states in the US are strongly different. Alberta and Wyoming resemble each other on a wide range of values and attitudes, and both are very different from Quebec and Mississippi, which in turn differ greatly from each other: Quebec is more liberal, and Mississippi is more traditional.

Both books show that certain historic similarities within a region, such as a shared history of settlement or connection to the centres of power, result in social and cultural similarities among its people. Ecological similarities have the same effects, largely due to their influence on the economy: that is, they strongly influence the source of wealth in the region. Economic historian Harold Innis said the history of Canada was the history of westward-moving resource extraction in one region after another. First, cod were fished (almost to extinction) from waters off Newfoundland. This was followed by beaver pelts from Quebec, then the timber from Quebec, New Brunswick, and Ontario. After this, minerals were extracted from northern Quebec and Ontario; then grain from Manitoba and Saskatchewan; then oil from Alberta; and more or less simultaneously timber, minerals, and fish from British Columbia. One result of this series of events is that Canadian history tends to be regional history.

A common ecology produces similar economic activities, which result in similar lifestyles and attitudes. There is more cultural similarity between the fishermen of Nova Scotia and Maine, for example, than between the loggers of New Brunswick, the garment-factory workers of New Hampshire, or the oil-patch workers of Alberta. Of course, there are also state-imposed policy differences between New Brunswick and New Hampshire (such as universal health care coverage in the former but not the latter). These policy differences have consequences for poverty, immigration, health, crime, addiction, and so on.

There are certainly social and cultural differences between Canada and the US, and these are both the cause and consequence of other differences. Yet we should not exaggerate these differences. Both countries are more alike than either is like Brazil, India, Nigeria, or Italy. The common cultural heritage—originating in British imperial settlement—has had a huge significance for both Canadian and US development in the nineteenth and twentieth centuries. That said, even within the domain of former British colonies, we see important social and cultural differences. As sociologist Seymour Martin Lipset points out in his classic work *The First New Nation* (1961), the US is very different from Canada, Britain, and Australia; he argues that this is largely because the US had a revolution and the others did not. Clearly, Australia has never had a revolution; Britain did in 1640 and 1688, but Lipset discounts these. Although there was a Canadian rebellion of sorts in 1837, the Loyalist (anti-revolutionary) tradition was far more important.

In short, we need to account for both nations and regions, both of which are largely ecological, economic, and cultural units. By contrast, empires are largely political and economic units, while nation-states are political and economic units that may not be culturally unified.

These different geographic units—regions, nations, and empires—are differently constituted, so discussing them all in the same chapter can be awkward. But they do have several features in common. First, we can analyze all of these units according to whether they are powerful core (or central) units or weak peripheral units: that is, whether they dominate other units or are dominated by them. Take the example of Canada: some believe that central Canada—Ontario and Quebec—has historically monopolized economic and political power, and the other provinces or regions have been on the periphery. At the same time, Canada itself has always been a peripheral or semi-peripheral member of the British Empire and, later, of the American Empire.

Within Canada's regions, certain key cities—mostly Toronto and Montreal—have been core cities, financially, politically, and artistically. Others have been peripheral. In turn, Toronto and Montreal have been peripheral to London, New York, and other global centres. We can at least in principle identify all places as dominant over some locations and subordinate to others.

Second, two features that characterize locations are worth discussing together: exchange and domination. Locations tied together by large-scale flows of people, goods, capital, or information are effectively regions, nations, or empires. Locations that are mainly the sources of capital, manufactured goods, and political decisions are "the centre." Locations that are mainly recipients of capital, manufactured goods, and political decisions are the periphery. Further, these peripheral locations send labour, raw materials, and profits to the centre. Other evidence of the unequal connection between centre and periphery is seen in news reporting. News about the central regions is reported everywhere in the periphery, while news about the periphery is rarely reported in the centre.

This chapter is about geographic locations that are connected by exchanges (of people, resources, and capital) and relations (of power). Sometimes they are also connected by common values and attitudes, a common ecology, or common economic interests. But often they are not.

Conflicts are likely to arise between (and within) regions, nations, and empires for a range of reasons. First, inequalities of power, wealth, and influence are central to these relationships as a result of unequal exchanges. Second, important ecological, cultural, and social differences also divide them one from another. Often the inequalities of power and wealth are mistaken for, or entangled in, conflicts over social and cultural differences. Political or economic wars turn into "culture wars," for example. Because there are so many bases of difference, it is never easy to figure out the exact reasons two regions or countries or empires get into fights with each other.

Opportunities for Co-operation across the Line

Given so many reasons for conflict, it is hard to imagine how people might co-operate across geographic boundaries. Yet they have co-operated on many occasions and for many reasons.

These were all evident during the Cold War between the US and the USSR, roughly in the period from 1945 to 1990. One form of co-operation was through music. Music is an international language, often without political content. The exchange of musicians has often served to keep open lines of communication and co-operation across hostile borders. Sports events serve a similar purpose since, like music, sport has little inherent political content, though it can be used to symbolize national aspirations and inspire unity. Other forms of co-operation, such as exchanges of scientists, writers, or academics, are more politically charged. In the past, concerns have almost always been raised about the possibilities of defection, spying, or opportunities to score political points. In fact, even musical and sporting exchanges were sometimes used for these purposes. The country that performed best was likely to claim that this success proved its social or economic superiority.

Sometimes regions, nations, or empires co-operate against common enemies. They may make humanitarian efforts to deal with the effects of a natural disaster (for example, a famine, earthquake, or epidemic in an impoverished country). Or they may make political or military efforts to end violence in other countries.

In the second half of the twentieth century, the United Nations was occasionally helpful in mobilizing co-operative efforts around international concerns. These included preserving heritage sites, calling attention to the rights of women and children, mobilizing peacekeeping troops, and so on. Some common opportunities like co-operation in the exploration of space were shared between the major world powers. But equally many significant opportunities like the conquest of disease, poverty, peace, and human rights were squandered. Today, after the collapse of the Soviet empire and the rise to dominance of US power, we still see no international initiatives against epidemics, human trafficking, or organized crime, though the opportunities are still there.

George Orwell, in his 1948 dystopian novel *1984*, imagined a world in which three dominant empires kept realigning themselves, with a different pair always ganging up against the third. In the last seventy years, this fantasy has proven more real than imaginary, given the shifting coalitions among the US, Russia, and China.

However, new mechanisms of co-operation have arisen at the same time. In the last few decades, multinational corporations and non-governmental organizations (NGOs) have assumed increasingly more economic and political influence. This has reduced the historic influence of regions, nations, and empires as political actors. It has also provided mechanisms for sharing across regional and cultural lines. Today, the whole world has become familiar with internationally marketed consumer brands (Coke, McDonald's, Nike) and with their cultural and social meanings. This has provided some basis for co-operation through shared cultural understanding.

Opportunities for co-operation across regional lines are also much more common within nations. First, there is the possibility of contact and co-operation at the highest levels of national government, in political parties and in Parliament. Second, there is contact among the employees of national businesses. Third, there is cross-regional contact among students in post-secondary institutions and youth organizations. Additionally, business and vacation travel within a country all increase contact and communication among people from different regions.

Increasingly, people also rely on the Internet and cyberspace to bridge the distance from one region to another and one country to another. More and more people are setting up networks of virtual relationships as well as real ones. In recent years, Internet-based social networking services such as LinkedIn, MySpace, and Facebook have grown exponentially in popularity. These services collect information from an individual's profile and list of social contacts, and display his or her personal social network. They are often provided free to users, although individuals must disclose personal information to register.

What remains to be seen is whether these networks of cyber-relations are as meaningful or stable as face-to-face relations. The evidence so far is mixed.

Researchers disagree about the overall effect of information technology on family and community life. On the one hand, increased connectedness makes it easier to contact friends, neighbours, acquaintances, spouses, children, parents, and siblings; relations can be maintained even from a distance. On the other hand, the new connectedness may intrude on traditional family life, disturbing rituals and cohesion. Computers and other IT (for example, video games) can isolate families, individuate family members across generations, separate them from one another in individual activities, and even lead to addictive behaviour. Some researchers argue that extensive Internet use increases the risk of depression and loneliness by isolating the user from sources of support and sociability. It seems clear that communication technologies will have unpredictable effects, at least for a while.

The effects of technology on intimacy seem to depend on the *type* of close relationship. Among strongly tied (that is, closely related) people, easy and relatively cheap technologies such as email do not replace traditional communication media like face-to-face meetings or telephone calls. Closely related communicators use new as well as old technologies and communicate frequently. More communication (and more varied communication) strengthens a relationship. By contrast, weakly tied communicators rely on one medium and are less motivated to explore new technologies. Their relationships remain distant as a result.

Over the last one hundred and fifty years, changes in communications and transport technologies have made contact among kin and friends—whether they live near one another or great distances apart—less expensive, faster, and easier. As email and Internet use spreads, geographic constraints on social relationships decrease. Changes in technology that simplify contact among family and friends are likely to contribute to the quality and cohesion of relationships. The spread of easy communication shrinks distances, and we can expect this shrinking of distance to continue. Yet despite the constant changes in the technological context of social relationships, most social theory continues to assume that people will form and preserve close relationships mainly through face-to-face interaction.

One strategy for studying cross-national and cross-regional relations is to examine how technology has affected close relations in the past. New technologies rapidly traverse traditional social barriers and achieve wide adoption. Consider the history of two important communication technologies: the telephone and email.

From the beginning, telephones were used mainly for long-distance calling. Commercial interests advertised the telephone as a means to link family and friends; women were shown using it for "kin-keeping." The telephone improved communication: people expressed their views in their own voice, it was simple to use, and (once the private line replaced the party line) it was as private as face-to-face communication. As a result, the telephone was widely adopted and used to preserve close relations, even at a distance. People quickly became dependent on this new communication instrument.

Yet surprisingly the telephone's effects on social life have been modest. There is no systematic evidence that the telephone has changed close relations. At most, the telephone helped them by keeping people in touch in between face-to-face meetings.

And the telephone, like other forms of communication, has had both positive and negative effects on close relations. Researchers have studied the ways peacekeeping troops in the Sinai (in Egypt) used telephones on the frontlines. Talking to parents and spouses preserved close relations while on duty. However, after receiving a phone call or hearing disturbing news from home, a large minority reported feeling sad or angry about being in the Sinai.

Some of the advantages of email are similar to those of the telephone. However, email is not as disruptive as the telephone, nor is it dependent on both people being available at the same time. Unlike the telephone, email is print-based. Since it involves computer technology and some literacy, email is not quite as simple or inexpensive to use as the telephone. Beyond that, email carries a variety of dangers of its own. Faceless anonymity poses the risk of indiscretion, misunderstanding, and misquoting. The shield of visual and vocal anonymity may encourage blunt disclosure and self-misrepresentation. As well, people are more likely to express themselves intemperately and thoughtlessly through email and text-messaging.

Still, the lack of temporal and spatial boundaries associated with telephone and email frees relationships and makes new relationships possible. It also makes relationships with online communicators possible for people formerly prevented from socializing—for example, people housebound by illness or child care. The proven effects of email on social life have been modest so far. But one thing is certain: the telephone and email have both made cross-regional, cross-national, and cross-empire communication easier than ever before.

Forces Pushing People Apart

EVIDENCE OF CONFLICT: INTRODUCTION

The other groups we have discussed in this book—men and women, old and young, majority and minority groups, and owning and working classes—have all institutionalized their identities and concerns. So while the working class has built trade unions to press its interests, the capitalist class has its industry associations. Ethnic groups with high institutional completeness have their own schools, newspapers, churches, and communities. Youth have their own culture, while the elderly have segregated living quarters and associations for retired people. Even men and women have their own institutions, to some degree: the private versus public sphere is a traditional example.

However, in terms of institutionalizing difference, nothing compares with regions and nations. Far more than gender groups, age groups, ethnic groups, or classes, regions and nations comprise perfect institutional boundaries.

Consider the regions of Canada. Canadian provinces all have their own governments, and these governments have protected powers under the British North America Act. What's more, the jurisdictional powers of these provinces (such as the control of health care and education) touch on the most important concerns of the twenty-first century. The provinces also have taxing powers, the right to legislate on various topics, and their own courts. No wonder, then, that the Canadian provinces (and as we have seen, collaborations between provinces in the form of Canadian regions) have enormous importance in Canadian politics. Further, they are constantly battling the federal government and often enjoy considerable success in doing so.

The poster child for provincial success is of course Quebec, which has both provincial and federal secessionist (i.e., sovereignist) parties: the Parti Québécois (provincial) and the Bloc Québécois (federal). Neither currently holds power, but each exerts an influence on Canadian politics. And the western region is not far behind in its institutionalization of political grievances through politics. The Conservative Party, which is now the ruling party, is rooted in the ideology, personnel, and supporters of the former Reform Party. This in turn rose out of the Alberta Social Credit Party, which was originally a traditional, fundamentalist party of rural protest against the urban east. Today, the Conservative Party has virtually no support east of Ontario; conversely, the opposing Liberal Party has virtually no support west of Ontario. In Quebec, the current provincial government is Liberal, and the Liberals and Conservatives together drew more votes than the Bloc Québécois, which (however) drew 38 percent of the federal vote in Quebec last year. Some would argue that regionalism in Canada is exacerbated by our first past the post voting system. It is clear that politics in Canada are highly regionalized, and the result is that regional conflicts are translated into national political institutions.

Add to this the fact that regionalism in Canada is strengthened by the linguistic split between French-speaking Quebec and the English-speaking rest of Canada. (Of course, some parts of English-speaking Canada—for example, parts of Northern Ontario, Manitoba, and New Brunswick—are ancestrally French-speaking. However, these play only a limited role in Canada's regional conflict.)

Nation-states are even better at finding ways to differentiate themselves institutionally. The whole purpose of state-building is to create institutions that promote the interests of one country at the expense of other countries. This is why sovereign countries have governments, armies, foreign policies, trade policies, tariffs, and immigration rules. So it is to be expected that nations will come into conflict with one another; their core institutions depend on such conflict. As well, these

core institutions also come into conflict with international organizations (e.g., NATO, the UN) and treaties (e.g., NAFTA, the European
Union) that are aimed at creating pan-national institutions with their
own interests and resources.

SEGREGATION OR DISTANCE

In Canada, there is no segregation or social distance among people
from different provinces; for example, in Toronto you won't find a
neighbourhood populated mainly by people from Newfoundland or
Saskatchewan. In fact, one of the problems faced by poor Canadians in
Toronto who come from Newfoundland or Northern Ontario is precisely that they are socially, residentially, and institutionally invisible.
As Canadian sociologist S.D. Clark wrote, the "new urban poor" from
rural regions of the country have a much harder time, and much less
social support, than the so-called visible minorities who at least often
live together and build co-operative institutions together.

Likewise, it would be hard to find an expatriate "American community" in Montreal, for example, or a "Canadian community" in New
York City. However, most national communities are more visible than
this, and the more visible they are, the more segregated and distant they
are from other communities. Visible expatriate national communities like
the Ukrainians in Winnipeg can be distinguished through a distinctive
language, church, neighbourhood, and set of community institutions.

As for social distance, some national or ethnic communities are
especially distant from others, even when we consider the differences
in their income or language. Some have no occasion to meet each other,
owing to differences in residential location, language, and institutional
completeness. But others deliberately avoid each other, a result of differences of religion or ideology. For example, there is little contact these
days between Jews and Muslims in Canada, because of disagreements
over the conflict in Israel. And there is also little contact between Afro-
Canadian and Asian communities.

The social distance between national or ethnic communities is obvious in various ways, such as marriage choices. Today, ethnic inter-marriage is much more common than it was in the past, and people are much less reluctant to leave their own group to find a mate. What's more, they are much more willing to cross racial or religious bound-aries to do so. Today, people look mainly for a mate who is like them in age, education, interests, and aspirations.

However, people are still more likely than random chance to marry those who are socially like themselves—who live nearby, attend the same educational and social institutions, or work in a similar job. In effect, then, our social institutions still influence who we meet and who we marry, and some of these influences are based on national difference.

PREJUDICE AND DISCRIMINATION

In an earlier chapter, we discussed some aspects of social distance in connection with racism and ethnicity. The same is true about prejudice and discrimination among different nationalities in Canada.

International politics exert a major influence on national groups in Canada, so we should start by discussing that influence. As a rule, prejudice and discrimination between groups are increased by con-flict—for example, by war or the threat of a war. Some have aptly pointed out that truth is the first casualty of war. Newspapers start reporting atrocities perpetrated by the enemy; there is the covert or overt implication of moral inferiority. This has a huge effect on people's perceptions of one another, and on their feelings of prejudice.

Nowhere has this been more obvious than in the current treatment of Muslims by the Western media—or for that matter, of Americans by the Islamic media. Some conservative commentators have tried to depict the suicide bombings in Iraq and Afghanistan, and the 9/11 ter-rorist attack on New York City, as parts of a "clash of civilizations"—a "culture war" of theocratic, backward Islam against secular, progres-sive America. Islamic commentators, for their part, have been far more likely to see these acts as responses to American imperialism and America's foreign policy objectives—namely, to secure oil, to protect Israel, and to undermine Islamic national independence.

Such broad-brush depictions of political events seem to accuse all Muslims of being backward ideologues and all Americans (and their allies) of being venal hypocrites. As a result, they increase the distance between nations and make it harder to resolve differences. At home in Canada, such prejudiced depictions cause discomfort to those uninvolved members of the same national group who are vilified by association: Arab-Canadians and Muslims of all nationalities and political persuasions, for example.

Despite this, there has been no evidence of a Canadian increase in hate crimes around these national depictions; nor is there any evidence of increased workplace discrimination. There has not been an upsurge in jokes at the expense of Muslims or Arabs, for instance. As we noted earlier, the main sign of tension between Islamic and Western groups in Canada has been on university campuses, around the Israel-Palestinian conflict.

The *relative* absence of visible discrimination and prejudice in Canada suggests several things. At the risk of overstating the case, it first suggests the success of human rights legislation aimed at preventing discrimination, hate crimes, and the use of derogatory language against other groups. Second, it suggests that Canadians are by and large a moderate people who tend to avoid conflict (much more, say, than Americans).

Finally, it suggests that in Canada, efforts by mainly American commentators to label the conflicts in the Middle East as "culture wars" have largely failed. Canadians in general are skeptical about the motives and claims of American foreign policy, though they may feel a strong kinship with other aspects of American society. (For example, probably no other country outside the US celebrated as sincerely and enthusiastically the election of the first African-American to the American presidency.)

SUSPICION AND DISTRUST

If in a time of war truth is the first casualty, trust is always the second. When you can't rely on knowing and hearing the truth, you can't trust what you do hear. In such times, people develop a generalized distrust about political matters. Unfortunately, this distrust has been proven to be justified by the failure of the news media to report truthfully about either foreign policy (for example, the progress of wars abroad) or the economy. The long celebration of wealth and hubris that framed American government since 1980 has now ended in stunned silence. There is evidence of a drop in trust for government and the media in the US, and even in Canada. (In Canada, the result is low voter turnout and continued minority governments.)

Perhaps this is another reason why today one hears relatively little prejudice or distrust voiced against other nations. No one knows what to believe and everyone knows it is necessary to be cautious. Besides, the Orwellian scenario sketched earlier—namely, that nations change their allies with shocking regularity—gives us pause. When the USSR invaded Afghanistan, the US supported so-called freedom fighters who, after the Russians left, came to power as the Taliban and are now viewed as enemies. Saddam Hussein's Iraq was at one time the West's ally against Iran. And our current allies, Pakistan and Saudi Arabia, are fully as theocratic, autocratic, and unpredictable as the Taliban, Iran, and Iraq. So how can we choose among them? (Don't even think about Russia, our ally in World War II, our enemy during the Cold War, and once again our ally, though headed by a former KGB agent who seems reluctant to give up power after his term of office has ended.)

We see then a generalized suspicion and distrust about politics and statecraft. But for this very reason, political leaders have a harder-than-usual time focusing hatred on any outside region, nation, or empire.

Add to this the political effects of the Internet, and you may imagine that we have entered a new era of international affairs. But contrary to the views of some, the Internet does not ensure that everyone knows the truth. The Internet merely ensures we know many different sides of every story, and so far we have no way of telling what is true from what is not. The information overload created by the Internet (and the mass media) has fed a general suspicion, distrust, and anxiety. Today, many people feel like they know *less* than they used to know, or thought they knew.

Confidence in some of the institutions responsible for international co-operation has also eroded. Westerners have relatively little confidence in the United Nations today, for example, and Canada no longer plays an important role there. The US has long refused to pay its membership dues, in a fit of pique against the many small developing nations that have repeatedly voted against (and scuttled) American resolutions. The UN is floundering for lack of money. This is worsened by competing views about the proper goals of the organization and a sense that it cannot be relied on to make sensible decisions or take timely actions (consider its failure to act during the Rwanda massacre). Both NATO and the European Union appear to be expanding, but it is unclear what goals they are pursuing, other than growth.

Violence and War

The only thing certain is that the twentieth century was a period of continued, sporadic war, and the twenty-first century has started out that way too. As a result we can have little doubt that these days the conflicts between nations and empires often take the shape of wars. Wars (including civil wars) are raging at this time in parts of Africa and the Middle East.

Most people consider war to be an openly declared armed conflict between two countries or between groups within a country. However, many would also expand the definition of war to include undeclared battles, guerrilla wars, covert operations, and even terrorism. Many countries even have a "war system." Here, social institutions, especially their economies and governments, and their cultural practices promote warfare as a normal aspect of life, even if no war is being waged at a given moment.

War is an institution of collective violence; it is a form of organized group violence used to promote a state agenda or resist the goals of another state. Unlike interpersonal violence, which is more episodic, unorganized, and impulsive, modern warfare relies on unemotional killing and advanced technology. Because of advances in military technology, the modern weapons used in combat are exponentially more deadly than ever before. A single precision-guided missile released by a B-52 bomber many thousands of feet above a war zone can kill hundreds of enemy soldiers and civilians. The nuclear bomb dropped on Hiroshima in the last days of World War II is estimated to have killed 80,000 people instantly. That was more than sixty years ago. Consider what we could do today.

Terrorism is war by other means, just as war is the continuation of politics by other means, as the military strategist Carl von Clausewitz declared in *On War*, published posthumously in 1832. A study by the Federal Research Division of the Library of Congress, cited in Mark Sauter and James Jay Carafano's book *Homeland Security* (2005), defined terrorism as "the calculated use of unexpected, shocking, and unlawful violence against non-combatants (including, in addition to civilians, off-duty military and security personnel in peaceful situations) and other symbolic targets." A simple, dispassionate definition of the term is difficult because "terrorism" is an ideological and value-laden term, as well as a description of events. However, a definition that is both broader and simpler characterizes it as any act by an individual or group that is intended to undermine the lawful authority of a government or state, usually through violence.

The roots of terrorism can be found in the religious, nationalist, political, economic, and social differences that prevent people from living together in peace. There is no evidence to suggest a single motive behind the use of terrorism, but the most accepted theory is that participants feel violence is the best course of action, after all things are considered. A rational cost-benefit analysis—not reckless impulse—leads people to this conclusion, often because of various frustrating or limiting social, political, and economic conditions.

Undesirable Outcomes

TERRORISM AND SUICIDE

Generally, terrorist acts are carried out by secret member(s) of a subnational group for what they believe to be the purpose of publicizing a political or a religious cause, or intimidating or coercing government(s) or the civilian population into accepting demands on behalf of the cause. Many of the terrorist suicide bombers in the Middle East, for example, have come from oppressed or relatively impoverished circumstances. One factor in accepting suicide is the promise of large cash payments to their families by supportive states and wealthy sympathizers—also, the promise of virgins waiting in heaven for the departed freedom fighter.

For the most part, however, terrorists—and especially their leaders, like the infamous Osama bin Laden—are men from middle- to upper-class backgrounds, typically with a higher-than-average education. They generally have specific skills and strong political motivation. Increasingly, terrorist organizations in the developing world recruit young members. Often, terrorists and guerrillas are the only role models available to these young people.

Terrorism is not a new phenomenon. Indeed, a recent book by Canadian historian Ana Siljak—*Angel of Vengeance*—examined its emergence in nineteenth-century Russia. However, the social construction of terrorism by the media through definitional and rhetorical processes has led it to be generally understood as an occurrence unique to our times.

Experts view terrorism as only a different form of soldiering, with the usual motives: protection of home and country. The limited data available on individual terrorists suggests that there is one common characteristic: "normality." What is unique about terrorists is not their abnormality so much as their degree of commitment and organization. Like other social movements, terrorist groups rely on existing social networks to recruit members. But because terrorist activities are organized and carried out in secret, social networks of friendship and kinship are particularly important means of maintaining control over the recruits—to ensure their reliability, as we noted above.

State-sponsored terrorism is the state-sanctioned use of terrorist groups to achieve foreign-policy objectives. The current US government has four countries on the "terrorism list": Cuba, Iran, Sudan, and Syria. Of these four, three are Middle Eastern or other nations with mainly Muslim populations. Other governments and groups might compile different lists. In the eyes of some, the US itself might be viewed as a state that sponsors terrorism, with the aim of destabilizing foreign governments and undermining progressive political movements.

In certain areas, state sponsorship remains an important driving force behind terrorism. This is likely true in Israel, the West Bank, and the Gaza Strip today, where state-sponsored groups have easy access to money, weapons, training, fake passports, and protection. Often, the US Central Intelligence Agency (CIA) has served as a go-between, providing such assets to US-friendly terrorists in various Central and South American countries.

The irony of state-sponsored terrorism is that, while it can be a powerful form of covert warfare, it can also be vulnerable to shifts in international politics. Terrorist groups in the developing world have on occasion found themselves suddenly deprived of support from foreign sponsors. We saw earlier how Iraq's Saddam Hussein was enlisted by the US as an ally against Iran, only to be later cast aside and ultimately vilified. Various religious fundamentalists, including the Taliban and

even Osama bin Laden, have also at one time received support from the
US and its allies in opposition to the Russian invasion of Afghanistan,
only to be later dropped and defamed.

Western governments have recently made many efforts to safeguard
their citizens against terrorist attacks. These measures often involve
tightening domestic security, sometimes at the expense of civil liberties. However, vigilance—even when combined with highly advanced
technology—cannot solve what is finally a social and political problem. Improved technologies are no guarantee against future terrorist
strikes or criminal sabotage. No amount of enhanced detection and
counterterrorism can fully secure a country against attack. Terrorists
will continue to adapt their tactics to exploit weaknesses in homeland
security measures.

Finally, note that on 11 September 2001, the terrorists used low-
tech weapons to take over the planes, which they also used as low-tech
weapons (i.e., bludgeons). It takes little imagination to see how dedicated terrorists might easily and calamitously bring about mass death
by infiltrating a city's water or subway system, the ventilation in a sky-
scraper, or a country's food distribution network.

What this means is that we must address the underlying motives
of terrorists, because we cannot control their opportunities. Without
understanding and changing motivation, no war against terrorism can
succeed. Preventing future attacks will mean considering the historical,
political, economic, and other factors that lead normal humans to see
mass terror as proper and death by martyrdom as appealing.

HEALTH EFFECTS OF WAR

As Thomas Malthus pointed out over two centuries ago, war—along
with disease and starvation—is a "positive check" on population.
Whether or not we choose to view war in this benignly clinical way,
there can be no doubt that to a dramatic degree wars have reduced the
population of humanity.

In the thousand years between 1000 and 2000 CE, wars killed about 175 million people. Of these, 111 million were killed in the twentieth century alone, owing to the increased scope and efficiency—the industrialization—of warfare. An estimated 9 million were killed in World War I and another 61 million were killed in World War II (of these, over half were civilians). The Soviet Union alone lost over 25 million people in World War II.

Projections by the UN and other groups estimate that had these 70 million people not been killed in World Wars I and II, the world's population today would have been 6.95 billion instead of 6.24 billion. Put differently, according to this reckoning, the deaths of 70 million people in two world wars prevented the births of 710 million people who, but for these wars, would have been alive today. Among the 710 million people who were never born, there might have been another Einstein, Mozart, Shakespeare, or Picasso; another Mother Teresa; or even your own uncle or cousin. Under some circumstances, you yourself might not have been born. Conflicts between regions, nations, and empires are matters of life and death—potentially even your own.

Not only has the nature of warfare changed over time, but so have the settings in which conflicts take place. Consider the growth of terrorist tactics that target civilian populations rather than military personnel. Warfare has shifted from secluded outposts and isolated bases to crowded urban centres. This has given rise to an increased incidence of what we call "war crimes."

WAR CRIMES

Despite the saying that "all's fair in love and war," signers of the Geneva Conventions formally declared that at least some actions are unacceptable even in the context of war.

The effort to impose legal norms on wartime behaviour has been ongoing for over a century. The First Geneva Convention concerned the treatment of battlefield casualties. The Second Geneva Convention extended the First Convention to warfare at sea. The Third Geneva Convention concerned the treatment of prisoners of war, while the Fourth and most important here covered the treatment of civilians during wartime. In 1949, all the conventions were redrawn and codified. Protocol I, a 1977 amendment, addressed the protection of victims in international conflicts, while Protocol II, in the same year, addressed the protection of victims in non-international armed conflicts.

Defining wartime atrocities against civilians as "war crimes" may seem strange, given the fundamental goal of combat—to defeat your enemies—and given the barbarous way people are killed during war. However, many nations hold the view that slaughtering soldiers is an acceptable cost of war, but the intentional slaughter of civilians is indefensible.

War crimes differ from other forms of violence in that representatives of one nation or empire inflict this violence to achieve self-interested political goals. An example of this is an attempt to challenge the political power of another nation or to prevent that nation from achieving its stated goals. Rationalizations and excuses are commonly devised to explain the extent of violence, its effects, or its lack of fairness.

Usually, these rationalizations begin by distinguishing "us" from "them." A group defined as outsiders or strangers is easily defamed and attacked—easily written off as a means to an end, and fully expendable. The most horrific manifestation of this is genocide, the systematic and planned execution of an entire national, ethnic, racial, or political group. The most notorious case of genocide was the attempted extermination of Jews and gypsies by Nazi Germany during World War II. Many others, including Slavs, homosexuals, and people deemed "mentally defective," were also murdered. In all, six million Jews were killed, many in concentration camps like Auschwitz, where an estimated one million died.

Though many vowed after 1945 that such an atrocity should never be allowed to happen again, genocides continue to take place.

Rwanda and the former Yugoslavia are two recent and notorious cases. However, procedures have been developed in international law to deal with genocidal war criminals. The International Criminal Court was created in 2002, although it is worth noting that both the US and Israel have not ratified it, and as such are not bound by its provisions.

There are also other important international legal bodies to prosecute such crimes. In 2001, Slobodan Milošević, president of Yugoslavia during the 1998–99 conflict in Kosovo, was indicted by the International Criminal Tribunal in The Hague, Netherlands, for committing war crimes against ethnic Albanians. Among other things, he was accused of ordering soldiers to dump at least fifty Kosovo Albanians into the Danube River in 1999, of approving the deaths of hundreds of others, of displacing up to 700,000 more, and of carrying out other "ethnic cleansing" policies while in power. Milošević was the first sitting head of state to ever face international war crimes charges. He died in prison before his trial was concluded and a verdict was rendered.

Most recently, Sudanese President Omar Hassan Ahmad al-Bashir was indicted on war crimes. On 4 March 2009, the International Criminal Court issued an arrest warrant for the sixty-five-year-old on charges of war crimes and crimes against humanity in Darfur—the first warrant ever issued by the court for a sitting head of state.

Other war crime tribunals, established on an ad hoc basis in contrast to the permanency of the International Criminal Court, are sporadic. Another issue is that war crimes tribunals are physically unable to process hundreds of thousands of trials. Nevertheless, it is clear that all such tribunals—for example, the Truth and Reconciliation Commission hearings in South Africa—are superior to acts of vengeance by the aggrieved parties. Right actions following wrongdoing, such as changing institutions, reparations, or apologies, may help to bring about healing and peace.

Wartime violence against civilians often targets women. Despite prohibitions outlined in the Geneva Conventions, rape, assault, and enforced prostitution of women have all continued during armed conflicts. For example, in the years of World War II, the Japanese military forced up to 200,000 young women into prostitution as "comfort women" for military personnel, with many eventually dying from sexually transmitted diseases and torture. During the recent conflicts in Bosnia-Herzegovina and Rwanda, and in most other hostile actions as well, roving bands of soldiers raped, beat, and killed women.

This has given rise to the concept of "gendercide"—genocidal acts committed against women as women and men as men—as human rights violations. Gendercide against women typically involves rape, which has come to be recognized as a war crime. Against men, such crimes involve the selective separation of young civilian men "of military age" (that is, between eighteen and forty-five years) from old men, children, and women of all ages for punishment, torture, and execution.

For centuries, warriors have considered captive women to be part of the booty of warfare. However, today many believe that a systematic campaign of rape against civilian women is designed to humiliate and break the resolve of an enemy nation, and in some African conflicts it has been used intentionally to spread HIV. It also destroys families by turning husbands, fathers, and brothers against the young women—wives and daughters—who have been raped.

Finally, when rape results in pregnancy, it changes the ethnic composition of a conquered society, a further source of humiliation and conflict that will continue for at least a generation. In some countries, such as Korea (which over the years has been occupied by Mongolian, Chinese, Japanese, and American troops), this has resulted in the subsequent shunning and social isolation of people of mixed race.

International feminist activists and women's organizations have played an important role in recent prosecutions of war crimes committed against women, especially rape and sexual enslavement.

Another strategy of modern warfare has been to destroy the environment of the opposing country. The wilful destruction of the environment as a strategy of war, practice for war, or punishment for the defeated occurred at least as early as Roman times, and it has persisted to the present. Roman armies routinely destroyed crops and salted the earth to ruin the land's fertility. A millennium later, Russian soldiers burned their own crops and homes not once but twice, as a means of denying them to the invading armies of Napoleon and, later, Hitler.

When the Allied forces pushed the Iraqi army out of Kuwait in 1991, Iraqi soldiers set fire to 732 of the country's roughly 900 oil wells, producing one of the worst environmental disasters in history. Black smoke from the fires blocked out the sun and produced record low temperatures along a 950-kilometre tract of land. Rescue operations recovered over 22 million barrels of oil. But more than this is thought to have leaked from the destroyed oil fields into the local environment, contaminating soil and water supplies. Saddam Hussein also ordered the release of an estimated 11 million barrels of oil into the Arabian Gulf, damaging local marine life.

Modern warfare and the innovative war technologies of the twenty-first century have recently given rise to "nanopollution," a type of pollution never before encountered that relies on tiny, almost invisible attack weapons. The impact and health risks of nanopollutants—such as dust at the nanoscale—have become a concern for researchers. These microscopic particles can enter the bloodstream, disseminate throughout the body, and cause new diseases with unusual symptoms and other yet-to-be-studied health problems, such as damage to unborn fetuses and male fertility. By directly limiting population growth, nanopollution would represent a crime against future generations.

By one estimate, military conflicts in the twentieth century led to the deaths of over 100 million soldiers and civilians—more than the total number of casualties in all previous wars in human history combined. If these numbers seem appalling, they pale in comparison to the possible death tolls in the event of a full-scale nuclear war. Currently, the nuclear weapons in major military arsenals are more than four thousand times as powerful as the atomic bombs dropped on Japan. A nuclear war today would instantly kill an estimated 160 million. Another billion would perish in the first few hours from radiation poisoning, environmental devastation, and massive social chaos. Hundreds of millions more would die slowly over the ensuing years.

Just as death is an unavoidable outcome of war, so too are physical and psychological injuries. The number of military personnel and civilians who are injured or maimed during a war usually exceeds the number of deaths. Indeed, one common military strategy is to maim rather than kill the enemy since it takes more resources to care for the wounded than to discard their bodies.

Anti-personnel land mines are particularly well suited to this task, given that they are largely undetectable by civilians or enemy troops without proper equipment and do not need a soldier present to "pull the trigger." Cambodia has been called the "land of the one-legged men": more than thirty thousand individuals, mostly rural farmers, have lost limbs from accidentally detonating a mine.

Many veterans of war suffer the slow torture of psychological disorders. Much of the mental health literature on the effects of war focuses on post-traumatic stress disorder (PTSD), which researchers previously called "shell shock," "concentration-camp syndrome," "survivor syndrome," and "war neurosis." Victims of terrorism are especially at risk of psychological trauma because of the unexpected and severe nature of the event and because civilians are usually sheltered from such levels of violence and death.

What to do? Military conflict has occurred so consistently throughout human history that it is unlikely our generation will be able to propose any practical solution to reverse millennia of past practice. Still, if warfare and other lesser forms of conflict cannot be ended, at least we can try to develop policies to help *reduce* conflict and preserve peace. That is what we will discuss in the final six chapters of this book.

Families

"Families" are well-known to us from personal experience. We all have views about what a family is and what its function should be. Indeed, every group and every culture has characteristic ideas about families and family life. But personal experience should not close our eyes to four general facts.

First, there are widely held ideals about family life. Second, in spite of this, very few families behave like the ideal or normative families we see in the mass media. Third, cultures and groups differ widely in what they idealize as family life, and this creates some conflict and confusion. Finally, family forms are changing rapidly, in Canada and elsewhere, with increasing numbers of what we perceive to be traditionally unconventional forms: single parent families, adoptive families, same-sex families, cohabiting families, and so on.

It makes sense, then, to ignore supposedly simple and well-known norms about families and family life. For a start, instead of focusing on *family forms*, we should focus on *family processes*. If we do, we can define a family as any social unit, or set of social relations, that does what families are popularly imagined to do, however it actually manages to do so. This process-oriented definition is especially valuable because this chapter is concerned with one particular family process: the socialization of children. As well as discussing families, this chapter will discuss socialization as one means by which societies achieve social integration, as well as some measure of equality.

What, then, are the social processes that define what we in Canada like to think of as "family life"? The social groups we think of as families typically share a few key features, and that commonality can help us understand the nature of modern families. Because families are extraordinarily diverse, it is difficult to generalize about them. However, it is possible to focus our attention on these common processes.

- *Dependency and Intimacy.* All idealized family relations emphasize attachment and some kind of interdependency. These are not unique to families; most friendships also include some degree of emotional dependency, based on familiarity and exchange. Family relations are special in that they tend to include long-term commitments, both to each other and to the family as a social unit. In reality, however, many families lack these idealized attachments and commitments; as a result, interdependency is limited.
- *Sexuality.* Adult partners in families ideally have, or are expected to have, a long-term, exclusive sexual relationship. By contrast, among friends, sexual relations are either absent or of short duration. In families, sexual relations are allowed and expected between certain members (for example, spouses) but outlawed between other members (for example, parents and children). Norms of sexual propriety are also much stronger in families than they are in friendship or work groups. Taboos against the sexual exploitation of children are aimed at preventing sexual relations with a family member other than a spouse. Nevertheless, the sexual abuse of children does occur within families.
- *Protection.* Idealized families guard their members against all kinds of internal and external dangers. Parents are supposed to keep children safe from accidents and household dangers, for example, and away from drugs, alcohol, and predators. As well, spouses are supposed to protect one another, and adult children are supposed to protect and help their parents. But in real life, of course, some family members sometimes fail to

protect each other; what's more, some people neglect, exploit, or abuse other family members.

- *Power.* Given the large differences in power, strength, age, and social resources among members, ideally the more powerful family members protect less powerful ones. However, this imbalance in power has made patriarchy—control of the family by a dominant male (typically, the father)—a central fact in the history of family life in most known societies. Simply put, men have dominated because they owned and controlled more of the resources. In much of family law and policy, this domination over family by men was seen as a right, sometimes even a duty.

- *Violence.* Families—though ideally peaceful and loving—are also often marked by violence, perhaps to a higher degree than any other long-lived groups. Although violence has always existed in families, in the last few decades it seems to have been on the increase in North America, perhaps because it is more reliably reported than in the past. Usually the violence consists of a husband or boyfriend against his partner. I mention violence here not because it is an idealized or normative aspect of family life, but because it is a common feature. What's more, like the other features of family life mentioned here, it has a bearing on socialization.

The term "socialization" means the life-long social learning a person undergoes to become a viable member of society. The process is "social" because it is through interaction with others and in response to social pressures that people learn the culture—the language; perspective and skills; likes and dislikes; and cluster of norms, values, and beliefs—that characterizes the group to which they belong. As a result, socialization is one of the most important processes by which social structure constrains and transforms us. Besides, it is bidirectional: society shapes us and we shape society.

Primary socialization is learning that takes place in the early years of a person's life. It is important in forming an individual's personality and charting the course of his or her development. Usually, primary socialization takes place within the context of a family. Here, a young child learns many of the social skills needed to take part in a wide variety of social institutions. More important, this is the process by which many of the basic features of character are formed.

Primary socialization is fundamental for both individuals and society as a whole. First, primary socialization is the mechanism by which people are integrated into society, coming to take their allotted role and learning to fulfill socially required roles. From this perspective, human babies are blank slates waiting to be imprinted with socially meaningful information. It is through this effective social imprinting—for example, the teaching and learning of language—that society manages to reproduce itself into the future.

Second, socialization perpetuates domination by maintaining and legitimating inequalities in the society. Socialization is influenced by the dominant class through schooling and the mass media, a process of teaching people their "place" in society and convincing them that this place is indisputable. Poor people learn to blame themselves for failing while praising the rich for succeeding, for instance. In this way, socialization contributes to the survival of dominant groups.

Microsociologists study the processes by which people are socialized, especially those that lead to the development of a social "self." Through these processes people come to view themselves as good or bad, competent or inept, normal or deviant, and so on. In this context, feminist sociologists focus especially on gender issues—on learning gender identities (or gendered selves) and gendered patterns of domination and submission.

Socialization does not end with childhood. We undergo new experiences throughout our lives and change in response to them. But the socialization that occurs after childhood, called secondary socialization, is much more limited than primary socialization and usually involves learning specific roles, norms, attitudes, or beliefs. Secondary socialization has less effect on self-image or sense of competence than primary socialization does, but at the same time we should not underestimate its importance.

Our focus in this chapter is on families and their contribution to primary socialization—the fundamental learning that takes place earliest in life.

Forces Pushing People Apart

Even institutions like the family that are essentially integrative are also unequal and experience conflict. For example, we have already noted that family (or domestic) violence is far from atypical. In fact, it is statistically not uncommon, although it is not culturally normative or considered acceptable. Often it is hidden and families develop deep secrets about the violence and accompanying problems: addiction, mental illness, incest, infidelity, and so on. The public disclosure—or even open admission to one another—of such secrets is rare and often shadowed by shame and guilt.

The best-known fact about family conflict is that some families experience more than others. Families that are under the greatest stress—social, economic, and otherwise—are most likely to descend into conflict. Even given these stresses, however, some families cope better than others. In general, families that are the most cohesive and adaptable (or flexible) are best able to deal with stresses. By "cohesive," researchers are referring to families in which members feel the strongest personal identification with the family and with one another. By "adaptable," we mean those families that are most used to making changes easily and most prepared to set about changing.

Not surprisingly, the families that are most cohesive and most adaptable share certain traits. First, they have the most open patterns of interpersonal communication. They make a practice of sharing and discussing their concerns. Second, when they disagree, they have accepted ways of making decisions—tactics for resolving conflicts in ways that seem workable and fair to all members of the family. Third, they have democratic or semi-democratic processes for setting group goals. Every individual has a voice, and compromises are reached when necessary. Finally, they have a group or family culture that ties everyone together: a culture that includes shared values, beliefs, and even rituals (such as family dinners and outings).

By contrast, the most conflictual families have few or none of these characteristics. They don't communicate openly, solve conflicts well, identify with one another, set goals fairly, or preserve a group culture. Not only do they fail to conduct their affairs in ways that would ensure cohesion and adaptability; often, they also fail to set themselves apart from the outside world. Put differently, poorly functioning families have porous boundaries; they are easily infiltrated and influenced by people and ideas from outside. And put in yet another way, in these families, members receive no greater affection or attention—and have no more influence over one another—than friends, acquaintances, or media messages.

Of course, no family can or should be completely separate from the outside world or from other families. However, families do vary in the degree to which they take part in "outside" activities and encourage their children to do so. They also vary in the degree to which they praise their own values and denigrate those of other families.

Some parents, for example, will encourage or discourage their children from playing with particular children, or visiting their homes, fearing the influence of these children on their own. Other parents may take steps to segregate their children from other outside influences, for example, by controlling the television programs their children watch or the Internet websites they visit. Some parents may also enrol their children in private schools, not wanting them in the public system, or enrol them in schools outside the neighbourhood, not wanting them to play with local children.

Parents also vary in the values they promote and in whether they promote inclusionary or exclusionary attitudes to children of different backgrounds. Some parents, based on their own upbringing and experiences, warn their children away from mixing with children of different class, ethnic, racial, or religious backgrounds. Indeed, some parents teach a generalized mistrust of other people, while others teach a generalized trust. I'll come back to this important difference shortly.

We have known, for at least sixty years, that prejudice and discrimination are learned in the family home. However, these are not merely attitudes taught and modelled by parents; they are part of a broader personality or character type that sociologist Theodor Adorno has called the "authoritarian personality." Parents, through a range of socialization and parenting practices, can create authoritarians and, in so doing, can endanger the world.

This finding comes from a massive, multi-year, multidisciplinary study conducted in the US after World War II to discover the psychological roots of fascism and to answer the question: could Nazism have happened anywhere? After interviewing thousands of Americans all over the US, researchers concluded that fascist—even Nazi—tendencies are present everywhere and, yes, Nazism could have arisen in the US.

Based on their research, Adorno et al. (1950) identified nine characteristics of the authoritarian personality that served as the basis for the California "F-scale," a measure of authoritarianism. The nine component characteristics, distributed into thirty items, comprised the following:

- Conventionalism: a rigid adherence to conventional, middle-class values;
- Authoritarian submission: a submissive, uncritical attitude toward idealized moral authorities of the in-group;

- Authoritarian aggression: a tendency to be on the lookout for, and to condemn, reject, and punish people who violate conventional values;
- Anti-introspection: opposition to the subjective, the imaginative, or the tender-minded;
- Superstition and stereotypy: the belief in mystical determinants of the individual's fate; the disposition to think in rigid categories;
- Power and "toughness": a preoccupation with the dominance-submission, strong-weak, leader-follower dimension; identification with power figures; overemphasis upon the conventionalized attributes of the ego; exaggerated assertion of strength and toughness;
- Destructiveness and cynicism: a generalized hostility, vilification of the human;
- Projectivity: a disposition to believe that wild and dangerous things go on in the world; the projection outward of unconscious emotional impulses; and
- Sex: exaggerated concern with sexual "goings-on."

To summarize, the first finding of this study was that prejudice is a generalized tendency: people who hate Jews also tend to hate blacks, gays, immigrants, and other minorities. Second, prejudice is linked to political and social conservatism of various types. An example of this would be a tendency to hold people responsible for their own problems and prefer a government that stays out of people's lives. Third, prejudice is related to a wide range of personal beliefs (distrust of others, superstition, and fatalism, for example) and anti-introspection (an unwillingness to explore one's own or other people's deeper feelings, anxieties, and concerns).

Research has shown that the most important influences in shaping the authoritarian personality are family relationships during childhood.

A child is most strongly influenced by his or her parents' characters, not by particular individual experiences. Cold, inaccessible fathers have an especially strong effect, creating a repressive household environment. The typical authoritarian has experienced a harsh and pedantic upbringing during childhood. This experience of subordination and repression in the family home teaches the child to suppress and repress his views, impulses, and emotions. The child socialized in this way learns to seek satisfaction in obedience and submission. Socialization of this kind also plays an important role in forming negative attitudes toward minorities and other powerless people. The family shapes and teaches these attitudes, and also condones or rewards discriminatory behaviours. Finally, the harsh and repressive upbringing associated with authoritarianism results in rigid, "black-and-white" thinking, a heavy reliance on rules, and intolerance of moral doubt.

We have all seen the historical effects of authoritarianism on the world stage, including Nazism, fascism, or homegrown racism and gay bashing. We know that authoritarian parenting practices can have huge social and political consequences.

Related processes work even more directly, as abuse and violence can be taught within the family in other ways as well. A mass of evidence shows, for example, that children who see their mothers or siblings abused grow up to tolerate or practice abuse themselves. Girls who see their mothers abused are more likely to grow up to mate with abusive partners. Likewise, boys who see their mothers abused are also more likely to grow up to abuse their partners. As well, some children who are abused grow up to abuse their own children. So under certain conditions, socialization—otherwise known as parenting—can produce violence and hatred. And under other conditions parenting can produce peace and co-operation.

In summary, socialization—by training and preparing the next generation of citizens—has an immense impact on the future of the family, community, country, and world. Yet anyone can become a parent and socialize children. No licence is needed, no training is required, and virtually no state oversight is permitted. What an immense right and responsibility society has placed in the hands of untrained and potentially unqualified citizens! Incredibly, we demand more of people before allowing them to drive cars or catch fish than we require of people who are setting out to parent.

Contributions to Integration

Let's take a positive approach now and ask: how can we raise children so they will be peaceful and co-operative, law-abiding and productive? Fortunately, we already know the answer to these questions from decades of research on parenting practices and their effects.

However, before discussing parenting per se, we should start with a brief review of what researchers know about the conditions that promote peaceful co-operation—that is, successful living together. These conditions fall into three main categories that I have called familiarity, interdependence, and civility.

In a wide variety of domains, the integration of people, and their peaceful coexistence, is promoted by a simple increase in familiarity. Familiarity often begins with increases in mutual visibility, then with communication and interaction, preferably of a non-competitive kind. Out of these communications can come a growing sense of likeness and the development of shared views and beliefs. Finally, with continued positive interaction and communication, familiarity can lead to trust, intimacy, and a wish for closeness.

A second element of integration, often related to familiarity, is interdependence. People who are familiar with one another often become dependent on one another. And sometimes interdependence can come first, before familiarity. Consider the actions of common friends or common enemies. Both common friends and common enemies can help people to see the value of co-operation. An exchange of resources such as information or support can also create interdependence, promote co-operation, and lead to the establishment of friendships.

A third element of integration, related less obviously to familiarity and interdependence, is civility. The common synonyms for "civility" are "politeness" and "courtesy"; other terms might include "consideration," "tact," "good manners," and "amiability." However, these are not merely character qualities; they are also societal accomplishments. Research by historical sociologists (Norbert Elias is a good example) suggests that there are macrosociological factors that promote and preserve such qualities. In particular, these are state or governmental guarantees that promote and protect good behaviour in private as well as public settings. It is no accident that the rise of public safety and table etiquette both accompanied the growth of nation-states in Europe.

In general, we associate "civility" with a sense of fairness and equity: in civil company, people feel that they are being treated fairly and respectfully. They feel safe and protected in their dealings with others. They do *not* feel degraded or humiliated, whether at school, at work, in public places, or otherwise. At least three public arrangements increase the chances that people will enjoy these experiences: the rule of law, justly enforced; suitable boundaries between contending groups; and a culture of human rights and dignity.

Canada has taken many steps toward ensuring all three experiences in order to encourage civility. These steps include an unbiased judiciary, laws against discrimination and hate crimes, professionally trained police, a human rights code, and a positive orientation to multiculturalism, among others. To be sure, many are critical of Canada for falling short, and by the strictest international standards we are not paragons of virtue. In particular, many have criticized the country's various police forces, from CSIS and the RCMP down to provincial, city, and town police units. Some have also criticized our immigration tribunals, labour tribunals, criminal courts, and ombudsman offices. Still, it is clear that an effort is being made.

FAMILIARITY

Childhood socialization gives people their first taste of intimacy and the other aspects of familiarity that can lead to social integration. But as we have already seen, the outcome depends entirely on *how* parents teach their children. Certain styles of parenting plainly produce antisocial authoritarians, while other styles produce good citizens and good neighbours.

In the last few decades we have seen much research on parenting and its outcomes, so we know a lot about what good parenting looks like and how it works. The general finding is that good results require what researchers have come to call "authoritative parenting." This is parenting that controls the child, sets and enforces rules, but is loving and seen to be loving.

Bad parenting falls into three main categories. As we saw above, so-called authoritarian parenting controls the child and is not loving or seen by the child to be loving. Two other types of parenting that produce bad outcomes are "permissive" parenting (loving but without any limits set or enforced), and "neglectful" or "unengaged" parenting (lacking both love and limits).

Research on parenting shows a great deal of consistency across a variety of outcomes. In general, good parenting—that is, authoritative parenting—leads to obedience, high self-esteem, good school performance, good mental and physical health, and good social skills (for example, friendships). Bad parenting leads to situational (i.e., superficial) compliance, disobedience (including running away from home), poor school performance (including dropping out), delinquency, risky behaviours (e.g., early use of drugs, alcohol, cigarettes, early and unsafe sex, and dangerous driving), depression, and low self-esteem.

Recent research shows that having only one authoritative parent is still better than having none in terms of child outcomes. These results tend to hold up over time, across societies, and across cultures.

However, bear in mind that the way a child perceives his or her parents' motives makes a difference. Parental consistency is important too.

Research repeatedly shows that what a child needs is love and attachment to his or her parents; emotional stability; family cohesion; an absence of family conflict; protection and control; and finally, fair and moderate discipline. We know the child needs these things because when she receives them, good outcomes follow (i.e., good mental and physical health, good adjustment in school, and so on) and when she does not, bad outcomes follow. And everyone agrees about which are the desirable outcomes.

Research also shows that *how* parents teach their children is just as important as *what* they teach them. In a sense, to quote Marshall McLuhan, "the medium is the message," in families as on television. The bad ways of teaching or socializing children—the authoritarian ways—are by power assertion. Using the power assertion method, a parent or other caregiver threatens a child with punishment for non-compliance. The child complies only to avoid this punishment. The conformity therefore is externally, not internally, driven. The child has no real sense of why he is doing what he is doing, and usually he will do the opposite when there is no fear of being caught and punished. A second bad way of teaching children is by means of love withdrawal. Here, instead of the punishment taking a physical form, it takes an emotional form—producing in the child anxiety, shame, or guilt over the loss of love. As with power assertion, the child complies with parental demands to avoid this punishment. However, the child punished in this way resents the emotional blackmail: so the result is a lethal combination of superficial conformity, guilt, and resentment.

Induction, the best way to teach or socialize a child, stresses the possible benefits of the child's behaviour. It includes teaching good behaviour by setting a good example, then rewarding imitation. It also explains the reasons why one way of behaving is better than another, and often points out the social benefits of proper behaviour. The goal is for the child to internalize the social rules, to make the rules his or her own. This leads children to exercise internalized moral control over their behaviour. In short, inductive discipline, combined with parental affection, promotes deep moral learning; power assertion and love withdrawal do not.

Socialization through inductive disciplining also teaches a child how to communicate, interact, and reason fruitfully with others. It encourages communication, trust, a sharing of beliefs and ideas, and even intimacy. By creating emotional equality between the parent and child, moral induction encourages the child to explore emotional equality with others and trains people to look for their similarities, not their differences. It also models a thoughtful, reasonable, and respectful way of resolving conflicts. In every possible way, moral induction is the opposite of the kind of parenting that produces and supports authoritarianism. And it promotes familiarity, intimacy, and sociability.

Some traditional cultures, however, impede this kind of positive parenting. They encourage men to think that they are superior to women and adults that they are superior to children, and that family authority should be exercised in a forceful, even brutal manner. Such patriarchal societies typically hold black-and-white views about morality, views often rooted in traditional religious teachings. In these societies people believe it is the right and duty of the parent to pass on "self-evident" moral, cultural, and religious ideas with little explanation or discussion and to enforce these traditional rules unwaveringly. In doing so, they are merely reproducing the authoritarian, brittle parenting to which they were subjected themselves.

On immigrating to Canada or another liberal Western society, parents from a culture with very different views on parenting may have trouble understanding or accepting an alternative way of raising children. This sometimes brings them into conflict with school, the law, or child protection services. Often, these parents find themselves embroiled in conflict with their children, who are readily learning new norms from the children they meet at school (and the parents of those children), as well as from the mass media. The resulting intergenerational conflict has been studied for well over eighty years, starting with a classic work by sociologists William Isaac Thomas and Florian Znaniecki, *The Polish Peasant in Europe and America* (1920). Often, such parents adapt and develop new ways of practicing parenthood, much to the benefit of their rapidly assimilating children. When this fails to happen, everyone suffers.

INTERDEPENDENCE

Émile Durkheim was convinced that social order and integration in a modern industrial society would come about through what he called "organic solidarity"—cohesion or co-operation based on interdependence. If so, what do children learn about interdependence in the family home, through observation and direct teaching?

First, they can see that family members are indeed interdependent. There are bills to pay, and one or more family members bring in the income to pay them. As well, there are household tasks to perform. In every household there is what sociologists call a domestic division of labour. This division of labour is often unequal and unfair. The work is unequally divided between parents and children, and between husbands and wives. Bear in mind that this *is* work, and people do it by sacrificing their free time and leisure, sometimes reluctantly.

Often children witness a conflict between their parents over the division of domestic labour, and they may also witness a conflict between the demands of domestic work and paid work among parents who do both. So they learn something about the problems of negotiating and completing unwanted duties, often under physical and mental stress.

Children are often told that their "job" is to go to school, do their homework, and get good grades. Some children are also expected to take part in after-school learning activities (music lessons, or ballet, or tutoring, for example), which their parents believe will improve their minds and their life-chances. In this way, children learn and observe several things. First, that everyone has work to do, and in principle, everyone should try to work as co-operatively as possible to minimize strain and conflict in the family. Second, children learn that family members also contribute to the extended family and the wider community in various ways. For example, they may witness their parents providing care to aged and infirm family members who live elsewhere or providing help to neighbours and friends. Some even see their parents taking part in community volunteer or charity work.

Third, in the home children may learn how to join groups. They see their parents interacting with friends and learn what friendship looks like in practice. They join in activities with their siblings and with neighbouring children, and when they are old enough to attend school, they learn how to extend these friendships more broadly to include a larger and more varied group of children.

Finally, children learn how to make alliances at home: with siblings plotting one against another or together against their parents, or with parents plotting one against another or together against another family member. So people get their first taste of politics and "horse-trading" within the family context. They perfect it at school, where they encounter cliques and larger friendship groups (not to mention teams, bands, and gangs). Socialization, then, is not merely about learning practical skills (how to tie your shoes or eat your food); it is also about learning social skills (how to dress and speak to adults) and political skills (how to judge people and distinguish friends from enemies).

Through co-operation, exchange, common friends, and common enemies, members of the same family teach each other the pleasures and duties of interdependence. These are practical matters, often learned by trial and error. As Robert Frost said so unsentimentally about family life, "Home is the place where, when you have to go there, they have to take you in."

So well do families teach interdependence that, when children come to school and then out into the larger world, they often imagine that the same rules apply "out there" that apply within the family. In that sense, socialization within a well-functioning family is a poor preparation for real life, where attachment, co-operation, and generosity cannot be taken for granted. In large part, that is why people continue to need socialization—secondary socialization—throughout their lives as they meet new situations and new social groups.

One reason that people cannot be relied on to provide the attachment, co-operation, and generosity that usually takes place within a family is that they are unaware of its importance for a modern and diverse society. While families teach people the value of interdependence in a family context, they don't teach people the need to seek and cultivate interdependence wherever they might be. Instead, families (and many of our other institutions) teach people to be ambitious, self-interested, and individualistic. Our society places too little emphasis on teaching civility. That is, children are not generally taught to extend worthier, more socially conscious qualities to the larger world.

CIVILITY

Recall that we defined "civility" as politeness and courtesy, as well as consideration, tact, good manners, and amiability. From a societal and sociological perspective, civility also includes an absence of degradation or humiliation; boundaries (i.e., fences that make good neighbours); a culture of human rights and dignity; safety (i.e., protection and rule of law); and a sense of fairness and equity.

In keeping with this definition, we might ask the following questions: how often, and in what ways, do Canadian parents teach their children to behave publicly in civil and polite ways? And how are children taught to honour public space? For example, consider how they might be taught to foreswear graffiti and other types of casual vandalism. Beyond that, what do parents teach their children about social responsibility, good citizenship, human rights, or how to behave in ways that are fair and equitable to others? Do Canadian parents discuss ethical or moral issues at all with their children or assume that this will be dealt with in school? Or do they suppose that church attendance and religious ritual provide as much morality and ethics as their children need?

Not knowing the answers to these questions, I reviewed the sociological research on socialization as it applies to morality, ethics, politics, altruism, and citizenship. I found very little of interest. This surprising lack of material suggests that researchers are either not studying this question, or that after exploring it, they find nothing to study; in other words, perhaps there is little evidence that parents are addressing these tasks. Using *Sociological Abstracts*, the continuously updated report of all sociological research findings, I looked at sociological research published since 1999. Normally I would expect to find hundreds of relevant studies on every topic when I search in this way; on this topic, I found only thirty-three studies published after 1999. Of these, none was Canadian. Roughly half were from the US, and the other half from Europe or Asia.

I quickly found a clear distinction between the ways that Americans and non-Americans discuss the topic of value socialization—indeed, between the ways that Americans and non-Americans socialize their children. American and Spanish parents stress different values in socializing their children, for example, placing a different weight on qualities like responsibility, imagination, or perseverance. Not surprisingly, the highly individualistic Americans produce high levels of ambition in their children, with resulting high levels of economic development. There is, however, much less sense of collective responsibility.

Values like ambition and independence, responsibility and perseverance, are transformative—a mechanism by which families prepare their children for the transition to adulthood. Families shape children's occupational ambitions and values largely by influencing their value structures. No doubt middle-class American socialization is mainly concerned with ensuring that children develop high educational and occupational ambitions, stay in school, and get good grades. According to American sociologist Annette Lareau's 2000 study, middle-class American parents emphasize the systematic cultivation of their children (providing French immersion, ballet lessons, and so on). Working class and poor families, by contrast, prefer to accomplish natural growth. As a result, working class and poor children often lead more childlike lives, with more autonomy and less control from adults.

Parents are also important sources of their children's views on issues relating to inequality. In raising their children, many parents spontaneously raise the issue of fairness when discussing wealth and poverty, but many do not. As a result, many elementary school children are inclined to accept great disparities in wealth and poverty, based on a belief that people deserve their economic situation in life and a conviction that efforts to help the poor are misguided or futile.

Children do, however, change their views over time, depending on their engagement with the news media and with voluntary associations. Some adolescents engage more actively than others with family, peers, teachers, and the media around questions of fairness, inequality, politics, and citizenship. Adolescents are not mere passive recipients of information from parents and teachers. Active citizenship requires knowledge and cognitive skills as well as commitment. The news media, interpersonal communication, and participation in school and community volunteer activities all offer opportunities to learn active citizenship, and in this way, can all contribute to the moral development of adolescents.

Some political socialization occurs during adolescence through participation in school politics. Such political engagement mimics adult civic life and is available to adolescents regardless of their social class. In this respect, any organized involvement in extracurricular activities is important. However, speaking in public forums, providing community service, and helping to create a communal identity most encourage future political participation.

There is a tendency in North America to leave much or all of the civics education to schools and take little responsibility for it at home. We see a much stronger dedication to societal responsibility, both in terms of teaching and practice, in parts of Europe. There, political socialization is widespread among adolescents, who tend to engage politically, are knowledgeable about the politics around them, and express a desire to vote in elections. The mass media, particularly newspaper and television news, as well as interpersonal communication, play a critical role in political socialization. In addition, parents have a strong influence on their child's political socialization, through practices of family communication. It seems that outside North America, political socialization occurs in a variety of ways, involving parents, schools, and the media both independently and interdependently.

And schools also remain an important source of the values that are vital for good citizenship, community building, and economic growth. Schools exert an important influence on the ethnocentrism and ethical liberalism of their pupils. In this respect, they do far more, and do it far better, than families. I will have much more to say about schools in a later chapter.

Even government (on which more is also to come) is doing much better than families in teaching people how to live together with others who are different. This, too, is especially evident in the regions of Europe that are grappling with large numbers of new, very different immigrants. In the Netherlands, for example, immigrants from outside the EU are obliged to take a one-year citizenship training program, in which they are taught the Dutch language and are introduced to Dutch culture. In the lessons, priority is given to the practical knowledge immigrants need to function in Dutch society.

Dutch norms and values form part of these lessons, both implicitly and explicitly. These are categorized into various themes:

constitutional rights like gender equality, freedom of sexual orientation, non-discrimination, freedom of speech, opinion, and religion.
Newcomers are urged to accept values like tolerance and respect for
differences, because these are seen to be indispensable for living in
Dutch society. While teachers are averse to telling immigrants how to
live or how to behave, they nevertheless attempt to teach self-control,
self-reflection, and managing emotions given these demands.

This kind of program, so foreign to Canadian "multicultural" thinking, views political socialization as essential for good citizenship; it is
seen as key to the maintenance of civil liberties, security, justice, and
prosperity. You cannot rely on families—or perhaps even schools—to
teach values like tolerance and universalism, apparently. For this reason it falls to the government to ensure that people are aware of society's norms and values, and that they are expected to obey them. Good
citizenship means knowing the values or virtues applicable to various
situations, internalizing them, and practicing them. Family and school
should assist in this crucial awareness-raising process, and perhaps
"problem families" should have access to a family coach.

What these studies show is a much higher awareness in Europe than
in the US (and let alone Canada) about the value of teaching civility.
Families at best can do part of the job, though they are probably doing
too little in North America. Of course, this may not be totally disastrous. Children do grow up, and in doing so, they will be influenced
by a variety of people and situations, some of them more socially progressive than their own parents. It may turn out to be a good thing if
(many) children are shaped not by parental socialization, but instead
by extra-familial influences. Perhaps this is especially true in parochial
or ethnocentric communities.

As a sidebar, it might be noted that while parents can be a source
of emotional stability and love—good things—they are also a source
of societal inertia. Parents by and large promote the last generation's
views, beliefs, and prejudices—the ones they learned as children or

developed themselves as young adults. That's one reason why societies take so long to change, for better or worse. As Freud pointed out in *The Future of an Illusion* (1927), that's one reason why religiosity persists in society: the religious tendency is handed down from one generation to the next. So, for that matter, is sexism, racism, and domestic violence.

What can be said with some certainty is that many, and perhaps most, Canadian families are not socializing their children for co-operation. This may be especially true of what we are calling civility, citizenship, or altruism. We may be doing better on the dimensions of familiarity and interdependence. The fact, though, is that we have never measured this. We have no good data to show how Canadian families—especially Canadian parents—are performing. Perhaps, as we gear up to measure schoolteachers to assess their effectiveness in Canadian classrooms, we ought to similarly measure parents to assess their effectiveness in Canadian homes.

We noted at the beginning of this chapter that everyone knows something about families and about socialization. Many of us currently live in family households; we all grew up in families and we were all socialized. However, the danger of "common knowledge"—of taken-for-granted, what-everyone-knows knowledge—is that it is often wrong because it is uninspected.

We don't know how many Canadian families are working well, by the standards stated in this chapter. The government doesn't study this; many Canadians would likely view it as prying into their private lives. There is the assumption that, unless one practices the most extreme and visible forms of abuse, every adult is free to bear and raise children by any method judged appropriate. However, we have already noted that the results of bad parenting are consequential for all Canadians, and for the future. You, I, and everyone else pay the long-term costs of bad parenting. (I discuss some of the larger social processes that produce bad parenting in another book, *Close Relations*, co-authored with Susan McDaniel.)

We know that, in some societies, parents are more socially conscious—that is, more concerned with civility and good citizenship—than we are in North America. We also know that some societies—typically, Western and Northern European societies—are more dedicated to helping families succeed in their lives together. This includes overseeing and protecting the children of vulnerable populations like the poor and helping immigrants to assimilate culturally into national standards of ethical behaviour. In Canada, the embrace of "multiculturalism" hinders our ability to do the same. What originated as a plan to signal tolerance and increase social inclusion has turned into moral laziness. It is time for a national discussion of socialization practices if we are to build a co-operative society.

Clearly, when compared to more progressive social-democratic societies in Northern and Western Europe, liberal Canada shows a great deal of tolerance for conflict and antisocial individualism. That said, we cannot ignore the role that families can and must play in a changing society.

NINE

Education

Just as we have all had family experiences, we have all had school experiences. You, gentle reader, may even be in the middle of a school experience right now. In a certain sense, most of us are experts on the topic of schools and formal education. But as with all first-hand experiential knowledge, it may be necessary to dig deeper to find out what we really know.

In Canada, public elementary and secondary education has been available to everyone—male and female, rich and poor—for over a century. But it is only in the last few generations since the 1960s that large numbers of women, low-income Canadians, and immigrants have been able to continue their formal education up through secondary school and into college or university. Today, unprecedented numbers of people from every background are obtaining college diplomas, bachelor's degrees, master's degrees, doctorates, and other advanced training. And we can anticipate that the numbers of people receiving higher education will continue to grow.

The reason is that for fifty years there has been an increasing demand for higher education and an increasing ability for colleges and universities to supply it. Furthermore, the work world has demanded ever-higher educational credentials of its job applicants. There is less need for workers whose main qualification is a strong back. We still need all the trades like mechanics, construction, and transport, for example, and they do require some physical strength. But increasingly there seems to be a significant and rapidly growing need for people with problem-solving skills, writing skills, literacy, numeracy, and interpersonal competence. The latter, in theory, are people who have learned how to learn—the prime requirement in what we like to call an information society, or knowledge society.

Of course, we know that schools are not quite what we would like them to be. In large classrooms, for example, it is hard to teach problem-solving skills, writing skills, literacy, numeracy, and interpersonal competence. And a great many students gain much of their education, even their higher education, in large classrooms. So the real Canadian school has roughly the same relation to the ideal school as the real Canadian family has to the ideal family: each falls short in important ways, much of the time.

Also, the "world of work" is not quite what many have advertised it to be: it is not always full of interesting challenges and opportunities for brainy, ambitious people. In fact, some research has suggested that nowadays there is a tendency toward over-education, given the reality of available jobs. People with far less education could largely accomplish these jobs, and would have done similar jobs in the past. You don't need a PhD to sell real estate or industrial logistics services or drive a cab, a BA to flip burgers, or a college diploma to sell cosmetics. Ivar Berg has called this over-education for work "the great training robbery."

Like workplaces, schools actually fall far short of the ideal. As well, there are many reasons for the poor fit between ideal and actual, both in schools and in the workplace. There are also many reasons why people today may be over-educated for the work they are doing. This goes back in part to fallacies in the premise of the "knowledge society" that our society values information and problem-solving skills above all else. Some might say that, as in the past, our society values conformity and consumerism above all else. Capital and technology are still important. The rest is window dressing.

The question here is what *do* schools teach people, and what bearing might that have on their ability to live with other people? How might that improve their ability to co-operate and prosper as members of the same society? This chapter will try to answer these questions. As we will see, elementary schools have a mixed job, partly a result of the practical problems they face in transforming young children into "students" and partly because of conflicting views about the true purpose and best methods of education. (We will not even try to discuss the shortage of funds. In general, most schools—and especially those in poor neighbourhoods—have too few funds and too large classrooms. This always makes a difference.)

These disagreements about the purpose and method of education continue up through elementary, secondary, and into post-secondary schooling. Even in universities, the debate continues about whether the goal of formal education is to prepare people to think or to force-feed them specialized information and skills. Let's start with a brief definition of terms. Consider the origins of the word "education." "To educate" comes from the Latin word *educare*, which is related to *educere*, meaning "to bring out" and *e(x) ducere*, meaning "to lead out of."

In the last chapter, we saw that over the life course socialization is a key part of the process by which we become products of our experiences. As we pass through life, we have many learning experiences, and these collectively create the person we become. Socialization, in this way, fills us up with society's rules and roles.

You might then ask: how is education related to socialization? What are students being "led out" of when they are educated? What methods do educators use? What are the consequences of leading people out of ignorance? And how is education (and its outcome) different from "training"?

"Training," sometimes used interchangeably with the word "education," actually means something different, and again we can look to the origin of the word for more understanding. Historically, it derives from sources meaning "to drag along," "to draw forward," or "to trail along after a great man"—that is, to belong to a retinue. Training, unlike education, means pulling or pushing someone into a particular role rather than leading a person out of ignorance and revealing his or her true, best self.

If we compare the two ideas, we understand that "education" involves teaching concepts, principles, and accepted knowledge. It is intended to develop a student's general capacity for thinking, to teach students how to learn, and ideally to grow a capacity for self-understanding and self-reliance. By contrast, "training" is the identification and practice of specific routines that achieve desired results. These routines are immediately useful but cannot always be applied to *new* problems, and as a result, training promotes intermittent, continuing reliance on other people's expertise.

Most educators, including myself, believe that education more than training is important in modern societies, and that it is critical to other aspects of our culture, such as economic development. More than that we will see that formal education—schooling—is critical for the development of good citizens and ethical human beings. It plays a key role in integrating self-centred individuals into society.

Also, *formal* education is central to the operation of the "knowledge society." We expect education to provide students with a wide range of skills that will prepare them for an uncertain future. Communities of disadvantaged people especially *need* the educational system to help them surmount social and economic obstacles. Today, we are even more reliant than in the past on formal education—on institutions that provide knowledge and credentials (like universities). However, we also continue to depend on *informal* education, the learning that people undertake themselves to gain new knowledge on their own. Even today, when people receive a great deal of formal education, many continue to educate themselves throughout life.

In the past, a greater proportion of a person's learning was informal. A century ago, only three out of five young people enrolled in schools and attended regularly. Today a formal education is available to virtually everyone. In fact, most people today are able to obtain both formal and informal education, and most people delay entering full-time paid work until they have completed a significant amount of formal education.

A century ago, most left school in their teens to go to work. They matured into adulthood at work, not at school. In general, childhood and adolescence were shorter than they are now. Schools were also different. In nineteenth- and early twentieth-century Canada, schooling in smaller communities and rural areas remained uncertain and irregular. Pupil attendance was sporadic. Many schools suffered from a crippling lack of funding and an inability to attract qualified teachers. This problem has not disappeared today, but it is less acute in most parts of the country.

Today, schools in Canada are larger and more bureaucratic than a century ago. They follow a clearly defined curriculum, set largely by the provinces. Many more students today complete primary school and secondary school, and virtually all Canadians today are literate. Unlike students of the past, today's students delay working full-time often until five to ten years after their teens. Increasingly, they are adults at school. As a result, many marry or become parents while still students, and many come back to school after starting full-time work. What this means is that schools, colleges, and universities serve a more experienced and demanding population. Students also have access to extensive learning resources outside schools (a good example of this is the Internet). They bring much more information into the classroom.

All of this means that schools, colleges, and universities need to work harder to serve a more diverse and experienced population.

Forces Pushing People Apart

As we saw in the previous chapter, in North America middle-class parents drum into their children strong needs for achievement. They socialize their children to be ambitious, independent, and successful rather than promoting more traditional qualities such as duty, generosity, or piety. And children internalize their parents' values. They know—and this is well established after decades of research—that in modern industrial societies, educational credentials more than anything else give people a foothold in the middle-class. In the competition for good jobs and good careers, educational credentials largely erase differences in class of birth. People with the same educational credentials are roughly on the same footing when it comes to acquiring good jobs.

Of course, other factors matter too, such as social capital (valuable social connections) and cultural capital (knowledge of "high culture," for example). In Canada and the US, as well as elsewhere in the economically developed world, these play a large part in securing good jobs. In fact, they are key influences at the highest levels of society—alongside people's BAs, MBAs, MDs, and other relevant credentials. Educational background puts you in the running for good jobs and good careers—especially if you have little social or cultural capital to start with. And once you have the credentials, differences in social and cultural capital are metaphorical icing on the cake.

But given all this socially structured ambition, many middle-class children come to school with huge anxiety about obtaining good grades, pleasing the teacher, and getting ahead—gaining scholarships and admissions to desirable schools and jobs, for example. From childhood on, they worry a lot, and the worry often leads to high rates of depression, panic, obsessive behaviour, anorexia, and even suicide. This issue is thoroughly documented in Richard D. Kadison and Theresa Foy DiGeronimo's book, *College of the Overwhelmed: The Campus Mental Health Crisis and What to Do About It* (2004). (Kadison is chief of mental health services at Harvard University and well situated to comment on this.)

Many parents intensify this anxiety by pushing their children to take extra training—to pad their personal resumés, even in childhood.

The pressures and anxieties that children feel in school over performance and grades, caused by their parents, are likely to drive a wedge
between them and other children, many of whom are viewed as potential competitors.

These anxieties increase in adolescence when young people also
become concerned about their popularity and attractiveness to others.
Self-esteem issues and emotional surges, fed by hormones, intensify all
the concerns described so far.

SEGREGATION OR DISTANCE

At school, students also see new and often marked variations in social
and cultural capital associated with class. They also often see ethnocultural differences associated with different ancestral backgrounds. All
this is challenging to young people; some adjust well, but others do not.

Some schools minimize or control the variation by segregating different "kinds" of students. One common type of segregation is "ability
grouping," more often spoken of as "tracking" or "streaming." And
much has been said in favour of ability grouping: for example, that
it ensures the best students receive the most challenging and enriched
education, while the less gifted students are spared the humiliation of
struggling with materials they can't master and competing against students they can't match.

Yet in school systems all over the US and Canada, a debate continues to rage over whether students, especially at secondary level
(junior and senior high schools), should be segregated into classes
according to ability.

There are three main types of ability grouping. Under the first,
common in elementary classrooms, students may be divided according to differential ability to handle materials, for instance as "slow,"
"average," and "advanced" readers. The second type of grouping is
in Britain termed "setting." Different classes exist in each subject, and

students are assigned to classes that cover the ground more or less rapidly, according to ability in that particular subject. This system is often found in North American high schools, where classes may be distinguished as "honours," "academic," or "general," the level often signalled by the registration number assigned to the class.

In the third level, variously referred to as "tracking" or "streaming," students move together from one class to another, as members of a "general," "vocational," or "academic" group. The advantages of streaming have been known for years: indeed they were summarized as long ago as 1931. Streaming allows pupils to advance according to their abilities. It adapts instructional techniques to the needs of the group. It reduces failures, and it helps to preserve interest and incentive, because bright students are not bored by the sluggish participation of the dull. Likewise, slower pupils engage more when not eclipsed by those who are much brighter. So streaming makes teaching easier and it makes individual instruction possible to small, slow groups.

All of these points, when studied by present-day researchers, still hold. Teaching a class of mixed-ability students is regarded by many teachers as a nightmare. Bright children from any race or class deserve to be challenged with materials that will broaden their horizons and extend their abilities. This is not possible within mixed-ability classrooms. It is for this reason that some believe that tracking does not perpetuate inequality, and if used properly it will actively reduce it. However that is not the end of the story.

Not only have the arguments *for* tracking been current for nearly eighty years but so have arguments *against* it, and recently a few others have been added to the list. Some argue that slow pupils need the presence of the able students to stimulate and encourage them. A stigma attached to low sections or classes works to discourage the pupils who have been placed in these categories. Teachers are unable, or do not have time, to specify the work for different levels of ability. Often high-ability classes or groups receive simply more work, rather than a different level of work. Teachers object to the slower groups, and do not want to teach them.

As well, there is evidence that streaming or tracking reproduces existing social inequalities. Ability grouping discriminates against minority and lower-class students, since they are more likely to end up in the lowest streams. And low-stream students typically receive instruction that is slower-paced and of lower quality than that available to higher-track students.

This last point bears expansion. The instruction of low-stream students is not only slower-paced than, but indeed different in kind from, instruction aimed at college-bound students. Students not only cover less material but do so with less concern for detailed analysis—also, with less social analysis. Low-stream students, who are often disproportionately poor and from minority groups, leave school with fewer of the skills necessary for employment. They also leave school with less knowledge of how their society works, and less faith in their ability to effect changes in their own lives.

"Ability grouping" is only one way of segregating students. Another is the creation of separate schools: faith-based schools for people of different religions and private schools for rich people are examples of this.

Some parents choose to segregate their children in private schools where the class and ethnic or religious variety is much less than it is in secular public schools. Parents have various motives for placing their children in such schools. Some believe the children will receive a better education than they do in the public system, or that the private system will better prepare their children to compete for top university and occupational positions; of course, in parochial schools, they will be taught suitable values and religious dogma.

Currently, there is even a move in Toronto, Boston, and other North American cities to enrol black students in "black schools" where, some believe, they will do better than they would in the mixed-race public system. The goal is to halt high dropout and failure rates by building schools that meet the academic and emotional needs of black boys—boys who in the past have often had to learn in crowded schools with inexperienced teachers, cope without fathers at home, and contend with pop culture's negative images of them.

However, such single-race (or single-gender, or single-anything) schools can face legal and political opposition. In addition, separate schools minimize contact among students from different backdrops or different demographics. At worst, separate schools can also limit public visibility and accountability. At the extreme, this makes children in separate schools more vulnerable to the harm and neglect associated with total institutions. For example, it was in the isolated, segregated residential schools designed for Canada's First Nations children that the worst abuses were committed against children who were there against their will in the first place.

Worried about the public system, some parents choose to home-school their children. Home-schooling has been increasing in popularity in the US and Canada over the past few decades. Rather than attending a state school or registered private school, children remain at home to receive their schooling from a parent or another relative. Many states and provinces have adopted the position that children may legally receive instruction at home, as long as they are registered with the school system and as long as their curriculum of study is approved. However, in some quarters, there remains much hostility to home-schooling, and some home-schooling parents report difficulties in having their curricula approved.

Compulsory schooling is a development of the late nineteenth and early twentieth centuries. By the end of the nineteenth century, every Canadian province (except Quebec) had enacted compulsory education laws; every Canadian child had to attend school. The rationale for compulsory schooling was to give children the skills that they would need in the workforce and to make them good citizens. The latter was especially highlighted in areas where immigration made for a mix of cultural values and norms. Many of the nineteenth-century reformers who called for mass public education were concerned with producing an obedient workforce that would be suitably deferential to factory owners and management.

Home-schoolers often see themselves as resisting this social control. But this can work two ways. Parents say they do not want their children "brainwashed"; they want their children to "think for themselves." Of course, many people (including schoolteachers) would wholeheartedly agree with this sentiment. Some parents, however, choose home-schooling because they do not wish for their children to be exposed to ideas of multiculturalism and the equality of all peoples. Likewise, some parents choose to isolate their children from the opposite sex, preferring to send their children to boy-only or girl-only schools. There has been much research about whether girls (for example) do better in same-sex or mixed-sex schools and colleges; the debate is still inconclusive on this point.

Whatever the academic merits of segregating school-aged children—in public schools, private schools, parochial schools, same-sex schools, or home-schools—it seems clear that segregation has the social effect of separating people from others who are different. In this way, it is likely to increase suspicion and distrust, or at the very least, fail to build competence and familiarity in dealing with people who are different—this among young students who may already be having trouble dealing with the unexpected differences based on sex, class, and races.

The US went through a long and painful history of legally desegregating its schools racially, although in practice many schools are still mainly white or mainly black. So we know plenty about the correlation between school segregation and racism. But nowhere is the harmful effect of school segregation clearer than in the case of wartorn Vukovar—a city in the former Yugoslavia. The Battle of Vukovar was an eighty-seven-day siege of the Croatian city of Vukovar by the Yugoslav People's Army (JNA), supported by various Serbian paramilitary forces, between August and November 1991 during the Croatian War of Independence. It ended with the defeat of the local Croatian National Guard, the near-total destruction of Vukovar, and the murder or expulsion of most of the Croat population of the city and surroundings. Though estimates vary, it is clear that thousands of military personnel and civilians were killed in this battle.

The cruelty of this battle destroyed what had been an integrated multi-ethnic community. The suffering, death, and destruction left many Croats with feelings of betrayal by their Serb neighbours. As a result, the city and surrounding area is now a divided community; people do not readily cross the ethnic lines to communicate or interact.

After the war, schools also became divided; Serb and Croat children went to separate schools. As a result, their opportunity to meet one another across the ethnic divide became and remained severely limited. The effect on the younger generation has been revealed in a study of students aged twelve to sixteen and their parents. The study found that children have even more out-group biases and negative attitudes, and are more likely to discriminate against peers from the other ethnic group, than their parents. Paradoxically, Croat parents—who were more viciously betrayed by their Serb neighbours—continue to hold stronger feelings of attachment to the other group, learned in childhood.

This shows what happens when schools fail to play their socially integrative role in the community. Schools were powerless to prevent the genocide, but in childhood, they build feelings of attachment and identification that even survive murder. Separating ethnic groups at school today will not prevent future genocide, but it will ensure a growing distance between the groups.

PREJUDICE OR DISCRIMINATION

The problems associated with segregation are bad enough, but they are complicated by clique formation—a normal part of children's development as well as a normal feature of school life. For example, not only does streaming identify students to teachers as below- or above-par, it identifies them in the same way to students who are looking for ways to ridicule their fellow classmates and, by lowering their classmates' status, to raise their own.

As we saw in an earlier chapter, cliques separate people and set them against one another. In most schools, there are well-known cliques—the jocks, the nerds, the popular kid—and tension among them is always high. Streaming further intensifies the tension and hostility between these groups, as it too conveniently identifies some students as "brainy" and other students as subnormal or handicapped in some way.

ABUSE OR VIOLENCE

A source of increased concern today is bullying—especially the use of violence or threatened violence against children at or near school. And with the evolution of the Internet, much bullying has taken on the form of psychological rather than physical abuse.

Bullies win power over their victims physically, emotionally, and socially. They do this in many ways: by physical size and strength, by status within the peer group, by knowing the victim's weaknesses, or by recruiting support from other children, as in group bullying. Emotional and social bullying may perhaps be the most frequent and harmful forms. Bullying can be physical or verbal. It can be direct (face-to-face) or indirect (gossip or exclusion). With repeated bullying, the bully's dominance over the victim is established and the victim becomes increasingly distressed and fearful.

Bullying is a serious problem for those who engage in it, for its victims, and for the communities in which it takes place. It can make children feel frightened, sick, lonely, and unhappy. And childhood bullies are also more likely to develop antisocial behaviours. Studies show that 30 to 40 percent of children with aggression problems grow up to have problems with violence as adults.

A review of the literature notes that the motives for bullying originate at home, where children's behaviour patterns are first established. Bullies often come from homes that are neglectful, hostile, or use harsh punishment; it can also be learned from observing conflict between parents. Fighting among siblings to solve problems can unintentionally support bullying when it is accepted as a normal part of growing up.

Bullies tend to be hyperactive, disruptive, and impulsive. They are aggressive toward their peers, teachers, parents, siblings, and others, and tend to be assertive and easily provoked. They are attracted to situations with aggressive content and have positive attitudes about aggression. Boys who bully are physically stronger and have a need to dominate others. They have little empathy for their victims and show little or no remorse for bullying.

Children become victimized for many different reasons. Boys and girls are equally likely to report being victimized. Another interesting fact is that victimization decreases across grade levels. Children in lower grades are more likely to be victims of older bullies, whereas children in higher grades are more likely to be victims of same-age bullies. Victimized children have a tendency to be anxious and withdrawn, and they often report low self-esteem, likely because of repeated exposure to victimization. Both boys and girls who are victimized report symptoms of depression, such as sadness and loss of interest in activities. Boys and girls who are victims also report symptoms of anxiety, such as tension, fears, and worries.

Most bullying episodes occur in the context of a peer group. Although five out of six students say that watching bullying makes them feel uncomfortable, observations also suggest that peers assume many roles in the bullying episode: joining in, cheering, passively watching, and occasionally intervening. Peers give positive attention to the bully, rather than the victim. Their encouragement of the bully may serve to uphold the bully's power over the victim and within the peer group.

Bullying is embedded in cultural norms and values common to the whole community. It can be largely hidden, since often only pupils in the community can understand the meanings given to bullying. This is why bullying is possible even in the presence of the teacher and during lessons.

Bullying behaviour, a way of gaining power and status in a group or school class, often includes calling the bullied pupil a name. The pupil singled out for this treatment is often "different" in some way that has cultural meaning. Telling stories and calling the bullied pupil names increases the group's cohesion. The treatment of the bullied pupil also creates fear in other pupils, who do not dare to intervene. In a community where bullying occurs, fear and guilt are endemic.

One study examined the effects on adolescent males of being bullied with verbal taunts related to gender nonconformity—that is, they were routinely called "gay." In this study many students from the ninth, tenth, and eleventh grade in a private, all-male college preparatory school reported being bullied at some time. Of these, one-quarter reported that they had been called "gay." These boys experienced greater psychological distress, more verbal and physical bullying, and held more negative opinions of their school experiences than boys who were bullied in other ways.

All forms of bullying—direct and indirect, and even including cyberbullying—can have significant negative outcomes for health and well-being that may persist into adulthood. Many children do not tell of their bullying experience or seek help and support. Peer support programs have increasingly been identified as an important approach to tackling and preventing bullying. It has been suggested that these programs contribute by building resilience, promoting friendship, and challenging negative peer group roles in bullying behaviour. Bullying by a child considered a friend can be especially upsetting. It can be difficult for the child to recognize that a friend is bullying and for parents and teachers to identify these interactions as bullying.

One model to address bullying is using focus groups to address the behaviours of the bully and the victim. Positive social interaction can be reinforced through role-playing, literature, journal writing, open discussions, and team-building activities. This helps students realize the seriousness of bullying; they learn that it cannot be brushed off as typical middle-school behaviour. Though this intervention may not reduce the number of incidents, it gives victims "tools" to handle bullying situations and makes them feel sufficiently empowered to let the bully know that his or her actions will not be tolerated. Students became more confident in their ability to handle bullying situations. They feel more comfortable coming to an adult, and more able to handle these situations independently. A feeling of safety at school increases as a result.

Rooted in a group culture, bullying focuses on certain culturally supported stereotypes and prejudices. This includes singling out people who are handicapped (for example, deaf, blind, obese, or given to stuttering, and therefore socially isolated), unpopular, or homosexual. We have already noted that bullying often employs homophobic epithets—"you are so gay!" for example—even against boys who are not homosexual. This tendency is supported by aggressive, sexist, and heteronormative subcultures.

Though some homophobia is learned at home, some is learned and perpetuated at school, in peer groups; this is clear even after controlling for the predictive effect of individuals' own previously reported attitudes and behaviour. Aggressive peer group social climates increase the use of such epithets. In an aggressive, homophobic social climate, all students—whatever their tendencies—are likelier to call other students these names. Research has shown that lesbian, gay, bisexual, and transgendered (LGBT) students are commonly bullied at school. Such students experience name-calling, teasing, and bullying in their everyday lives. The LGBT population is always "at risk" of school bullying. Homophobic bullying should be highlighted as a concern in teacher training and should be reviewed in any school anti-bullying policy. Paradoxically, efforts to instill more tolerant views about homosexuality often seem to support binary concepts of (hetero- and homo-) sexuality.

Hyper-masculinity associated with certain contact sports such as football is especially likely to increase bullying. This is because of the values and attitudes that circulate within such contexts, with their historical leaning toward character qualities aligned to hardness, solidarity, and stoicism. Tensions and social anxieties around modern masculinity emerge in schools where a hyper-masculine sporting identity flourishes. Added problems in these schools are cultures of entitlement, abuse, and exclusion—also, homophobia and heteronormativity.

Opportunities for Co-operation across the Line

Under the conditions described above—competition, streaming, difference, inequality, and bullying—it is hard to imagine children and youth forming attachments at school. Yet many of them do. It is in the school environment that children form and broaden their base of close friendships. Often, these turn into long-term relationships and some even turn into marriage. So clearly school is helping to integrate people after all, teaching them how to live with one another.

This suggests that school is doing something to bring people together, despite the many ways in which it also drives them apart. Something about the school experience is evidently increasing familiarity in various ways. In particular, it is helping to wean students away from their parents and in the direction of the peer group.

Early in life, we are most concerned about relations with our parents. Our childhood home is the culture and society we know best, and we measure everything else—including our wishes, hopes, and self-esteem—against what we have learned there. As we age, all this changes radically. We become aware of a much larger world at school; the peers whom we encounter there are much more varied than our parents and siblings. For the first time, we feel moral doubt. The question we face is not "should I obey the rules?" but "what *are* the rules?" In adolescence, our needs for peer acceptance are increasing when we are searching for an identity and purpose of our own. We often feel torn between the conflicting goals of finding our own true selves and gaining social acceptance as "one of the crowd."

Our cultural norms invite this rejection of family life and reintegration into it as part of normal development and the passage from childhood to adulthood. For similar reasons, teenagers rate success and comfort more highly than adults do. To adults, material success and comfort are indicators of family well-being and security. To teenagers, they are means of freeing oneself from family constraints, as well as proof that they have achieved full membership in adult society.

Schools contribute to this process of independence and integration. First, and most obviously, schools bring together large numbers of young people, giving them an opportunity to communicate and interact easily. Schools are like factories: occasions for interaction and sociability, as well as for work. To some degree, this interaction is simplified by likeness and shared beliefs. Remember that most children attend neighbourhood public schools, and most neighbourhoods are socially homogeneous—at least, more homogeneous than the city population as a whole. And those children who go to a private school are also likely to be homogeneous in some respects—whether economically, ethnically, religiously, or otherwise.

Second, most children want to make friends. They don't want to be isolated loners, excluded from everything that is going on. They would even rather be a member of an unpopular group than be a member of no group whatsoever. This is, again, part of the developmental cycle we discussed above.

Psychoanalyst and researcher Erik Erikson described eight stages of development in the human life cycle, and of these, two are especially important for our discussion of schools. In stage four, from age six to twelve (often called the Latency stage), people are learning many new skills, developing a sense of industry and competence in the process. This is also a social stage of development; children often experience feelings of inadequacy and inferiority among their peers. At such times, they may develop problems of self-esteem. Their most significant relationship is with the school, neighbourhood, and peer group. Parents are no longer seen as the complete authorities they once were, although they are still important.

This becomes even more marked in adolescence. In stage five, from twelve to eighteen, development comes to depend on mainly what we do, not on what others do to us. The adolescent is neither a child nor an adult. Life gets more complex as young people try to find their own identity, struggle with social interactions, and grapple with moral issues. Finally, their goal is to discover who they are as individuals, separate from their family of origin and as members of a wider society.

In doing this, many teens withdraw from responsibilities, which Erikson called a "moratorium," and some may also suffer role confusion. At this stage, young people tend to think in black-and-white, idealized terms, terms which are clear-cut and conflict-free—little resembling the messy reality around them. Because they lack experience, they substitute ideals for experience. Seeking support for their ideas, they also develop strong devotion to friends and causes, wanting to idealize them and cling to them. It is no surprise that their most significant relationships are often with peer groups at this age, although families continue to hold importance for many.

Schools help children by developing occasions for peers to watch one another and even to work together on group or classroom projects. These opportunities to watch one another, interact and communicate with one another, and develop skills for trust and conflict resolution are all fundamental benefits of classroom education, whether private or public. These are also benefits denied to the home-schooled child, who will likely develop other less social and more academic skills instead.

INTERDEPENDENCE

Schools also integrate children into society by teaching them about their interdependence. They do this in several important, though often hidden and unintended, ways.

First and most important, schools often unite students against their teachers and the school staff. School is the first authoritative—sometimes authoritarian—environment run by strangers that children will have had to deal with. The classroom is run by a stranger, the teacher, who is intent on teaching rules and punishing noncompliance. Unlike a parent, the teacher is not easily seduced by compliments, tears, threats, or appeals to another authority. In fact, sociologist Harry L. Gracey has even compared kindergarten to a marine boot camp. The purpose of kindergarten—continued in the later grades—is to accustom students to taking and following orders, and working to the clock.

In this sense, the school can be like a total institution described by Goffman—intent on dissolving the child's former identity and building a new student-based one. Important in this are what Goffman called "degradation ceremonies," close discipline, constant surveillance, and the depersonalization of rules. These degradation ceremonies sometimes make the teacher seem like an enemy. And as we know from chapter 1, common enemies are as important as common friends in establishing social linkages among people. The hated or feared teacher can perform as important a role in a student's life as the beloved one.

Second, schools are a seedbed for teams, bands, and gangs (TBG) that we saw in chapter 3. There is probably no institution anywhere that contains more team, band, and gang members than a typical secondary school. This means that a great many students will have their first, or only, taste of TBG life—with the consequent issues of leadership, team spirit, group competition, and organized rivalry—during their school years.

Related to this is the role of the school in a system of schools, as the promoter of "school spirit." This is the youth-version of patriotism that pits all students collectively against the students of schools who are rivals in hockey, basketball, football, or other league competition. Spirit-building indiscriminately and purposely pits all members of school A against all members of school B—unifying each student body across differences in gender, class, race, ethnicity, religion, interests, aptitudes, and other socially, psychologically, and spiritually meaningful features. What better training for unthinking adult patriotism could there possibly be?

CIVILITY

It may seem odd, at this point, to look for signs of civility-education in schools. As we have already seen, schools—especially secondary schools—do not lack for degradation and humiliation. And although schools try to provide safety in the way of physical protection as well as the rule of law, the prevalence of bullying makes us doubt how successful they are. Schools, no doubt, try to instill a culture of human rights and dignity with multiculturalism and fairness, but they have a hard time succeeding. There are too many competing goals: notably, the goal of regimentation (discussed above), coverage of a mandated basic provincial curriculum, and the endless struggle for order and resources seen in any formal organization.

Yet what is remarkable about schools and educators is that they plainly keep trying. They remain aware of a professional duty to promote the basics of civility, despite evidence that efforts to do so are (often) largely unsuccessful. We know of these continued efforts from work carried out by educational researchers.

Some schools do better at this than others. Just as poorly functioning families—families lacking in cohesion and adaptability—fail to cope well with new stresses, so too do poorly functioning schools fail to respond well to the challenges posed by budget cuts, new provincial rules, losses of key personnel, and the arrival of at-risk students. Among the common inappropriate responses are a failure to reorganize the division of labour, poor staff development, increased class size, overreliance on untrained helpers, and an expansion of rules and harsher punishments. (In coping with a given problem, organizations always multiply rules and punishments when they can't think of anything better to do.)

Well-functioning schools overcome these problems. These schools, diverse in their philosophical approaches to education and socio-economic composition, foster the critical capabilities of students with an explicit "citizenship framework." In all of these schools, students are granted rights and responsibilities within the school community. These schools view rules as statements of principles rather than an extensive list of dos and don'ts, and they keep their flexibility rather than taking a "one-size-fits-all" approach to the discipline of students.

Good schools promote ethical relationships in the interactions of the student, instructor, and institution. Teaching there is based on moral and ethical principles, as opposed to technical ones. Students are called on to recognize and resolve various ethical issues, some of which focus on the instructor's actions, and the institution, as it supports its students and instructors, is ethically involved.

Traditionally, theories of education have focused on how children are socialized from the top-down, according to a values-transmission model. In good schools today, however, children are not just passive recipients but active agents in their socialization. They are invited openly to do what they have been covertly doing for generations: criticizing some school rules, distrusting teachers' explanations of particular rules, viewing some school rules and teachers' interventions as unfair and inconsistent, and often feeling they have no power over the construction of school rules.

Good teachers use open class meetings to set and revise class rules, asking students to accept collective responsibility for those rules, and working together to solve classroom problems. Informal feedback from others such as preservice teachers is also solicited.

Other good teachers use discussions of language—vocabulary lessons—to explore important ideas about civility. Teaching vocabulary can enrich students' understanding of words or ideas for which they may already know basic meanings—concepts such as courage, honesty, loyalty, maturity, justice, prejudice, and so forth. These occasions can also be used to engage students in exploring ideas such as loyalty (including misplaced or misguided loyalty), friendship, justice, fairness, maturity, bullying, and so on. Lively discussion and debate on these ideas can improve students' understanding of them as well as of their school lives.

One good teacher used a box of chocolate chip cookies, which he divided among his students: crumbs for the majority, two cookies for a few, and most of the box for one person. Turmoil erupted after this unequal distribution. The next day, the teacher took a different approach, placing a box of cookies in front of the students and telling them to divide the cookies among themselves. After brief discussions, the class devised a solution, but again turmoil erupted. Over the next few days, students continued to discuss cookie sharing, and in this way discussed resource distribution, power, and truth and reconciliation. In doing so, they learned a basic lesson on the fury of those who are deprived, as well as on greed and violence. They also learned that democratic decision-making is possible through prolonged, patient give and take.

These strategies all promote civility while preserving the engagement of the students. Not an easy task. One study by Amy Azzam, "Why Students Drop Out" (2007), found that although high school dropouts blame themselves rather than their schools or teachers, there are specific actions schools can take to increase students' likelihood of staying in school. Here's what the dropouts advised: (1) make school more engaging through real-world, experiential learning; (2) improve instruction and supports for struggling learners; (3) improve the school climate (that is, work for more civility); (4) ensure that all students have a relationship with at least one adult in the school; and (5) improve the communication between parents and schools, to gain parental support for school initiatives.

Good schools need order, respect, and connection. But respect for individual teachers and for the school as a whole must be earned, and it must be bidirectional. The students must also be shown respect. And, difficult as this is, the school must balance adolescents' needs for autonomy with teachers' needs for authority. Fortunately, a respectful environment feeds both goals.

Recent research by Lindsay Matsumura et al. (2008), based on observations of grade six and seven classrooms in high-poverty neighbourhoods, found that the degree of respect that teachers showed students significantly predicted students' behaviour toward one another. In other words, when teachers behaved respectfully, students behaved respectfully. Order was also important: clear classroom rules requiring respectful behaviour also increased the number of students who participated in discussions.

Civility depends on rules, but not all rules enjoy the same status among students. Robert Thornberg (2008) separates school rules into five categories: (1) relational rules; (2) structuring rules; (3) protecting rules; (4) personal rules; and (5) etiquette rules. Students view some of these categories as being more reasonable and important than others, and they are more willing to accept the reasonable, important ones. According to the students, relational rules are the most important in school. By contrast, etiquette rules are valued as the least important, if not in fact downright unnecessary, by the students.

Group tasks can help students discover the value of different types of rules and practices, while learning about the value of co-operation, division of labour, and mutual respect. For example, one teacher assigned groups of students the task of creating a web page together. She points out that "creativity" is not a gifted individual capacity; it is a group achievement, an everyday act that is achieved through social participation by members of a community. In creating something together, students negotiate new ideas and working arrangements within the general context of task completion. This supports the findings of research on students who worked together to compose and arrange music: through the act of collaboration, they learn about the co-construction of creative decisions.

Even competition—often involving some disruption of civility—can be made constructive. One art teacher notes that just as coaches never let athletes prepare without a clear understanding of the rules, teachers must ground their students in how art competitions work. Preparation for an art competition begins in the sixth grade. Not only do the students evaluate their own work with each project, using suitable standards, they also agree to class-wide reviews and critiques. By eighth grade art class, the students have a firmer idea of how the opinions of others can foster their artistic growth or at least provide help in thinking through a rut. In this way, by the time they get to the eighth grade, students are ready for more formal outside evaluations. Before entering their own work in an outside competition, students evaluate each other "blind," using the same standards and categories as the outside judges. To prepare for potential rejection, the teacher asks her students to keep a file of favoured comments and positive reviews of their work.

What do we learn from this and other research? We learn that co-operation breaks down barriers between students, teaches them the value of rules, and teaches them to surmount individual differences. It even breaks down barriers between students from different ethnic backgrounds and students of different skill levels. Respectful and participatory rule-making and fair, consistent rule enforcement reduces teacher stress, increases student engagement, and improves learning.

As we have seen, education—true education and not simply training—is concerned with bringing out the best in people and helping them to live well with others. This happens by showing children, through familiarity and first-hand experience, that different kinds of people are just as good as other kinds of people, and that we are all interdependent. In many domains of life, we have common friends and we also have common enemies—for example, today's environmental and economic dangers.

More than that, at their best, schools teach students lessons in civility that they may not learn at home. These lessons are the grounding of an educated citizenry and therefore a good society. In short, we have delegated to schools a task that no other institution in society is able or willing to take on: teaching people to be their best possible selves, in relation to the needs of other people.

Well-functioning schools work toward building a civilized society of students and teachers. The psychologist Lawrence Kohlberg coined the term "Just Community" in 1985 to describe a social grouping built on trust and resolution, in which each member engages democratically in developing the rules that govern their lives together. In a just school—a good school—students and teachers both take part in discussions about ethical issues that involve the relations between students and teachers. Each member of the community is held accountable to the group. So, the Just Community represents a moral laboratory: an opportunity for students to discuss ethical issues that arise and to act conscientiously under the rules set forth by the group.

For Kohlberg, the Just Community is based on ideas of justice (fairness and equal rights) and benevolence (social responsibility and altruism), and inspired by a sense of group solidarity. This community represents a humane experiment in participatory democracy. Such ideas about civility and democracy fit well with other liberal ideas that govern our society. They work toward what philosopher John Rawls called an "overlapping consensus" about political principles among people who hold widely varying cultural and personal conceptions of "the Good." Developing a public school curriculum that is suitable for such a civic education demands social tolerance and reflection on society's history and goals. It also means teaching children to understand the events and policies of their nation as following from general ethical principles.

While these goals may sound high-minded and impractical, schools are doing these things all the time. Like Molière's foolish "bourgeois gentilhomme," who was delighted to learn he had been speaking prose all his life, we may be surprised to learn that we act on social principles throughout life. It is the job of schools to bring these principles to light—to lead them (and us) out of ethical darkness, and in this way, help us live together.

TEN

Media and Mass Communication

Business success depends on finding and persuading the largest possible number of consumers. And political success depends on finding and persuading the largest possible number of voters. Finding and *rapidly* persuading large numbers of people relies on technology that was simply unavailable just over a century ago. The radio really only came into widespread popular use eighty or ninety years ago. Modern mass communication—movies, television, and the Internet, for example—are all much more recent than that. We have to realize that the modern mass media have changed human life dramatically since the birth of our great-grandparents.

Mass communication is the communication of a message from a single source to multiple recipients who receive the message at the same time. This kind of all-at-once communication is only possible using the technology that we call "mass media," a collection of tools including the printing press, the radio, television, the photocopier, and the camera. All of these, individually or working together, can reproduce and disseminate thousands, even millions, of copies of one original message.

The age of mass media began with the invention of the printing press around 1447 by German goldsmith and inventor Johannes Gutenberg (1398–1468). With his use of movable type, Gutenberg changed the world. By 1500 his printing technology had spread throughout Europe; in a very short space of time, ordinary people were reading the first widely distributed reading matter—the Holy Bible. Since then, we have come to associate civilization with literacy, and modernity with the media. Today communications technology is central to our culture, politics, and society.

Because of its capacity to reach millions, nothing in society is so integrative *in principle* as the media and the information that it carries. If there is anything that can help us live together well, surely it is the mass media. After all, television, radio, movies, newspapers, magazines, CDs, DVDs—all these are dedicated to serving society at large.

"Mass," as any good dictionary makes clear, means not only large but undifferentiated and unnumbered. We find a massive quantity of sand on the beach, for example, but no one teaches a mass (that is, an uncountable number) of undergraduates or buys a mass (that is, an uncountable amount) of groceries. The task of the mass media is to carry communication (information and entertainment) to the "masses." But since most of the mass media are owned by private individuals or groups, the purpose of this mass communication is to make a profit by advertising consumer products—Coca-Cola, McDonald's—that interest the largest possible number of undifferentiated, undistinguished people. (We will see below the role of marketing in targeting ever smaller segments of the population.)

Given this tendency to view the masses as indistinct and undistinguishable, and to be motivated by profit-making, it is no surprise that the mass media often carry shoddy, unremarkable goods and entertainments—that is, play to the lowest common denominator. Despite occasional pretensions and any earlier hopes to the contrary, the mass media provide the "circus" part of what the Latin poet Juvenal called "bread and circuses," a recipe for despotic control in the late Roman Empire. The mass media, and particularly television, are a "vast wasteland," as FCC commissioner Newton Minor famously remarked in 1961. In fact, the media are a wasteland with homogenizing, levelling effects. By design, the mass media bring everyone down to the same intellectual level.

Forty years ago Marshall McLuhan drew attention to the homogenizing effect of mass media with his famous dictum: "the medium is the message." Part of McLuhan's meaning is that how media affect people depends largely on whether the medium is printed (like books) or visual (like television). The impact of television is much more direct and visceral, less favourable to clear, deep thinking, and more emotionally provocative than print media. When a mass of people receive televised communications, they are all being stimulated—massaged psychologically, if you like—in a similar, often uncritical but emotionally arousing way.

But there are limits to the homogenizing effects of mass media. We have noted several times already that industrial societies are much more diverse than pre-industrial ones, owing to the division of labour and specialization this entails. As Durkheim points out, this fact is central to the problem of social order in modern, complex societies. And we saw earlier how certain social differences and inequalities separate people in important ways: by gender, age, race, ethnicity, class, region, nationality, and so on. Broadcasters and advertisers take note of these differences and use them in advertising, which places a limit on the overall potential for homogenization.

This insight has led to a vigorous development in the last few decades of niche marketing by advertisers and broadcasters. Media messages are targeted to specific demographic groupings. Think of an NFL football game: it is watched by mainly young and middle-aged men. The accompanying sports commentary and advertising strategies are all shaped with this viewing demographic in mind. In fact *all* media "products," whether television programs, movies, books, magazines, newspapers, or websites, target particular audiences in a range of artful ways.

Communications technology has been influenced by increasingly sophisticated marketing research in recent decades. People spend their money differently, although certain commonalities are visible. Items that were once considered to be luxuries are now necessities. Today almost everyone has a telephone, refrigerator, and television set. Back in 1940, however, only a minority of North American homes owned telephones; in 1950 the same was true of refrigerators, and likewise the television was still a relative rarity in 1955. Most households have come to first value, then *need*, a second telephone, a second television, cable TV, and a VCR. And since 1980, there has been a rapid surge in the ownership of smoke detectors, clothes dryers, and of course mass media devices: big-screen colour TVs and DVD players, among other items. High-income families own more of all these things than low-income families. But as they have become more common and their prices have fallen, these goods have also crossed the class line from luxury goods (available only to the few) to necessities.

In general, however, the poor have less disposable income for luxury goods and leisure. People with a more modest income spend a greater portion of their money on a small variety of goods and services, like food and rent. This leaves them with a distinctive spending pattern whether they live in Toronto, Los Angeles, or Bangladesh. And given that they have less money and less choice, the poor hold less interest for market researchers, who are more concerned with using communications technology to persuade well-off people to part with their money.

The mass media have played a key role in the promotion of consumerism and neediness. In the influence they wield over consumers, market researchers—manipulating the mass media like orchestra conductors waving batons—are "captains of consciousness," in the words of social historian Stuart Ewen. They mould the desires, needs, and intentions of the spending public. Market research has become ever more sophisticated with repeated surveys of purchasing behaviour and the development of demographic and psychographic models. The focus is on consumer spending patterns by age, income, education, and gender across multiple market sectors. The purpose is to guess who will buy SUVs, frozen meat pies, Asian-style cooking sauces, vacations in the South Pacific, or Viagra, and with what inducements.

Sociologists have played a (not always glorious) part in market research. For example, to promote household products more effectively, three sociologists in the early 1960s helped the publisher of romance magazines find out the secret fears and desires of working-class wives. They advised the publisher to play on women's fears of becoming unattractive, losing their husbands to other women, and losing the love and respect of their children (this research is described in Lee Rainwater et al., 1962).

Today it is likely that mass communications have a less homogenizing effect than in the past. The reason for this is that they are more "multicultural": that they target market segments rather than everyone at once. As a result, they play a less integrative role in society than they once did, and arguably they may actually reproduce society's social divisions and inequalities. This, however, comes from a new and improved sales strategy, not a change in the media themselves.

Not only do the mass media provide poor quality information and entertainment, but according to critics, they often misinform the public. In newspapers, magazines, and television programming, it is often difficult to distinguish news reporting and commentary from political propaganda. The information provided is so incomplete and slanted that one can only suppose it is aimed at achieving a political goal. (More on this in the next chapter on politics.)

We must avoid becoming "technological determinists," narrowly imagining that the media have their own logic of development. The mass media, like other tools, are a result of human ingenuity, and their use reflects the goals (and morals) of the humans who control them. The media make possible certain types of social change, for better or for worse, but they do not make these changes inevitable. In the discussions below, then, we must keep in mind that people—not media—are producing the social effects that we study as sociologists.

Forces Pushing People Apart

The need to reach different groups with different messages means that, increasingly, the mass media provide different news and entertainment for people from different ethnocultural groups and socio-economic classes. We can see this on the cable channels that provide programming in dozens of different languages in any major metropolitan centre. In effect, the mass media are multicultural and multilingual, just like society itself. This multicultural programming tends to preserve the segregation and distance that exists between different social groups. For example, immigrant-language programming reduces people's exposure to Canada's official languages and lessens the speed with which they learn them. This, in turn, increases the likelihood they will cocoon themselves in ethnic neighbourhoods and maintain their traditional lifestyle.

The media also encourage separation, distance, and distrust between the genders by promoting stereotypes and gender discrimination. Many observers have commented that media representations of men and women tend to reproduce conventional stereotypes and prejudices. They do so mainly by dramatizing the differences between popular conceptions of masculinity and femininity, and often by objectifying women as sexual commodities.

As well, the media routinely depict conflict and violence. Both news shows and dramas depict violence in a variety of forms, including rape, murder, gunplay, and fist fights. Many efforts have been made to evaluate and measure the impact of these depictions on actual behaviour. There is some evidence that young people mimic violence shortly after viewing it.

However, it has been difficult to prove that in the long-term violent actions are direct results of long-term exposure to violent media. The media desensitize people to violence and, in this way, make violent behaviour seem normal and socially acceptable. But it still isn't clear how much this contributes to actual violence, compared with other social factors such as childhood experiences, peer influences, and parental abuse.

The point is that the media often portray people using violence to deal with problems; less often do we see them dealing with problems in a peaceful, co-operative way. There is a journalistic dictum that applies here: "if it bleeds, it leads." As well, the mass media play a major role in setting the agenda for a public discussion of current events, and research shows they tend to do so in a narrow, biased, and conflictual fashion. One need only watch Fox News to see a combative conservative (or right-wing) portrayal of US events, compared with CNN, whose presentation is much more centrist or liberal, if sometimes equally combative. (CNN is viewed as the most centrist of the cable news channels, though a traditional network news division like NBC News or ABC News probably makes an even better contrast.)

This is not to argue a conspiratorial point of view about journalists and journalism, as though a few powerful media owners are consistently quarterbacking a particular political agenda (although this would seem to correctly describe the role of Rupert Murdoch in relation to the Fox network). Rather, mainstream newspaper and other media are conservative—that is, reflect the dominant ideology of the ruling class—due to systematic processes such as reliance on powerful individual and "expert" representatives of groups as news sources. In fact, only a small number of people are frequently called on to give their views about current events, and often little effort is made to determine how closely these views approximate those of the larger public. Let's consider each of these media effects in closer detail.

Media and Politics

The mass media today make the news available to all interested consumers. The news as it is presented in the morning paper or evening television broadcast, however, is not just a neutral assortment of facts. Increasingly, it is a carefully designed commercial product that promotes a particular political and cultural ideology. In subtle ways, news media is involved in disseminating propaganda and perpetuating mainstream capitalist ideology.

News stories are coded messages about the nature of society and the nature of social life. To achieve their ideological goal, stories are simplified and slanted. During elections, political strategists—aware that voters respond best to messages delivered in simple language—advise their candidates to keep statements brief and punchy. The result is that more and more politicians speak in "sound bites." During the 1968 US presidential election, for example, the candidates' evening news sound bites lasted an average of forty-two seconds. By 1996, the average sound bite had shrunk to eight seconds.

Providing the public with a true picture of current happenings no longer seems possible. News space and time are limited and competitive, and force editors and reporters to make choices about who and what to cover.

However, it is not just the impracticality of lengthy stories that leads to brief or fantastic versions of the news. Another central issue is that news media are privately owned. News outlets are constantly being consolidated into massive multimedia empires, controlled by an ever smaller handful of increasingly powerful and influential players. Time Warner, for instance, is the largest media company in the world, with interests in the Internet (AOL), television (CNN, HBO, TBS, and many other networks), and film (Warner Bros.). It also controls Time Inc., the largest magazine publisher in the world, whose 115-plus titles—including *Time*, *Fortune*, *People*, and *Sports Illustrated*—reach a worldwide audience of over three hundred million.

In the US, three of the four major television networks, the source of daily news for most Americans, are part of multimedia giants: ABC is owned by the Walt Disney Company (Miramax Films, Hyperion Books) and Fox Television is controlled by Rupert Murdoch's News Corporation (the *New York Post*, HarperCollins). NBC is (along with Universal Studios) owned by the huge industrial conglomerate General Electric. CBS owns numerous other media properties, including book publisher Simon & Schuster, and in turn is controlled by Sumner

Redstone, who also holds the reins at Viacom, owner of Paramount Studios and MTV Networks. Viacom was split into two companies several years ago: CBS Corp., which owns the TV network, also owns Simon & Schuster and various other properties; the movie business and cable networks were left with Viacom. Sumner Redstone holds a majority stake in both companies.

In Canada, ownership is concentrated as well—a fact well documented over several decades. Creation of a Royal Commission (popularly known as the Kent Commission) was provoked by newspaper closings in Winnipeg and Ottawa in August 1980 that eliminated direct competition between Canada's two largest newspaper chains in those cities. (An earlier government inquiry, the Davey Commission, had in fact predicted such loss of competition.) Tom Kent, a former newspaper editor, civil servant, and academic, was chosen as chair of the commission, which collected a vast amount of information on newspapers and journalism in Canada and produced a nine-volume report outlining the structure and operation of the newspaper industry.

In its 1981 report, the Kent Commission made the following statement: "Concentration engulfs Canadian daily newspaper publishing. Three chains control nine-tenths of French-language daily newspaper circulation, while three other chains control two-thirds of English-language circulation." The report also found that there was little justification for the ownership of newspaper chains by conglomerates with major interests in other sectors like television. Such "cross-ownership," the commission felt, would compromise journalism's social responsibility to the reading public, and also resulted in lower spending by newspapers on editorial content and investigative reporting. All these factors were driving good journalists out of the profession as a result of inadequate pay, failure to train newsroom managers properly, and sometimes the favouring of profit at the expense of responsible journalism. The commission also found that the public (rightly) believed that the quality of political journalism had declined, and that diverse interests were not as well represented as they had been previously.

The report praised smaller news services such as United Press Canada, but was unsure that they would survive in the face of so many newspaper closures and mergers. These concerns proved justifiable. As well, the commission predicted that the growth of electronic publishing and telecommunication information, in addition to the rapid development of the electronic media, could present a critical problem for the future of the newspaper industry. This, we now know, was another fully warranted concern.

Recommendations that legislation be devised to reduce the power of conglomerates—to solve the problems that the commission had identified—were largely ignored. Newspaper publishers fiercely opposed creating the proposed Press Rights Council, arguing that this would promote government interference with a free press. They attacked the Kent Commission's research, contending that it had not proven that chain-owned monopoly newspapers are worse than the old individually owned competitive newspapers. For this and other reasons, interest in the commission's findings soon faded.

Though some recommendations did reach the stage of draft legislation under the Liberal Trudeau government, most disappeared during the Conservative Mulroney government. The exception was a 1982 government instruction to the Canadian Radio-Television and Telecommunications Commission (CRTC) to deny new broadcasting licences or renewals to applicants who owned daily newspapers in the same market. However, this allowed for exceptions "in the public interest," and these exceptions were found to apply to almost every case heard by the Commission. In the end, there was no net effect.

As most major media outlets are owned by large business enterprises, the goal of producing revenue for shareholders' parent companies influences what gets published. These companies are motivated by two goals: immediate profit and service to political and corporate friends, which will result in longer-term profit. As a result, dissenting opinions and alternative voices are marginalized—reduced to a decentralized network of activists. Meanwhile, the massive mainstream news services increasingly condense the political landscape into a two-party competition, represented by catchy sound bites.

We saw above that much journalism today is biased, supporting one political party or ideology over another. In general, newspapers can be classified as either conservative or liberal, based on content analyses of their editorials and commentaries. Biased journalism erodes the quality of political debate because it divides public opinion and forces conservatives and radicals to their respective extremes. Biased journalism not only disgraces the profession of journalism, it also simplifies complex issues.

Increasingly, the media coverage of politics is based on polls rather than in-depth analysis of issues. On the one hand, this reflects an underlying concern with public opinion—the *vox populi*. But on the other, it sidesteps a comprehensive analysis of the issues at hand. Politicians give a televised speech; it is instantly "spun" by partisans and analyzed by journalists. Public opinion is instantly polled to determine if the politician pushed the right buttons in his speech or the wrong ones.

Polling, especially when used to highlight the "horse race" aspect of a political contest, subverts the concept of democracy as a deliberative process in which citizens evaluate ideas and elect candidates whose notions of government and the just society most closely align with their own. Instead, by devoting most of the coverage to who is leading the race, news agencies increase rates of "bandwagon-ism." When this phenomenon occurs, undecided voters simply cast their ballots for whoever is projected to win, rather than engaging in the political debate.

More subtly corrosive still is "agenda-setting," which focuses attention on some issues at the expense of others. In this way, news agencies can influence what voters think about. The media also shape views toward candidates in an election. Some report more on candidates' characteristics, while others focus more on policy issues. Always, the goal is to show the favoured candidate in a positive light and the opposing candidate in a negative one. Whether positive or negative, such pointed coverage often has the intended effect of influencing the views audiences hold toward candidates. The media also set the "tone" in which people talk about public issues—whether this tone is a civil one or not.

So it seems that very often the role of the media in politics is neither informative nor integrative. It serves the interests of the media owners and their political friends; in addition, it also promotes the illusion of conflict and doubt where there is none, or not much of one. It diverts attention from important issues to trivial ones. And in this way the existing structure of power and opinion in society is reproduced.

MEDIA AND GENDER

The media also generally maintain existing gender relations. Consider children's television that runs 24-7: "boys' shows" often have commercials for action figures, while "girls' shows" have commercials for Barbie dolls. Media advertising tends to be gender-specific, aimed at men or at women. Even in the newer media such as computerized adventure games, traditional stereotypes remain. Although we see the feisty fighting woman, her appeal is still primarily sexiness. In newspapers and television, women continue to be described by the number of children they have and/or their age; men, on the other hand, are often described by occupations or political affiliations. A woman who stresses politics in her life is pointed out as a curiosity, as is the man who describes himself as a child care provider. Neither is shown as a role model. (Compare the media treatment of federal politician Belinda Stronach with that of her former boyfriend Peter MacKay.)

Some branches of the media see their role differently, as forerunners and agents of change. They purposely present the female engineer or the male nurse not as curiosities but as experts in their fields. These programs and magazines show awareness of diversity in race and ethnicity, as well as in gender. But even so, it is clear that these programs are stereotyped by the rest of the media as "educational" or "feminist," and are watched, read, or listened to by relatively small numbers of people.

The continued gendering of media depiction has an effect on people. One of the oldest findings in social science is that people imitate others in order to gain vicarious (that is, second-hand) rewards. Certain kinds of people are more likely to be imitated than others: for example, we are more likely to imitate those who are closest to us or whom we see as powerful and important. Using attractive, well-known, or admired figures—who in advertisements seem to speak directly to the viewer—is a good way to influence our behaviour. These are people we look up to, and we are inclined to copy their appearance and behaviour.

Some efforts have been made to overcome the nastier and more stereotypical forms of gendered advertising. In fact, some socially conscious organizations are using commercial media (like television advertisements) to promote change. Occasionally, we see male sports stars talking about problems of violence against women, in an attempt to promote models of masculinity that are concerned, caring, and nurturing as well as strong.

And in a turnaround of traditional depictions, we often see women (especially wives) presented as sensible and competent, with husbands who are inept knuckleheads. But these gender anti-stereotypes are typically cast in the domestic realm, at home, not at the office or in Parliament. They simply confirm the deeply held notion that women's proper place is in the home. Most Hollywood films continue to present women, and women's bodies, as objects for the male gaze—even if today the women depicted are more educated and feistier. Few films are made for women, even when the filmmakers are female. Those that are have come to be set apart as "chick flicks."

It is still common to discover that newspapers are directed at male readers—perhaps male readers of a particular social class—with incidental pages containing what women are assumed to "want" (fashion and human interest stories, not politics). Most newspaper stories are about men.

The media also slant information to conform to a particular gendered approach that has come to be called "the male gaze." When a news story is told from a male point of view, especially that of a male European-American, the standpoint of the reporter or editor is effectively hidden. It is assumed to be unbiased and objective, speaking on behalf of all of us. However, the "point of view" subtly marks the tone and emphases in a news story.

In Canada, stories about the two most recent Governors General—Adrienne Clarkson and Michaëlle Jean—have focused on these women's style, glamour, and exoticism while, at the same time, hinting at their inexperience and inappropriateness for the role. Few if any male Governors General have been treated so dismissively. Whatever the merits of these particular criticisms, they remind us of a long-standing tendency to treat women less seriously and with less respect than men.

Media images of gender have a vast impact on the daily lives of women and men. It is not merely a question of a girl seeing on TV another girl playing with a dollhouse and choosing to imitate this behaviour, although of course sometimes this may happen. More importantly, the media images present us with ideas of how the world is organized, the social relations that prevail, and assumptions about men and maleness and women and femaleness that enter silently into our everyday behaviour.

Here we have used gendered social relations as the example, but the media separate people by age, class, race, ethnicity, and region in similar ways.

Contributions to Integration

Since the media reproduce existing gender and class relations through their advertising and their depiction of public affairs, we can rightly wonder whether they contribute to integrating people—to helping different kinds of people live together in our society. There is some evidence that the mass media are improving in this area. However, the biggest improvements are coming via the newest medium: the World Wide Web.

THE INTERNET

We are living today in what has been called the "information age." We have more information and more ideas than ever before in history. We make use of this information, exchange it, and transform it. Information is a commodity to be bought and sold. What's more, the increasing spread of access to information has the potential to integrate society—to help us live together better—more than ever before.

Information has truly exploded. Five centuries ago, scholars could agree on what made up the sum total of knowledge in a literate society, whether it was in China or in Western Europe. It was still possible for someone to imagine becoming an expert in *everything*. The Renaissance scholar Erasmus has been thought of in these terms, as a "universal" scholar; many would see Leonardo da Vinci in the same way. Even fifty years ago, scholars could still demarcate the boundaries of knowledge: that is, the boundaries of what was known and knowable. But by then the demarcated body of knowledge was far beyond the reach of a single person, so specialization was needed even within fields (for example, within chemistry, anthropology, or literature).

This idea of a body of knowledge, of what educated people should or could know, was limited by the technology of the day and by definitions of what constituted "knowledge." For a long time, most knowledge (such as how to grow food, to weave fibres, or to work with metal) was transferred orally and preserved by human memory. In medieval Europe, monks copied manuscripts, believed to be the word of God.

The act of writing underwent a transformation with the invention of the printing press, which changed all this by making fast, accurate copies that had previously taken months or years to do by hand. Knowledge became an item that could be spread among strangers. Printers sought out new material. Even so, it took several centuries for authorship to gain its modern form. The concept of knowledge that could be owned as a form of property was followed by a concept of standards. Eventually, in the popular mind, a standard of information became associated with what had been printed. Printing endowed a halo of authority or credibility.

Today we may be less gullible, but we still distinguish between knowledge producers and knowledge consumers. *Producers* are people who are seen as "experts" and who can get their works into print: this may be as academics through peer-reviewed journals and monographs, as "hands-on" experts through popular books, or as reporters in far-off places who tell us through newspapers and magazines what is happening elsewhere in the world.

Consumers, by contrast, are people who use the knowledge produced in these ways. They buy "how-to" books. They go to school and college to gain knowledge, and from there to the world of work. In the workplace, at least in theory, they use this knowledge. Often they may find that they need more knowledge and information. And producers are themselves consumers, obliged to make clear, in academic publications, what is "their" knowledge and what has come from other people. Clearly the ownership of knowledge is important, both for its own sake and for its market value.

The Internet has been altering this link between consumers, producers, and knowledge. Indeed, the web has changed the whole way we produce information and understand the concept of knowledge; in short, it changes the relations of its production. By 2008, an estimated 84 percent of Canadians were using the Internet (internetworldstats .com provides comparisons here: this is apparently true of 73 percent of Americans and 19 percent of the rest of the world). The growth of Internet use has increased in Canada by 121 percent since the year 2000. Most important, many of these Internet users are both information consumers *and* information producers.

The revolutionary potential of the Internet is that it recreates information as something that is commonly shared and exchanged, not as a commodity to be owned. The Internet was described by Howard Rheingold as the "agora," after the ancient Greek word for "marketplace," the social space in which people walked and talked. In our contemporary terms, this information marketplace is huge; some see it as spinning out of control, impossible to map accurately, and used far beyond its original aims. The size and chaos of the Internet is indeed worrisome from some standpoints. Without quality checks and quality controls, we are all at risk of something that we may call "mind pollution" whenever we set foot in cyberspace. However, the upside of cyberspace is that it gives ordinary people the chance to return to being producers, rather than only consumers, of knowledge. Indeed, of today's Internet users, nearly half are estimated to contribute actively to web *content* rather than just reading. Some of the material contributed in this way is ill-informed and ridiculous, but much of it is no worse than the material supplied by professional journalists and spin doctors.

Another important aspect of the electronic agora is that it is made up of people who have probably never met each other face to face, yet share beliefs and ideologies, give one another support, and regularly exchange ideas. The result is a creation of worldwide virtual communities: communities of interest and shared viewpoints, unhampered by distance and many of the social factors (age, race, gender, class) that often keep otherwise similar people from meeting or interacting with one another.

So the Internet is somewhat anarchic. There is no centralized control, including quality control, but many believe that this fact is both good and healthy. If access to the Internet is free and open, anyone can post what they want. This leaves scope for new ideas to surface. But it also leaves scope for hate literature and obscenities, plus an immense amount of sludge. Many wonder how the Internet community can control the latter without limiting free speech.

Some Internet providers have tried voluntary controls, asking that people not post offensive material on their sites. This does seem to work to an extent. However, there have also been campaigns to censor whole categories of material, and some countries have even gone beyond this. China, for example, controls Internet access in and out of the country through gateways with the complicit involvement of international telecommunication giants. The US has tried several methods of state censorship. Some of these have been struck down. There have been challenges and counterchallenges related to spam and to free access of legal minors to the web. It seems clear that any censorship of the Internet has the potential to prevent important ideas from being openly debated. In an information economy, this amounts to societal suicide.

And too much control also poses political dangers. Without vigilance by users, the Internet could be transformed from an anarchic network of information providers and communicators to a means of political surveillance. Already authorities have the potential to track the messages and website addresses of individual users, and in some countries are already doing so. The threat here is that the Internet could become a "panopticon": the all-seeing eye that allows those in authority to oversee people's actions, thoughts, and communications. Some Internet users are campaigning on issues of privacy and security of information, including the information they pass on when they connect to any site.

Internet communication is changing society, and it is also changing the mass media. There is no room for the traditional media to be complacent when not-for-profit information producers are making available material that is (sometimes) more entertaining, informative, honest, and insightful—for free. True, a lot of the material in cyberspace is illiterate rubbish, but at least it is (usually) honest rubbish. Will the Internet remain a free marketplace? Or will it become a forum that is ultimately controlled by a larger power? And will it exclude startling or sensitive material in the interests of protecting vulnerable members of society?

What the Internet issue does is throw into clear relief the abstract issues of rights to information property, liberty versus authority, geographic community versus virtual community, and technology-in-theory versus technology-in-social-use. Much of the twenty-first century will be taken up with democratically resolving issues that, before the rise of the Internet, were mainly of theoretical interest.

FAMILIARITY

Recall that, in discussing issues around living together, our goal is to consider contributions to familiarity, interdependence, and civility. On the first issue, familiarity, there can be no doubt that increased Internet use has increased global familiarity. First, it has increased the sheer volume of communication between individuals, between institutions, and between individuals and institutions. The Internet is the first place we go now to seek information—not to printed telephone directories, encyclopedias, or local wise people. And increasingly we trust the information we get in this way. Take the example of Wikipedia, the first-ever fully collaborative encyclopedia. Although lacking a hierarchy of resident experts, Wikipedia is widely used and increasingly widely trusted as the source of reliable information.

Beyond that, the Internet has revolutionized mass communication by making possible simultaneous communication between multiple receivers and multiple senders. Consider Facebook: this tool allows ordinary people to keep their entire network of friends and acquaintances continually informed about their current activities and thoughts. Or consider the role of blogs, which transfer the thoughts and musing of ordinary author-publishers to countless anonymous readers. Both of these new "publishing" strategies are bound to increase the sharing of ideas and beliefs, and the growth of intimacy and trust. We may not agree with everything we read in cyberspace, but I suspect (though I can't prove it) we come to understand our fellow humans far better than we did in the age of one-way mass communication.

INTERDEPENDENCE

The same processes that increase familiarity also increase inter-dependence. In large part, this takes place with the construction of social networks of communicators. Here, again, Facebook may be the best example. By creating and preserving networks of directly and indirectly tied people, Facebook clarifies who are common friends and, often, who are common enemies. These networks of cyber- or virtual-relationships lay the groundwork for an exchange of resour-ces—particularly information and support—and increase the likeli-hood that people will co-operate, even at a distance.

Of course, such social networks in cyberspace are no guarantee of co-operation and exchange, or even of trust and intimacy. But they are a necessary (though not sufficient) basis for this. Research shows that building and tending virtual relationships through the Internet sup-ports other forms of communication. Relations in cyberspace, whether by email or Twitter, do not substitute for face-to-face or even video tele-phone (or Skype) communications. They may even increase the likeli-hood and volume of such communications, in effect training people to be more communicative. Internet communications "merely" lower the cost and increase the speed of all communication.

Of course, this increase also carries costs and dangers. Many have written about problems associated with new cyber-communication—for example, with text messaging and twittering. They note a tendency for such messages to be too brief, lacking in nuance, sometimes hard to understand or interpret as they were intended, and liable to express volatile and even offensive emotional extravagance. In short, people have not yet perfected an etiquette associated with text messaging. Many have been so thrilled by the ease of communication that they have failed to consider the possible fallout of miscommunication. This will be corrected eventually, as with every other form of human communication (for example, we have learned to use telephones politely and informatively—leaving out telemarketers, of course).

CIVILITY

Finally, we want to consider the role the Internet—and other mass communication—might play in increasing civility. Here we are concerned with issues of fairness and equity, human rights and dignity.

Will the Internet, along with other forms of mass communication, improve public debate and give more people access to political conversation and decision-making? And will it do so in a way that increases people's respect for one another? Will it, for example, protect and be protected by legal rules of behaviour, or will it merely unleash disreputable attacks and cyberbullying? Finally, in breaking down the old "fences" of cost and distance that have historically separated people, will it erect new virtual fences—based on good sense and good manners—that will keep people feeling safe from one another, even while they interact and communicate widely?

Clearly, on these matters, we will have to await the final evidence.

CLAIMS-MAKING AND SOCIAL MARKETING

Two important ways that mass communications continue to affect social civility are through claims-making and social marketing.

Claims-making is a social strategy associated with what sociologists call "social constructionism." The concept of social constructionism rests on a sociological theory of knowledge stated by Peter L. Berger and Thomas Luckmann in their 1966 book *The Social Construction of Reality*. The social construction of reality often involves the work of what have been called "moral entrepreneurs"—members of the grassroots community, elites, or interest groups—to motivate political action. In this process, social problems are framed and identified. "Constructing" problems in this sense involves claims-making, a procedure that describes, explains, and blames people who are involved with the problem.

The goal of social constructionism as a sociological enterprise is to examine the ways people interact to create a shared definition of social problems. Berger and Luckmann argue that *all* knowledge—including the most taken-for-granted knowledge of everyday life—is created, preserved, and spread by social interaction.

In the eyes of social constructionists, human beings react not to physical objects and events themselves, but to the shared meanings of objects and events. These meanings are not essential features of the objects and events; rather, they are socially imposed or erected meanings. In our society, a red rose is considered beautiful and romantic, while a daisy is simple, and a cabbage, ugly. That's a social construction. (If you question this, present your loved one with a dozen Brussels sprouts on Valentine's Day.) The meaning of anything, including a social problem, is the product of the dominant cultural and symbolic practices in a group or society.

In a 1995 study, social psychologist Vivien Burr identified four basic assumptions of the social constructionist position:

- The world does not present itself objectively to the observer; instead, it is known through human experience, which is largely influenced by language.

- Categories of understanding are situational and emerge from the social interaction within a group of people at a particular time and in a particular place.
- How reality is understood at a given moment is determined by the conventions of communication in force at that time.
- Within a social group or culture, reality is defined less by individual acts than it is by complex and organized patterns of ongoing actions.

In short, when people interact, they share their views of reality and act on these shared views. Since people negotiate their shared common-sense knowledge, it can be said that all reality is socially constructed. As an approach, social constructionism looks at the ways people create and institutionalize social reality. And when people act on their interpretations and their knowledge of this "reality," they reinforce it or lock it in. It becomes habit and seems natural, even unavoidable.

The social constructionist position is that social problems exist when claims-makers or moral entrepreneurs succeed in persuading the public that they exist. The social constructionist approach is interested in answering certain questions. How do claims-makers make successful claims? What kinds of problems or situations support claims-making? What kinds of people, with what kinds of motives, make claims? What leads people to hold certain kinds of belief and not others? And under what circumstances (if any) is it possible to argue with or disprove these beliefs? And finally, and most obviously relevant to our current discussion, how do the mass media—including the Internet—influence the construction of social problems?

The social constructionist position is valuable because it helps us understand why public attitudes about social problems change over time. It also leads us to explore the reasons why people behave in such seemingly irrational ways—developing "manias" about some supposed problems while ignoring other problems in their midst that may be obviously more important.

The social constructionist approach to social problems is valuable for having called our attention to this problem and for giving us the tools to understand how the process of claims-making works. The approach gained major ground with Malcolm Spector and John Kitsuse's 1977 theory of social problems as claims-making activities. These authors proposed a natural history or chronological model, in which a problem goes through stages of development, that has proven to be especially useful.

Early social constructionists in the tradition of Spector and Kitsuse often did little to place claims-making in its social context. They paid little attention to the motives, meanings, and intentions that went into claims-making. And we also have to be aware of the use and abuse of statistical data to provide claims with an aura of precision and accuracy. In this way, social statistics become rhetorical materials in a scientific and supposedly fact-obsessed age. Social constructionist Joel Best, in his 2001 book *Damned Lies and Statistics: Untangling Numbers from the Media, Politicians, and Activists*, has written persuasively on this very topic.

While many issues that we are concerned about today are issues that also concerned people fifty years ago, others have gained our attention in a way they have not done previously. Today we consider family violence and child sexual abuse to be legitimate social problems in need of public attention. They "became" problems not because they were happening more or less often, but because people became more concerned about them. Social issues are constructed by claims-making to invoke intense feelings toward sensed harm in the community. What's more, the mass media were important tools in publicizing the extent of these problems.

However, the media have also been complicit in promoting silly concerns, simply because doing so catches the public attention for a brief time and sells product. Discussions of welfare fraud fall into that category. Other, more extreme examples include the preoccupation with witchcraft, devil worship, and satanic rituals that produced a flurry of concern in the 1990s. More recently we have seen preoccupations about child pornography. Sociologists refer to short-lived, intense periods of concern as moral panics and to the people held responsible for the sensed threats as folk devils. Though moral panics, like fads, are short-lived, they leave a legacy, whether as laws, stereotypes, cultural beliefs, or changed attitudes. A good example is the health care debate in the US with its talk of death panels, killing Grandma, and so on. This debate also seems to me to be symptomatic of the problems with the Internet: idiocy now spreads far faster and more nastily than ever before.

In the paranoid mid-twentieth century, "Commies," "subversives," "agitators," "foreigners," "outsiders," and "hippies" were all viewed as folk devils. Today, only "terrorists" and "suspected terrorists" fall easily into this category.

Recent Issues

As we read reports of recent research on the role of media in the public sphere, we can see recurrent themes. First, some governments continue to use the media to influence and manipulate public opinion with propaganda; it has been used to tranquilize discontent and promote political support. They also use the mass media to market new ideas and behaviours that are important for modernization and social development. In Canada, public health promotion is often carried out through the mass media.

The mass media play somewhat different roles in different societies. In many societies—especially developing ones—political, religious, economic, media, and regulation actors compete in the public sphere for influence and control. Here, the media sometimes succeed in promoting democratic politics. But equally often they are the tools of competing groups and merely reproduce existing conflicts. In many countries, the outcome of such conflicts depends on transnational flows of information, resources, and influence. For example, outside support was important in the successful media campaign to oust Chilean dictator Augusto Pinochet from power.

We have seen how in some societies a powerful central government continues to use the media for propaganda. Take the example of the People's Republic of China. In the last decade or so, China's economy has shifted from communism to neoliberal capitalism, and as a result economic inequality has increased dramatically. An affluent new middle class has developed in many of the larger cities. To accommodate these changes, the state has used mass media to model new ways of thinking and talking about society. Gone is the socialist jargon of the Maoist period. The Marxist language of "class" has been replaced by Weberian (that is, American) notions of "social strata."

Transformations from socialism to capitalism have taken place elsewhere, occasioning similar uses of the media to soften the changeover. For example, in Lithuania—a former Soviet republic—rural poverty has been re-imagined in the media to serve political goals. During the 1990s, the media coverage of rural poverty was associated with a failure by the rural population to achieve "moral modernization." Then, the rural population was stigmatized as being morally deficient, stuck in the grip of Soviet-style thinking and state dependency, and thereby unable to take advantage of the opportunities created by capitalism. However, in the early 2000s, the economic situation in Lithuania improved significantly and the country began negotiating for membership in the European Union (EU). The media coverage of rural life was transformed in EU terms to call attention to local policies that promoted the diversity, well-being, and active citizenship of rural communities.

Here in the West, the media continue to give us a skewed coverage (and understanding) of other countries. In keeping with the centre-periphery pattern discussed in chapter 7, media coverage continues to focus on some countries and ignore others. A recent analysis of human rights reporting by *The Economist* (UK) and *Newsweek* (US) from 1986 to 2000, covering 145 countries, found that these two media sources cover human rights abuses more often when they occur in countries with relatively high levels of state repression, economic development, population, and Amnesty International attention (for example, China and Russia). Poorer and less populous countries with equally serious problems are often ignored—think of Sudan, Myanmar, Rwanda, and the Democratic Republic of Congo as examples of such blind spots.

The Western media also continue to create celebrities—in sports, entertainment, crime, business, and elsewhere—in a way that promotes what sociologist Chris Rojek (2006) calls invasive egoism: an over-close identification between fans and their idols. This tendency continues a media tradition of celebrity culture, commodifying sports culture. It also promotes what historian Daniel Boorstin has called the media creation of "pseudo events," incidents or activities that serve little purpose aside from being reproduced through advertisements or other forms of publicity. Boorstin is famous for having defined "the celebrity" in his book *The Image; or, What Happened to the American Dream* (1961) as "a person who is well-known for his well-knownness," which is often misquoted as "a celebrity is someone famous for being famous." Interestingly, the Internet seems to have made this tendency even worse (think of Twitter).

The Continuing Search for Civility

Far more complicated than the celebration of non-events is solving the problem of what we mean by (and desire from) civil society and citizenship. What should be the role of the mass media in creating a "public sphere" and empowering "citizens" within that sphere?

Obviously, most people are not just passive recipients of mass communication, if they ever were. There are too many sources of competing information and too many ways to resist. Even back in the 1950s, mass communication researchers knew that. A classic work in this area was by sociologists Paul Lazarsfeld and Elihu Katz with their theory of two-step communication. They showed that people use their personal networks to discuss and evaluate media messages before acting on them. Today, they likely also surf the Internet, adding a third step to the process of interpreting and responding to advertisements, news reports, and political opinion. So we must look beyond mere information acquisition to explain how and why citizens use political information, and we must also recognize that we live in a culture of mediated engagement with politics that organizes our political lives in new, ever more complex ways.

Consider, for example, the role of transnational influences—the effects of pan-national media on people's perceptions. Increasingly, we pay attention to how other countries and other media view us: how they look at our lives, our politics, and our leaders. The South African anti-apartheid movement relied on transnational media to promote its goals. What were the main strategies of public communication of the anti-apartheid movement, and why did they succeed as well as they did? And how can we apply our understanding of this case to current issues that are just as pressing? Think of the movement to achieve global justice.

Increasingly, national public spheres are being penetrated by outside influences (as with the furor about the 2005 Danish cartoon depictions of Muhammad). The world's attention was caught up in this episode, which seemed to focus the anger between Islam and the West. In that sense, we are all living in a "porous public sphere." Yet despite economic globalization, there is little sign of a global consciousness around political, social, or moral issues. There is not even much evidence yet of a European public sphere, or European identity—the creation of which would require a non-commercial transnational media strategy.

The German social theorist Jürgen Habermas (b.1929) concludes that

mediated political communication in the public sphere can facilitate deliberative legitimation processes in complex societies *only if* a self-regulating media system gains independence from its social environments and if anonymous audiences grant a feedback between an informed elite discourse and a responsive civil society.

The mass media will play a politically significant and useful role only when it has freed itself from its current biases and preoccupations with profit-making. Another necessary factor noted by Habermas is the point when informed elites are willing to honestly discuss policy issues with an informed public.

We have seen that the mass media already play an important, though not always positive, role in our society. The media, for example, bring supposed problems to the public agenda through the process of claims-making. This kind of claims-making relies on common rhetorical idioms and styles that reflect and legitimize core cultural values. Particular images or icons may be used to sway public opinion. Given that popular views and beliefs today are more often shaped by media depiction than by first-hand experience, it matters a great deal how the media depict a problem.

We have also seen how part of the media's influence comes through placing "problems" on the agenda for repeated discussion in news reports. Some of this influence arises through a depiction of the problem in particular ways, with heroes and villains in exaggerated stories. Some media portrayal is also implicit, as in television talk shows. There, we learn the current standards of behaviour—what is considered deviant and normal, praiseworthy and shocking—as members of the viewing audience. These hosts are moral entrepreneurs and claims-makers, but the studio audience (and the home audience) is the court of public opinion.

Sometimes interest groups succeed in bringing new issues into the social realm by redefining and renegotiating previously unacceptable acts, making them more acceptable social practices. (Think, for example, about the growing acceptance of marijuana smoking and premarital sex.) Nonetheless, they rely on the mass media or the Internet (or even both) to mobilize public opinion around supposed problems and change public perceptions.

The framing of social problems clearly influences public opinion, and we all need to be alert to this. Media education is especially important for young people given the role of different communications media in the formation of youth at school, in the family, and in the community. Given the close links between media education and civic participation, we need to know as much as we can about the media, and how we can promote responsible coverage.

Our awareness of social problems is a function of claims-making, a social activity that relies heavily on the media. As this technology continues to develop, we will probably see more real and supposed social problems. It is not yet clear whether this hurricane of information flow will lead to a general increase in social integration—to more familiarity, interdependence, and civility. No one can tell yet whether the mass media will be a tool or an impediment in this civilizing project.

ELEVEN

Churches and Religion

In this chapter, I use the term "church" to refer to any social location or building—church, mosque, synagogue, or temple—where people carry out religious rituals. The term "religion" refers to any system of beliefs about the supernatural, and to the social groups, whether these are denominations, sects, or cults, that gather around these beliefs. The question of interest to sociologists is this one: how do churches and religions help to integrate a society? That is, how do these communities help people live together in better ways?

We know that religion can be a form of social control. Through religion and the "dominant ideology," people are encouraged to act in ways that benefit ruling classes of society: such behaviour may include meekness, submissiveness, or conformity. This is largely what Karl Marx meant when he spoke of religion as being "the opiate of the masses." On the other hand, religion can also help to foster resistance. The clearest examples come from situations where religion not only fosters identity as a group member—for example, as a member of the working class—but gives value and respectability to more traditional, humble ways of life.

Most of the time, however, religion is irrelevant to many people's lives. Our society is often called a "secular society," and by that we mean that people today are less religiously inclined than they were a century or two ago. People are less inclined to attend churches or think about the supernatural. By contrast, people today often speak of our society as being, among other things, a technological or scientific or—as Max Weber called it—a "rational-legal" society. This refers to a society in which people are "disenchanted" or demystified about the natural world, and disinclined to explain natural phenomena by invoking supernatural causes.

This is all true. In fact, we get the clearest idea about the difference between a secular and religious society if we contrast religion with science. Much was made about this contrast throughout the nineteenth and twentieth centuries. Indeed, there was virtual warfare between science and religion during that time, around topics like Darwin's theory of evolution. Darwin's thinking posed a significant challenge to a literal interpretation of the Old Testament. We will not go into this hoary controversy, except to note that it has resurfaced recently in fundamentalist portions of the Southern US.

What we do need to consider is the big gap in thinking between science and religion, and specifically between the ways science and religion carry out their enquiries. Science, you will remember, is a cultural and social orientation toward the search for knowledge. We noted in chapter 2 that advances in technology have come about largely through the scientific revolutions that began in Europe five hundred years ago. Recall also that these advances rest on empirical research that obeys the "norms of science" identified by Robert Merton as CUDOS: communalism, universalism, disinterest, and organized skepticism.

We have seen how science proceeds by peer review. So, in fact, does religion. Even religious scholars have their colleagues and coteries—for that matter, the same is true of astrologers, magicians, and jazz musicians. More important, science advances by independent disinterested research, a public review of findings, and the application of universal criteria of judgment. And most important of all, science demands organized skepticism. All scientific claims are critically evaluated and all conclusions are considered "tentative," awaiting disproof.

By contrast, religious scholarship is rarely disinterested. It is often organized and funded by religious organizations or by colleges with religious affiliations. For this reason, it is unlikely that, say, a Catholic scholar will conclude the Vatican is all wrong about papal infallibility or that the Gospels are a hoax. Scholars and other religious commentators who step too far outside the accepted institutional boundaries risk ridicule, exclusion, expulsion, excommunication, or even in Islam a *fatwa* (death sentence).

Religious debates are rarely public, perhaps owing in part to a lack of public interest. Often, they are carried out "internally," so the church can continue to present a united front toward the outside world. This is typical of a large business or governmental organization, not of an open inquiry. A final key point is that religions do not encourage or even necessarily approve organized skepticism. Churches and religions are built on faith. They do not regard their values, beliefs, and holy documents as current "best guesses" about the supernatural. So by and large they are unwilling to change these values, beliefs, or holy documents.

That said, every religion has procedures for "adapting" these when it becomes necessary. Like other organizations, churches always have a "Plan B." A prime example of such adaptability is the use of Hadiths in Islam. In theory, Islam is based on a literal interpretation of the Quran. However, Islamic societies differ widely in their social, political, and economic sophistication. As a result, Islam has historically made great use of Hadiths to allow flexibility in the "interpretation" of the Quran. Hadiths are supposed sayings and beliefs of Muhammad that were not written into the Quran but are known to us through later scholars. Typically, much effort is made to trace the genealogy, and therefore the legitimacy, of any particular Hadith. For example, scholars will try to demonstrate that a particular commentator might indeed have spoken with Muhammad and therefore been directly exposed to a given idea.

So religions do change and allow some flexibility. When they are too rigid they are likely to shatter or splinter. This is precisely what happened to Catholicism during the Protestant Reformation of the sixteenth century. Catholicism was irreconcilably fractured because, under pressure to change, it was incapable of bending its key principles like papal infallibility and divorce. Today, Catholicism runs a similar risk through its inflexible views about birth control, abortion, and premarital sex. Already, many in the West—especially in northwestern Europe, but even also in South America—have rejected Catholic teachings on these matters.

Religions, then, do vary in their flexibility and adaptability under pressure. But taken as a whole, a religion can never be as flexible and adaptable as a science, because science demands no commitment whatever to traditional beliefs. Indeed, science abjures such commitments.

Here's some evidence: in a religious book or textbook on theology, you will read a great deal about people who lived hundreds and even thousands of years ago. In a textbook about physics, chemistry, or astronomy, you will read next to nothing about people who lived hundreds, let alone thousands, of years ago. The older ideas have been left behind by the scientific community. When was the last time you heard a church leader discuss a religious figure who lived two thousand years ago? Many will reflect that you hear one such biography every Christmas at least! The same is not true of science. Churches revere their founders and worship their founding documents, while science faculties largely ignore the founders of science and any documents they left us.

Consider "phlogiston theory"—a theory about combustion advanced by J.J. Becher in the late seventeenth century and popularized by G.E. Stahl. It theorizes that in all flammable materials there is present "phlogiston," a substance without colour, odour, taste, or weight that is given off in burning. "Phlogisticated" substances are said to be those that contain phlogiston and, on being burned, they are "dephlogisticated." So, only the ash of the burned material is said to be the "true" material. This theory enjoyed strong, widespread support through much of the eighteenth century until it was disproved by the scientific work of A.L. Lavoisier (1743–94). He revealed the true nature of combustion is otherwise and there is no "phlogiston" involved. That is why you have probably never heard of phlogiston theory, J.J. Becher, or G.E. Stahl.

Is this a fair comparison? Surely, you might say, there have been religious philosophers who came up with ideas that became popular but were eventually dismissed. And you'd be right. Yet these religious thinkers were often treated quite differently from those whose scientific ideas had been dismissed. For example, religious philosophers with institutionally unacceptable views have often been characterized as heretics and punished with excommunication or fatwa. Nothing of the kind happened to Becher and Stahl, despite the rejection of their phlogiston theory.

Of course, this is something of an oversimplification. There are lots of religious beliefs that are just as dead and buried as phlogiston. And remember that Western science dates back only five hundred years or so, yet scientists still rely on the ideas of a founding figure like Isaac Newton, whose laws of motion still apply in non-relativistic settings. A different way of distinguishing between scientific and religious ideas is that scientific ideas are depersonalized. Scientists (as opposed to historians of science) still learn about Newton's laws, but not necessarily about Newton, because it is the depersonalized theory about the "real" world that matters in science—not the guy who thought of it. Religious beliefs, on the other hand, are by nature subjective and personal and so very hard to "depersonalize." In other words, the distinction is not between rigid and flexible modes of knowing, but between a subjective mode of knowing (which admittedly lends itself to inflexibility since it's hard to prove anything wrong if subjective feeling is the main criterion) and an objective mode of knowing that is subject to testing against the "real" world.

Where it has proven impossible to test a scientific view against the real world because of current technique—for instance, string theory in modern physics—inflexibility tends to persist until experimentation becomes possible.

That said, one cannot help being struck by the past-orientation of religion compared with the future-orientation of science. The saints memorialized by the names of Anglican churches in Toronto alone include: St. Aidan, St. Alban, St. Andrew-by-the-Lake, St. Andrew (two of these), St. Anne, St. Augustine, St. Barnabas, St. Bartholomew, St. Bede, St. Chad, St. Clement, St. Columba, St. Crispin, St. Cuthbert, St. Cyprian, St. David (two of these), St. Dunstan, St. George-the-Martyr, St. George-on-the-Hill, St. George Anglican, St. Giles, St. Hilda, St. James (two of these), St. John the Baptist, St. John the Divine, St. John (five with this name), St. Jude, St. Leonard (two with this name), St. Luke, St. Margaret-in-the-Pines, St. Margaret (two of these), St. Mark, St. Martin-in-the-Fields, St. Mary Magdalene, St. Matthew the Apostle, St. Matthew (two of these), St. Matthias (two of these), St. Michael and All Angels, St. Michael the Archangel, St. Monica, St. Nicholas, St. Ninian, St. Olave, St. Patrick, St. Paul (four of these), St. Peter (two of these), St. Philip (two of these), St. Saviour, St. Simon-the-Apostle, St. Stephen-in-the-Fields, St. Stephen, St. Theodore, St. Thomas, St. Timothy (three of these), and St. Wilfrid.

Then there are the saints memorialized by the names of Roman Catholic churches in Toronto alone—shall I run through this list too? It's even longer and includes some other names—Agnes, Alphonsus, Ambrose, Anselm, Anthony, Basil, Benedict, Bernard de Clairvaux .... You can complete the list yourself. Then there are the saints memorialized by the names of United Churches and Greek Orthodox churches. To avoid being tedious, my point is simply that science rarely memorializes its historic figures, while religion usually does. The tendency of religion to memorialize the past suggests that ideas and actions in the past should set the pattern for ideas and actions in the future.

This historical anecdote shows that, compared to science, religion is rigid and unyielding. Churches are often convinced that they have found the eternal and everlasting truth; they are also convinced that other churches, including other believers, are at best misguided and at worst infidels or pagans, doomed to eternal darkness. Such strong, unyielding, and exclusionary views have led to centuries, if not millennia, of hatred and bloodshed. So perhaps it seems odd that we should even consider churches and religions as candidates for helping people to live together. Yet a case can be made for doing so, because religions clearly also bring people together. What's more, they are universal, so they must be doing something socially important.

This chapter will argue that religions continue to exercise a hold on the human imagination. People continue to join churches and hang on to religious beliefs all over the world. What's more, churches and religions continue to exert powerful influence over political life in many parts of the world. This is obvious in Islamic countries, in Roman Catholic countries, in Israel (the only Jewish country), and even in Protestant fundamentalist regions of the US. And religions influence social life throughout the world.

Why are people (still) religious, given the enormous and persuasive importance of science in our lives? I do not believe that Freud was right in thinking that religion is nothing more than a symptom of neurosis, an illusion that people are unable to shed generation after generation. Evidently, religions give people a sense of meaning and purpose, a way of thinking about their lives and their sufferings, that science does not. No secular belief can do the same over an extended period, although in their heyday, Russian and Chinese communism, German Nazism, and Japanese fascism were powerful competitors. These political ideologies each provided people with what one sociologist called a "civil religion." Each was a celebration of the state, complete with imposing beliefs, rituals, and sacred objects—including persuasive versions of Heaven and Hell on earth. But in less than a century those civil religions have come and gone; meanwhile, Judaism, Roman Catholicism, Islam, Protestantism, and other religions persist.

Throughout the nineteenth and twentieth centuries "nationalism" provided many people with a sense of meaning and purpose. In some particularly patriotic countries like the US, nationalism and patriotism continue to be very powerful, and much more so than in Canada, for example. They have often been linked to religious belief and combined secular, nationalist, and other ideological elements in vast public rituals.

Think of major American sporting events such as the Super Bowl. These rival or even surpass religious events as occasions for ritual celebration. Indeed, one can view the Super Bowl as nothing less than a full-fledged civic religious festival, bringing together powerful elements of sports, politics, and myth. A recent Super Bowl halftime show even included militaristic and nationalistic aspects in its allusions to the post-9/11 "war on terror." The goal of this display was to justify the American war in Iraq by representing it in terms of "American" values and the virtues of democratic citizenship, all in the context of sports coverage.

Clearly religions help "the faithful" live together—not equally or always happily, but with a feeling that they belong somewhere. Science doesn't give people that sense of belonging. On the other hand, science also does not drive people apart and build walls between communities, as competing religions often do.

Forces Pushing People Apart

In the city where I live, you can see every kind of clothing and self-display. In one part of the city you will see members of a particular religious group—Orthodox Jews—living in self-segregated neighbourhoods, dressed in distinctive, archaic ways (for example, wearing large black hats), and consuming specially mandated (that is, kosher) foods.

In another part of the city you will see members of another religious group—orthodox Muslims—living in self-segregated neighbourhoods, dressed in distinctive, archaic ways (for example, burkas), and consuming specially mandated (that is, halal) foods. These two groups are equally devout, equally distinct, originate ancestrally in the same part of the globe (the Middle East), and are sworn political enemies.

This makes a simple point: namely, throughout history, churches and religions have pushed people apart. Two prime examples of the civil strife caused by religion are the historic treatment of religious minorities and of women. We will discuss each below, before going on to discuss the conditions under which religion might serve as a source of integration.

RELIGIOUS STRIFE

No one who has read history can deny that religions and churches have played a major role in creating conflict, often violent bloodshed. Anti-Semitism in Europe was historically approved, if not provoked, by the Catholic Church. More generally, few religious leaders have ever been willing to take the sides of religious minorities, whether of Protestants in Catholic countries, Catholics in Protestant countries, or Jews or Muslims in any Christian country.

The result has been continued social distance and segregation between religious groups, sometimes even resulting in the confinement of groups (e.g., Jews) in segregated ghettos. Into the twentieth century, prejudice and discrimination were freely expressed against religious minorities throughout Europe, culminating in the Holocaust—the biggest religion- and race-based pogrom in human history. We don't have to dig very far back in our history to come across instances of abuse and violence against religious minorities, let alone reasons for continuing suspicion and distrust.

This has not been limited to Europe. India, before gaining independence, burst into violent conflict between Hindu and Muslim groups; this led finally to a separation into two religion-based countries, India and Pakistan.

(Actually, the creation of the two separate countries out of the British Raj was simultaneous with the granting of independence. This came about because, in addition to the Gandhi-led independence movement in what we now call India, Muslim independence movements existed in what is now Pakistan. This region also wanted to be independent, but only if that meant independent from Britain *and* India. So the two countries existed from the moment of the Raj's dissolution, with Bangladesh [East Pakistan] of course winning independence from Pakistan proper in the early 1970s. The violence at the time of Indian independence involved minority Hindus and Muslims who found themselves in the wrong country after the British left.)

- In Ireland, religious violence between Catholics and Protestants raged for generations; it has only recently come to an uneasy halt. And in the former Yugoslavia, religious violence between Muslims, Catholics, and Orthodox Christians tore apart the country and resulted in thousands of deaths.

Given so much violence, many feel that religions and churches should not have any role whatsoever in political life. This principle has led to the constitutional doctrine of separation between church and state in many countries, including Canada and the US. According to this doctrine, religious institutions should never become key actors in political affairs. When religions *have* become key actors, the outcomes have often been disastrous. At the extremes, religious groups have promoted genocide (think of the Spanish Inquisition against Jews and Islamic Moors, for example) and suppressed particular groups (whether women, religious minorities, or others with "unacceptable" qualities). Many believe that Catholicism and Islam continue to support anti-democratic regimes in much of the world today. By contrast, other religions—Hinduism, Buddhism, and Confucianism—play little role in politics (although it is worth noting that Confucianism was an important religious basis for Japanese fascism during World War II).

Many churches have also taken conservative, anti-egalitarian stances on other social issues. Consider the role of fundamentalist religions in opposing same-sex marriage, currently legal in Canada and in some areas of the US. These religions maintain that marriage is a sacrament that can occur only between a woman and a man. Often, they view marriage as an institution for producing children; so traditional (often high-fertility) religions tend to oppose legislation to legalize same-sex marriage. Other religious groups are more liberal. Some even campaign to have same-sex marriages legalized. Clearly, it would be a big oversimplification to say that all religions are equally traditional, conservative, or anti-egalitarian.

In multi-ethnic and multi-religious states such as the US, the UK, or Canada, no one religion can claim that it has all the answers for society's needs. The separation of politics from religion in the West has been good for politics and it has also been good for religion, because religious groups have been protected by multicultural tolerance. The problem we face today in Canada and other multicultural nations is whether to give priority to religious tolerance over concerns about the rights of, say, women within religious groups.

This conflict was symbolized in the dispute over sharia courts in Ontario. In late 2003, the Canadian media reported that the Islamic Institute of Civil Justice would start offering arbitration in family disputes in accordance with both Islamic legal principles and Ontario's Arbitration Act of 1991. A (very vocal) two-year debate followed the introduction of sharia law in Ontario. This debate captured the problem of, first, handling religious rules within a secular framework; second, recognizing the cultural diversity of Muslim communities in Canada; and third, protecting from domination and subordination women who are embedded in a religious community to which they feel some loyalty.

Religions today chiefly help people develop and achieve fulfillment by exploring their spiritual needs, and some believe this goal is incompatible with partisan political involvement. Politics deal with the material basis of life and with power and its operation; religion deals with spiritual life and the relation of people to the divine. If religions are to advocate political courses of action, then they can no longer speak to all their followers, but rather only to those who belong to particular political parties or support particular secular causes. If religions enter the political arena, they become mere pressure groups for political causes. If they compete for political favours they lose the right, in the eyes of the public, to speak to higher moral issues.

GENDERED STRIFE

Giving religions a political role would also pose a great challenge to the safeguarding of women's citizenship rights. This is because many religious codes define civil, political, and social rights and duties in ways that systematically encourage different treatment of women and men, and girls and boys. And while we want to protect religious freedom, we don't want to give religious groups the right to discriminate in this way. The trick is to find a way of protecting both equal citizenship and religious accommodation. This has recently become the central issue in debates about citizenship: how to protect women's rights to non-discrimination when confronted with the protection of the right to religious freedom.

So far no society has addressed and solved this problem. In the past there was no corresponding concern with either religious (minority) accommodation or women's rights, let alone with both. As a result, women have been ignored and abused by organized religion throughout the ages. The Islamic fundamentalist Taliban in Afghanistan are the most recent in a long list of groups who, in the name of religious devotion, have subordinated women, depriving them of equal rights.

The discriminatory treatment of women spans continents and centuries. Consider also the notorious witch hunts of early modern times. Is it really so different in tone and scale from the Taliban treatment of women? During the period roughly between the fifteenth and seventeenth centuries, recently named "the Burning Times," large numbers of European women were condemned by the church and accused of "witchcraft." While men were also put to death, the vast majority of victims were women; estimates of some sixty thousand in Europe and North America in a period of some two hundred years. The men who were put to death were most often associated with women condemned as witches—fathers, sons, or husbands, or even men who tried to defend them.

It is no accident that this "craze" of witch burning led to (and simplified) the segregation and control of women. When it began, women were active in the public sphere, as farmers, traders, craftspeople, midwives, and folk healers. Toward the end, a woman's place had been firmly established as being in the home, as an adjunct to her husband if she had one. Whether intended or not, the accusation, trial, torture, and execution of thousands of women proved to be an effective method by which women's lives could be restricted. By the early 1800s, the lives of women in the Western world were more constrained than they have ever been before or since.

It was largely the theology of the times that made this witch craze possible (although the "witch craze" was conducted by civil authorities as well as by the churches, so it is perhaps unjust to blame the churches alone). Women were seen as the carriers of evil: they were considered to be susceptible to advances by the devil, from whom they took their powers through a pact. They were seen as being sexually unquenchable, and therefore the greatest danger to Christian society.

Today, some analyses of the witch craze still do not mention the intense misogyny instilled by Christian doctrines, or the determined hunting-out of folk-religious practices among women. Often, the witch craze is portrayed as quaint, belonging to the past, and irrelevant to modern society. Many feminist scholars, however, point out that the effects of the witch craze period are still with us, in popular images of older women, troublesome women, and disobedient women as "witches."

Even today, the organization, symbolism, and language of many churches are deeply misogynistic. Some religions, Orthodox Judaism among them, isolate women from men during worship and in many secular activities. Others, including orthodox Islam, place women under significant social and legal controls, at home and in public. And still other faiths, such as Roman Catholicism, continue to promote gendered hierarchy, with "God" at the top, followed by men, then women and children. A mundane example of the religious persecution of women is the Vatican telling women that sex is only for procreation and that they are not allowed to control their reproduction.

Protestant churches have also traditionally viewed men as being closer to God than women. Until recently, women were considered by mainstream Christian churches as being incapable of acting as priests or ministers. Although in many Protestant churches women can now serve as ministers, this change was not achieved without a struggle. The Catholic Church continues to reiterate its opposition to women serving as priests.

This gendered church hierarchy is strengthened and promoted by an overwhelming number of male images. In Christianity, "God" is still presented as male, images of Jesus abound in churches, and figures of the (male) apostles appear everywhere. Often, the only female image is that of Mary, displayed as mother and described in ways that make plain she is set apart from "ordinary" women, and so cannot be copied or imitated; an obvious example is virgin birth.

In some churches, women remain excluded from many areas of religious life, and their qualifications to speak as theologians and teachers are under constant review. Some feminist scholars and theologians argue that, given time, constant pressure for reform will bring change. Others, however, argue that women can best express their spiritualities outside established churches.

Today, some women are trying to develop feminist theologies that imagine divinity as female, or both female and male. There are groups in North America and Europe that are exploring their spirituality through practices based in the folk religions of Africa, America, and Europe. Aboriginal groups are working to re-establish indigenous North American religions. Others, looking to their own background or ancestry, focus on African traditions and beliefs, or on European

Celtic and Nordic folklore and mythology. And yet others still, sharing an idea of Earth (Gaia) as the mother of all beings, become promoters of environmental awareness. From this standpoint, the new environmentalism represents for some an effort to satisfy spiritual needs.

It is too early to tell what challenge these remodelled religions will pose to patriarchal Christian dominance within North America. Perhaps in a postmodern world, with more tolerance of religious diversity than ever, each religion (however small) can hold its own and empower its adherents. Yet women who speak out on religious topics are still viewed negatively, and followers of smaller sectarian religions may still find that others view them as a threat.

Contributions to Integration

Despite their many wrongs, religions have also played an important part in pulling people together around shared symbols and rituals. In this way, they have increased communication, interaction, intimacy, and trust among fellow believers.

We know from research by Max Weber that religion played a large part in the economic development of modern capitalist societies, and so helped mould the kind of society with which we're all familiar. In his book *The Protestant Ethic and the Spirit of Capitalism* (1905), Weber discussed the origins of capitalism in relation to religious theory, doctrine, and practice. Strict Calvinism was important in providing a value structure and promoting character formation— especially the virtue of hard work; this in turn supported the rise of capitalism in northwest Europe. That is a big part of the reason why capitalism arose there when it did, and not in ancient India, China, Israel, or Catholic Southern Europe. In this way, religious beliefs encouraged economic development.

Churches have also promoted interdependence by creating communities of believers: groups of people who co-operate, exchange resources, and share common enemies and common friends. On occasion, churches and religions have even promoted civility, serving worthy causes that advance the general interests of humanity. It is this last feature we will explore in the rest of this chapter.

Throughout the twentieth century sociologists predicted that religion would decline in importance, often basing their work on the ideas of Émile Durkheim, who made the assumption that religion and religious expression would change as society changed. Durkheim, concerned with what holds society together, defined two types of solidarity: mechanical and organic. The first referred to societies where people did much the same thing, so households were self-sufficient (as among foraging peoples or small-scale agriculturalists). The second referred to societies where people were interdependent: individuals' work differed greatly, but each person was reliant on many others for the needs of life (as in present-day industrial societies).

In short, mechanical solidarity was built on similarities of daily life—on shared norms, beliefs, and ways of thinking. Organic solidarity was built around reliance on other people, however different they might be.

Durkheim studied the religions of Aboriginal peoples of Australia and compared them with the religions he saw around him in Europe. He found that religions express the central values of a society: when people engage in religious practices they are linking themselves to each other as social beings. Even the totemic animals they worship—the snake or kangaroo or wolf—are ultimately symbols of their own society. In effect, when people worship a kangaroo, plant, god, or mythical figure, they are worshiping their own collective existence.

Durkheim was not interested in asking whether "God" really exists, as imagined in the Judeo-Christian tradition, for example. His interest was in how people connect to and worship their gods. According to Durkheim, different ideas of "God" are needed in mechanical and organic societies. A diverse (organic) society would be torn apart by religious tensions if the old, homogeneous ways of connecting with divinity were retained. A diverse, organic society—for example, an urban industrial society—needs a form of humanism: this is a set of beliefs that lets people see their common humanity, not specific religious beliefs, as interlinking them.

This shift to a more humanist orientation is connected to secularization. Many scholars have studied secularization in Western societies, noting a steadily dwindling influence of religion in public life. Three features of life in industrial societies lead toward secularization: social differentiation, societalization, and rationalization.

Social differentiation, the first feature of secularization, is the process by which a society becomes increasingly complex. People's activities become more varied and specialized, so the role of religion must also become more specialized. In the past, churches provided centres for worship and teaching about sacred things, but churches also taught children many basic skills, supported people in need, cared for the sick, served as meeting places, and organized social events. In modern societies, many separate institutions play these roles: schools, hospitals, government agencies, and social clubs, among others. This means the church is no longer central to daily living, but merely one institution among many. The church is also an institution with which many individuals have little contact. It is no longer necessary to belong to a religious institution in North America or Western Europe.

Societalization, the second aspect of secularization, refers to how people increasingly connect to an abstract "society," not to a community in which every person knows everyone else. In North America and Europe today, most people look to "society"—a large, shapeless unit made up of organizations run on bureaucratic principles—to provide for their needs. People regularly find and work at jobs, read and watch the news, attend school, and vote in elections. All of these activities put them into contact with a "society" that regulates their activities, often through the State.

Interaction with this "society" leaves little room for religion, which people increasingly view as personal (not societal) and marginal to their lives. For most people, religion is not an important part of their dealings with society. Even though many people continue to engage in prayer and worship and attend church, they engage in religion mainly as individuals committed to a lifestyle, following a private concern.

The third feature of modern life that undermines the importance of religion is *rationalization*, an effort to explain the world through the logical interpretation of empirical evidence. The Judeo-Christian religions themselves encouraged the spread of rationalization, to reduce people's earlier reliance on "superstition" and folk magic. By emphasizing rationality, modern religion stressed theology over myth. In most Christian denominations, church leaders encourage philosophical inquiry into the nature of people's link with the divine, not just a literal interpretation of Bible stories. This is, in fact, the basic difference between mainstream and fundamentalist churches.

In time, however, rationalization undermined the churches. The major Western religions are based on faith, and matters of faith have never really been open to empirical testing and logical analysis. The question "Does God exist?" cannot be answered using the scientific method. In the battle between science and religion, many people came to view all religion as superstition and faith as a psychological crutch to help people deal with problems in their everyday lives.

In response, religions have tried to make themselves more relevant. First, as states have demanded people's national loyalties, religions have increasingly sought people's individual, local (i.e., sub-national), and pan-national loyalties. With global migration and the creation of international religious communities—Jews of the world, Muslims of the world, Catholics of the world, and so on—religions have become less synonymous with particular nations or states. Societalization, instead of weakening the role of religion, has changed and strengthened it, making religion transnational. Some even believe this globalization of religion has led to more intergroup contact, more sophistication, more religious toleration, and a separation of religion from the political workings of any particular society.

As Durkheim had hoped, humanism has indeed emerged as another "religion." Many of today's religions teach people to be citizens of the world, to think globally. A prime example is Unitarianism. And new religions continue to emerge and compete with older, more parochial ones.

Throughout the world today we see examples of people, motivated by religion, fighting for improvements in the lives of others. These include Catholic nuns who campaign for increased status for women and an end to spouse abuse; religious leaders who campaign for peace; and other individuals who, as spokespeople for religious groups, become associated with civil causes. Think of Archbishop Desmond Tutu, who played such an important role in the fight to end apartheid in South Africa, or Dr Martin Luther King, who fought for civil rights in the United States.

Both Tutu and King were, originally, religious and not political figures, yet they used their religious connections and preaching skills to mobilize people for political causes. In Canada, religious leaders such as J.S. Woodsworth played an important role in the rise of the progressive CCF, the Co-operative Commonwealth Federation (known today as the New Democratic Party). Religion, through the Social Gospel Movement, also played an important role in many progressive causes in the early twentieth century throughout North America.

For many people, religious commitment today includes a strong portion of social activism. Many churches and other religious organizations promote the idea that all people are equal, regardless of ethnicity or race, and encourage their members to campaign for social equality. Anti-poverty issues also provide a focus for action that may include organizing charity events such as food bank drives. In fact, religion-based social activism can mean anything from lobbying at a local government level to mobilizing and supporting anti-government protest, as in the liberation theology of Latin American churches. For some groups (again an example is Unitarians), engaging in social activism is more important than adherence to a creed or belief.

Many campaigners against poverty, racism, or violence in society trace the strength of their activist commitment to their religious (including humanist) affiliations. Their religion gives them a philosophy and a sense of purpose, as well as a feeling that by acting on their principles they can help create a better world. They use their religious commitment to oppose trends in society that they feel are against their beliefs. People come together, as religious groups, to show their beliefs through marches, boycotts, political lobbying, or active participation. Often they join with other groups in doing this.

In the mid-1990s, after several black Baptist church buildings in the US were destroyed by arson, Unitarians and Mennonites joined forces to show their opposition to racism and intolerance by helping to rebuild the churches. And when the buildings were burned down again, many other churches and religions, from Catholicism to Zoroastrianism, added their labour and helped with funds.

Black Baptist churches themselves show how religious feeling can unite communities in political action. We have seen above how Martin Luther King, a Baptist preacher, acted as his community's spokesperson against a range of injustices. Interfaith groups have arisen in many countries to call for social justice, particularly in anti-racist campaigns. Environmental issues are also targeted by faith organizations. Not only are Unitarians known for supporting environmental causes, but a major interfaith campaign focusing on climate change is sponsored by mainstream Jewish and Christian churches.

Inter-organizational links between religious congregations and social service agencies also create bonds with the capacity to strengthen civil society. While some congregations set up their own social service programs, many do not. Instead, they provide public services by forming relationships with other organizations. In this way, inter-organizational partnerships have great potential for contributing to stronger local civic life.

In Canadian society, no single religious organization dominates, so none could possibly control the state even if it tried. Most Canadians follow a form of Christianity (though not all of these are church-goers) but belong to many different churches or denominations. Many belong to other religions, including Islam, Buddhism, and Judaism. Some groups even draw on the teachings of several religions and philosophies: Unitarians, for example, formally admit contributions and teachings from many religions and religious leaders, specifically naming Christianity, Judaism, humanism, and Earth-based religions.

In Canada, traditional Aboriginal religions have recently been experiencing a revival, much to the benefit of often-demoralized First Nations groups. Native religions interpret the relation of people with the earth, and with animals and plants, in ways that highlight human roles as caretakers and conservationists (this is often in stark contrast to the European-American idea of "making use" of land, animals, and plants). Many people discover in these Native religions ways to express themselves and identify with their communities, and to reinterpret political events and take political action. These religions are attractive both to many Aboriginal people and to growing numbers of environmentally minded European-Americans.

Some have claimed that a rebirth of faith in these traditional religions has been instrumental in helping many Aboriginals overcome addictions and other social problems.

SEARCHING FOR CIVILITY

Sociologists today are actively re-examining the relations between religion and citizenship, or what we might call "the search for civility" within a religious context. In present-day Europe there are many ways of taking part in the host society. This ranges from Northern

European democracies that encourage the coexistence of identities to the French Republic aiming to develop into a union of the differences. Also in North America we see the difference between an American melting pot and a Canadian multicultural mosaic. The question is this: which societal model works best to stimulate the civility that is nascent in religion?

Today, faith groups are increasingly viewed as important participants in British civil society. There, faith engagement is linked to policies of social inclusion and "community cohesion," potentially serving to defuse worrisome radicalization along religious lines. Increasingly, efforts are being made to find bridges between the different perspectives of national policy-makers, local stakeholders, and faith actors themselves. British urban governance is increasingly decentred and continues to blur the boundaries between the public, private, and personal. There is, in short, a redefinition not only of civil society but also of secularization.

Secularization has its roots in the eighteenth-century Enlightenment. The ideal "secular citizen" was a product of positivist science and social engagement and placed concerns about progress and public order above God-given rules. Obviously, this orientation deprived the Church of its social role, which was rooted in civil notions. It also deprived the Church of its previously dominant role in culture. In fact, culture came to determine the place of religion in people's thinking. Today a post-secular age is emerging: it is less overtly anti-religious than in the past, but it remains centrally concerned with political and individual freedom. This post-secular view opposes religious repressiveness not because it is religious, but because it is repressive.

Of course, some religions are more repressive than others, and this is reflected in their political tolerance or lack thereof. Ever since sociologist Sam Stouffer began to measure political tolerance more than half a century ago, US studies have shown that church attendance and denominational affiliation significantly influence whether individuals willingly extend civil liberties to fringe groups. Generally, a high degree of religiosity produces a low degree of tolerance. A wrathful image of God strongly predicts support for the denial of civil liberties to unpopular groups, even controlling for church attendance and affiliation. These recent US findings show that religious faith and civil liberties are in tension only when believers think that God actively punishes sinners.

Post-secularism, then, rejects the idea that religion is necessarily repressive. Key characteristics of flexible, cosmopolitan secularism might include the erosion of traditional religious notions and familiarity with various other religions. With globalization, the whole world has now encountered secular post-Christianity. The result is a growing opposition from cultures and societies that are *not* post-religious—that retain traditional, fundamentalist values—particularly in the Islamic world and other traditional communities in Asia and Africa.

This is where cultures collide over human rights versus group rights. Difficulties remain, for example, in resolving problems around the Islamic treatment of women. In 2008, for example, Saeed Rahnema showed that many leaders of Muslim communities in the West, and especially conservative religious leaders, oppose "cultural immersion" and prefer instead a stronger, more cohesive community that continues to follow a traditional way of life. From this standpoint, the idea of diaspora poses considerable problems when applied to ethno-racial and religious minorities in Canada. It seems to portray these minorities as outsiders, lacking full citizenship and cultural immersion. However, their differentiation from the rest of society is not always imposed by the host society. In fact, it has historically been preferred by the uprooted communities, who want to preserve a sense of belonging to their land and culture of origin.

What should women in these communities do to protect themselves while remaining members of the community in good standing? Some believe they must take the initiative to reform their own religion, within a civil context that encourages and protects them while they do so. In Norway, for example, Muslim women increasingly take part in mosque activities, with some encouragement from their community, and they are slowly achieving a larger presence in these institutions. They are also being granted new forms of participation there. However, despite pressures from both within and without the mosques, Muslim congregations in Norway are still patriarchal regimes, and the participation of women still depends on the willingness of men to include them.

It may be easier for women to achieve the needed changes where Islamic people are not a minority group. This is suggested by evidence from Indonesia, where Muslims are the majority. There, Indonesia's Islamic revival has coincided with the growing involvement of women in civil society. Muslim women's organizations are playing an important role in social and political change. The increasing role of Islam in the public sphere gives religious women a platform to air their views in national debates over issues such as sharia law, abortion, and pornography. Through their involvement in debates between mosque and state, Muslim women activists are participants in renegotiating the Indonesian nation-state.

From the middle of the sixteenth century to the end of the seventeenth, a new form of social life emerged in different parts of Europe. This heralded the development of civil society as we recognize it today: a separate domain of comparatively safe and free human interaction, the result of different efforts to secure civil peace in times of extreme inter-religious violence. These efforts included at least three measures: the development of new forms of public law, especially in Germany; the development of the absolutist state, especially in France; and the separation of private religious conscience from public legal conscience, especially in England. They were all, in one way or another, steps toward halting (and preventing in future) the flow of blood caused by religious hatred.

Napoleon, spreading French ideas wherever he conquered, took pains to separate Church and State during his early nineteenth-century conquest of Europe. In doing so, he was supported by many other revolution-minded Europeans. The goal was to eliminate religion from politics and ideally even from public life, and to relegate the activities of prayer and contemplation to a bounded-off realm of religion. But for many in religious organizations today, prayer and contemplation is not enough. They are not contented with speculating about an afterlife, and they feel a moral commitment to social action.

The global spread of the "nation-state" has, paradoxically, created a new model of multicultural citizenship. It has done so by decoupling state membership, individual rights, and national identity. The content of human rights has changed in the second half of the twentieth century. The close link between human rights and national self-determination was rendered out of date with the belief that in protecting human rights, states must recognize a diversity of traditional identity groups.

Take a simple example: the controversy over Muslim women's headscarves, which many Europeans believe signifies women's subordination under Islamic law. Conflicts over Islamic headscarves have created divisive national crises in several European countries. In France and Germany, as in Turkey, legislation has banned "conspicuous" religious symbols in government institutions. In Germany, eight federal states have introduced legislation to ban the headscarf. In the Netherlands, the Islamic headscarf meets with a more sympathetic reception.

These differences among states are due to national differences in citizenship tradition. While the Netherlands represents a multicultural model, Germany and France continue to embrace an ethnocultural model of citizenship.

In all of these countries, the headscarf issue is framed as a conflict between public neutrality and religious freedom, not gender equality.

They agree about the rights of women to equal treatment under the law. Recent amendments to German citizenship law have eased immigrants' adoption of citizenship, representing a shift toward the display of cultural competence. In both Germany and France, national belonging and loyalty to the state must be proven through linguistic competence and modes of bodily performance that mainly focus on women.

In today's world, people make their own decisions about their religious and political commitment. Some people believe that religion and politics can, and should, be separate. Others see them as inextricably intertwined, with religion pointing to political routes they feel obliged to take. For such people, political action becomes a necessary corollary to religious belief.

Social activism aside, religious people—both inside and outside churches—have a role to play in building a more civil, tolerant society. However, we cannot predict how they will do so. People use religion in different ways to define the boundaries of group identities and relationships. Whether volunteering to help community development projects in a low-income minority neighbourhood or organizing public events against racism, group members use religious terms to argue sharply over civic identity—even when they share goals and similar motivations for them.

In short, people use religion in different ways, to include or exclude others in civic relationships. As a result, religion can improve or hinder collaboration across social status and religious divides. We should not view religion as an impediment to civility—to living well together— and we need to learn how to harness the religious impulses that, visibly, remain strong in modern societies.

TWELVE

Politics and Ideologies

For me, writing this chapter is a way of reliving and relieving a youthful humiliation.

In 1965, I was in graduate school at Harvard, newly arrived from Toronto a few weeks earlier. My new friend, a fellow Torontonian named David Bell, invited me along to his favourite political science course, taught by Carl Friedrich, one of the "greats" in the field. Professor Friedrich welcomed me to the class, and then proceeded to interrogate me in front of the class about my chosen field of sociology. "Does it have its own subject matter, distinct from every other field?" (No.) "Does it have its own unique methodology?" (No.) "Well then, what *exactly* is sociology?" The subtext of this question was clear: why was I apparently devoting my career to an activity that seemed to have so little purpose or merit?

Over the last forty years, I've had time to consider these questions. In a way, this book is the answer I wish I had given back then, though I suspect Professor Friedrich knew the answer all along (an answer which at the time I could not adequately express).

After this experience, I learned more about political science. I eventually took a course with S.M. Lipset, a world-famous sociologist and political scientist. I continue to read books in the field. I can even say, in all honesty, that one of my best friends is a political scientist—that's still David Bell—and we wrote a book together about Canada's political culture.

I have also learned that it's easy to confuse the sociological study of politics—political sociology—with its close neighbour, political science. Both fields study the State and both study social policy, for example, but there are some important differences. Political science deals mainly with the machinery of government and public administration, and with elections, public opinion polling, pressure groups, and political parties. Political sociology is more concerned with the relationships between politics, social institutions (for example, families, churches, workplaces, ethnic groups, and social classes), ideologies, and culture. As well, sociologists study political processes *within* social institutions, and the ways that power is distributed and used in different social relationships.

The two fields also differ in their methods. Political scientists tend to do more library research, more textual analysis of documents and debates, and more examination of laws, rules, and procedures. Their work is more often philosophical and historical. Sociologists do more survey research and more often interview people and watch groups. Typically, sociologists are more numbers-oriented and spend more time with living people.

Both political science and political sociology are interested in power, but sociology is especially interested in authority and the social processes that make authority feel legitimate—processes that rarely need to rely on force. We noted in chapter 1 that Max Weber was the first and most influential sociologist to analyze the workings of authority. But Weber did more than classify different types of authority. First, he noted and explained important shifts in the bases of authority, shifts from traditional authority to rational-legal authority, or from charisma to routinized charisma, for example. He also showed that important social and cultural—in addition to political—shifts accompanied such changes in the bases of authority.

However, what most shaped my understanding of politics was something else that was going on at Harvard while I was there. I am not thinking here of the time that "Students for a Democratic Society" anti-war protestors arrived from New York and threatened to burn down Widener Library. I mean my exposure to three separate socio-logical approaches to thinking about politics, represented by three of my teachers.

One teacher was Barrington Moore, whose analysis of politics is evident in his classic work, *Social Origins of Dictatorship and Democracy: Lord and Peasant in the Making of the Modern World* (1965). Moore's special talent, using Marxist methods, was to analyze class relations and their effects on politics. Moore showed that, during the process of modernization, it matters whether the dominant class in society is the middle class, the peasant class, or the traditional ruling class (the landowning aristocracy, supported by military and Church). The first scenario leads to what we generally know as democracy, the second to communism, and the third to fascism. His theory, based on a close historical analysis of eight different societies, is important for our understanding of modernization, class analysis, and social change.

A second teacher was Talcott Parsons, whose analysis of politics is scattered through a variety of papers and books, including *The Social System* (1951). Parsons's special talent was finding similarities between different kinds of social systems, large and small. He asserted that all social systems—whether families, small groups, large organizations, societies, or empires—have a political process, which he labelled the "goal attainment function." This political activity, or function, is neces-sary for the survival of the system; it is not imposed and, generally, it is not evil. The political structure (or subsystem) is not so much com-mitted to control and oppression (as in Marxist visions of the state) as it is to management, administration, and political motivation. As its name suggests, the political system expresses, and strives to achieve, collective goals. This takes place through debate and concerted action. It is assumed that people in the society usually consent to this political process and its leaders.

A third teacher was George Homans, whose analysis of politics is found mainly in his book *The Human Group* (1950). He would probably have laughed at my inclusion of him in a discussion of politics, and particularly alongside discussions of Moore and Parsons. These three teachers famously did not agree. Moore was never seen in the sociology department. There were stories of hallway shouting matches between Homans and Parsons. But still, there were connections. Both Homans and Parsons were "functionalists": they both believed that groups follow stable patterns that contribute to their survival. In this respect, they were different from Moore, a Marxist theorist (who, though a Marxist and a theorist, had reportedly worked during World War II as an analyst for the Office of Strategic Services, a forerunner of the CIA).

Homans, however, was more concrete than Parsons. In a famous published attack on Parsons, Homans called on sociology to "bring men back in" to sociological analyses and do away with windy abstractions. Homans knew that if you watch groups, you can see them "doing politics." Before your eyes you can observe goal setting, resource distribution, rule enforcement, ritual creation, and tradition preservation. They do so not to meet "system needs" but because it is personally rewarding, and they know it. Regardless of the culture or historical moment, I seem to recall hearing the words "Men is men!" likely from someone speaking about Homans's work.

So this chapter will discuss whether politics are integrative *for people*, whether politics draw people together despite their differences and inequalities or whether the opposite is true. Or to pose the question in more refined terms: under what circumstances do politics have an integrative effect, and when is this effect disintegrating?

It is worth considering here the integrative role of *ideologies*. There are no politics without ideologies, though some ideologies are more blatant—more clearly stated—than others. Ideologies are important because, like religions, they give people meanings and goals that are bigger than themselves. So people crave ideologies, just as they crave religions, and often political leaders harness ideologies to legitimate their authority and mobilize the citizenry.

Forces Pushing People Apart

Let's take a moment to examine ideologies and their social role before discussing their effects on integration.

Despite the important role that elites play in society, most Canadians do not see their society as elite-dominated. In large part this is because most Canadians accept an ideology of Canada as an egalitarian society. An ideology is a coherent set of interrelated beliefs about the nature of the world and of people. It guides a person's interpretation of, and reaction to, external events.

Here is an example. Many people in our society believe they are mainly responsible for their own success or failure. They think, "I am free to choose my own path; if my choice turns out badly, I have only myself to blame." This thinking is part of what sociologists call the "liberal ideology." Ideologies "explain" how society is, or should be, organized. In North America, we are used to ideological debates on political and economic topics. Yet our liberal ideology tends to focus attention away from shared values and toward individual responsibility.

Liberal ideology affects the way people behave in many situations. On the macrosociological side, it influences which political party they will vote for and whether they will support welfare benefits for the poor or capital gains taxes for the rich. On the microsociological side, it influences how they will react if they are thrown out of work, battered by a spouse, or mistreated by the government. In general, liberal ideology encourages people to "blame the victim" and support the status quo.

Since it is the ideology of the dominant group, it is sometimes called the "dominant ideology," justifying its power and wealth. The rest of us do not rebel against social inequality, largely because we have come to believe in the dominant ideology. We teach young people this ideology in schools, churches, and through the media; we hear it repeated throughout life. We learn to accept it, to accept inequality as natural and normal, and to live with the status quo. As French social theorist

Michel Foucault points out, in modern societies power is exercised by setting standards and defining what is normal and abnormal, proper and improper. (He is not the first to have said this, but his analysis is particularly fitting in present-day technological society, where surveillance is central.) These standards are then enforced through a range of vigilant techniques of control that have social legitimacy.

And as we learned in an earlier chapter, these strategies of control—formulated at the top, serving the dominant or ruling group in society, and spread through ideologies and standards—are not wholly outside the individuals they control. We all internalize these beliefs, norms, and standards, and come to view ourselves as good or bad, normal or abnormal. And most of the time, we control ourselves. These beliefs form the basis for our self-image and self-esteem; they help to shape our goals and fashion our self-worth.

Dominant ideologies support the status quo, then. Whether an ideology is dominant is something we can learn only through empirical research. We consider it "dominant" if the most powerful or socially dominant groups in society sponsor it, and if it also supports the interests of these groups. Consider the popular belief in "winners" and "losers"—in people getting what they deserve and deserving what they get. This dominates us, but at the same time, it disempowers the weak and empowers the already strong. The dominant ideology is also an important part of popular culture and entertainment. In American culture, for example, a high value is placed on heroism and war. This makes it easy for American politicians to mobilize public sentiment behind activities like the Iraq War, and before that, the longstanding Cold War.

Everywhere, dominant ideologies influence political life by shaping public opinion. However, there is no single "public" in industrial societies. A wide range of social types—the result of a complex division of labour, large-scale immigration, and relatively easy social mobility—creates a variety of "publics." Each has its own opinions, values, and interests. In large part, politics is about mobilizing public opinion and unifying specific fractions of the electorate around specific concerns.

People also use ideologies to interpret and react to events in the real world. Ideologies are important for social change because they motivate and control people. Myths and trust play important roles in all of social and political life. Before people can change their political order, they must imagine a new order worth working for. They must have faith in that vision and in the leaders they expect to carry out that vision. This means that, in changing a society, people always create and accept ideologies.

In this way, ideologies can influence the distribution of power. Sometimes, they prevent social protest and social change; at other times, they promote it. Ideological debates arise in widely varying areas of life. Should Canada admit more refugees? Should marijuana use be decriminalized? Is a fetus a person, entitled to legal rights like other people? Such debates are hard to resolve. That is because most people are sure they are right and equally sure that the other side is wrong. Usually both sides fail to see that their opinion is just a belief, not the truth. In fact, ideologies can never be proven or falsified by scientific means. And when people adopt these ideas, they usually don't know they are learning or believing in anything at all. They think they are discovering the "truth."

As we said, any given public is an unstructured set of people who hold certain interests in, views on, or concerns about a particular issue; ideologies help to structure their participation in society. Normally, members of a public do not interact with one another and are rarely aware of belonging to the same group. By contrast to this, "public opinion" is central to any democracy, since what we mean by a democracy is government by the people.

A Latin proverb says *vox populi, vox dei*: the voice of the people is the voice of God. This proverb should be the guiding principle in a democratic society, and to some degree it is, given that polls measure people's sentiments and politicians follow the polls. Generally, polls do measure public opinion accurately. But at the same time they also manipulate or shape public opinion. As well, they impute certainty (or what comedian Stephen Colbert calls "truthiness") to opinions that often are in flux, creating something out of nothing.

The *bandwagon effect* is one example of the way opinion polls influence public opinion. People like being part of a group that has succeeded: they want to "get on the bandwagon." The bandwagon effect shows up in post-election polls, when a much larger number of voters claim to have voted for the winning candidate than actually did. After the fact, people adopt opinions that are popular because they are popular. They may even support a politician who seems likely to win (that is, according to the pre-election polls) just because they want to back a winner.

Political and other public opinion polls contribute to this illusion-making, but journalists play a far larger role when they report propaganda under the guise of news. Propaganda is any idea or doctrine that is spread to influence people's opinions and actions. In this sense, Sunday-school lessons, advertising, and election campaigns are all forms of propaganda. (In fact, propaganda can be defined as any information that represents itself as pure, unquestionable truth.)

Not surprisingly, people are becoming more skeptical about the information they receive and the people who control the government. Survey data show that Canadians distrust politicians more than almost anyone else (including advertising executives, who have never been famous for their honesty). The best way to protect against a blind acceptance of propaganda is education, openness to new information, and a tolerance for ambiguity. It is especially important to be willing to consider different views of a single issue.

Ideologies can dominate us, but they can also empower us by helping people to form protest groups. In this way, they increase the chance that people will protest against, and therefore improve, their life chances. Ideologies that propose change are either radical or reformist. Those who support reformist ideologies call for changes without challenging the basic ground rules. In Canada, the provision of medicare, welfare, and unemployment insurance are reforms that were based on this kind of ideology. These programs were intended as "safety nets" to help people who got into trouble.

Unemployment insurance, however, does not prevent unemployment. It does not create jobs. It makes unemployment less harmful without changing the factors that create unemployment. Radical ideologies call for a reshaping of society. This is what the Co-operative Commonwealth Federation (CCF)—the parent of today's reformist New Democratic Party—did at its founding in 1933, when it adopted the Regina Manifesto. This manifesto declared that "no CCF government will rest content until it has wiped out capitalism and put into operation the full program of socialized planning which will lead to the establishment in Canada of the co-operative commonwealth."

Sociologists call these "counter ideologies." They are "counter" in the sense that they challenge the bases of the dominant ideologies. They also expose the interests that dominant ideologies serve and offer people a different vision of society.

Often, counter ideologies develop out of people's responses to experiences of unequal treatment. Counter ideologies call the status quo to account and deny legitimacy to usual ways of treating people. Feminism, for example, is a counter ideology that denies the legitimacy of sexism and traditional patriarchal ways of treating people.

Groups that promote counter ideologies get their message out to people in many ways, especially through public meetings and the media. Intellectuals and other highly educated people (called the "intelligentsia") often play an important part in promoting counter ideologies. The Polish intelligentsia, for example, had a central role in the Solidarity movement during the early 1980s. And in both Poland and Hungary the intelligentsia has helped to create a civil society since the collapse of communism.

I argued in chapter 1 that conflict is normal and often constructive. It can focus attention on social problems and bring people together to solve them. Conflict is the source of the women's movement, civil rights movements, and trade unionism, among others. As a result, it serves as the vehicle of positive social change.

Marxists have claimed that the dominant ideology promotes "false consciousness," a view of the world that is out of sync with objective reality. We see this when blame is placed on victimized and vulnerable people for their problems, and fail to consider that the problem may very well be in the way society is organized. Some may think, "women who wear revealing clothes have only themselves to blame if they get raped." Or, "drug addicts have only themselves to blame for getting hooked." Views like this, which hold the victims responsible for their own misfortunes, reveal this false consciousness.

Often, victims of the system even blame themselves. Many chronically unemployed people subscribe to the dominant ideology. How else can we explain the large number of unemployed people who fail to vote for radical politicians, if they vote at all? Our culture teaches us to hate ourselves if we fail to grab the gold ring, fail to be beautiful, rich, and popular. That's one reason why every generation yields a new crop of criminals, drug addicts, suicides, sex workers, and homeless people.

In short, ideologies serve various roles in the system of Canadian politics. They are sometimes the cause or instrument of conflict, and sometimes the means of resolving conflict. Ideologies can push people apart or bring them together; can increase or reduce prejudice and discrimination; and hatch suspicion and distrust, or the opposite. At the extremes, ideologies can stir up violence or prevent it. What ideology does all depends on the particular ideology and on the groups that use it to serve their political goals. In this sense, ideology is just a technology—a tool of power, wielded most often by and for the powerful.

So in the end, so-called dominant ideologies—conventional or folk wisdom, as well as social tradition included—generally seem to pull society together. But more often than not, they simply mask the underlying differences and inequalities. Reformist ideologies identify these differences and inequalities and try to correct them, but they don't hope to remove them. Radical ideologies identify and inflame these differences, in hopes of mobilizing protest movements to erase them. (We will discuss such protest movements further in the next chapter.)

Contributions to Integration

In Canada, Stephen Harper's Conservative government has often been criticized for setting groups against one another and vilifying the opposition. Attack ads have been widely published to present the Liberal leader as a casual or amateur politician, or as someone only loosely and recently attached to Canada. The traditional animosity of western Canada toward Ontario and Quebec is being whipped up. Diplomacy and statesmanship are not on view in the Canadian Parliament today.

However, politics can sometimes also pull people together. No more dramatic evidence of this could be imagined than what we saw in the election of Barack Obama to the US presidency. For months, a vast constituency of hopeful, ordinary people came together to bring about social change through the ballot box, and they succeeded. So electoral politics do sometimes work the way they are supposed to—to set goals that are in the public interest and work hard at achieving them.

This next section will consider the ways that political systems contribute to social integration. And we will use some new ideas, not yet seen in this book—in fact, ideas only rarely seen in the past thirty years. They are Talcott Parsons's pattern variables.

Parsons was concerned with developing a language that would allow the largest (and smallest) possible comparisons between social systems—that is, a discourse that would allow sociologists to compare societies with other societies, cultures with other cultures, organizations with other organizations, and families with other families. Ideally, this language would also allow comparisons between large and small systems, like families with societies, and organizations with cultures.

To do so, he invented these pattern variables, which he believed were sufficiently general yet also precise enough to allow such comparisons. These variables capture many key systemic differences that other sociologists and anthropologists had already noted; their importance lies not in their newness, but in their useful comprehensiveness across systems. It was in pointing out their comprehensive applicability that Parsons made his great contribution.

Over time, Parsons took a few different approaches to framing the pattern variables, so I will choose from these. In general, they provide a way of looking at various forms that norms and social actions can take. We can best think of these pattern variables as the ways that people relate to given situations, the orientation they bring to these situations, and how they are likely to interpret social actions. Here, briefly, are the pattern variables defined:

- *Affectivity and Affective Neutrality.* "Affect" means emotion. This dimension addresses the emotion people are expected to bring to a particular action or interaction. People in intimate relations are expected to show affect, while people in business or legal relations are expected to refrain from doing so.
- *Collectivity or Self.* This dimension addresses how much emphasis is to be placed on self-interest as opposed to collective or shared interest in a given action. The interests of the collectivity may take precedence over those of the individual, as typified by altruism, charity, and self-sacrifice in wartime, for example. However, economic activity typically assumes educated self-interest.
- *Particularism and Universalism.* This dimension addresses whether people are to act on general norms or personal (that is, particular) relations with other people. For example, we are often expected and allowed to behave in particularistic, preferential ways toward our loved ones. But as professionals we are

expected to act in universalistic ways with students, patients, clients, and so on. (That's probably why we shouldn't have professional relations with loved ones: there is a clash of norms.)

- *Diffuseness and Specificity.* This dimension addresses the breadth or range of duties in an interaction. Friendships and parent-child relationships call for a wide, diffuse form of contact, almost without limit on expectations. By contrast, buying a loaf of bread at the convenience store needs a limited, specific interaction: hand over the cash, take away the bread.
- *Ascription and Achievement.* "Ascription" refers to those unchangeable qualities of individuals such as sex, ethnicity, race, age, or family background; "achievement" refers to features that can be changed or gained through individual effort—for example, your grades, prizes won, and hobbies. This is important, because prejudice is often based on social ascription.
- *Expressive and Instrumental.* In any system of interaction, "expressive" actions refer to actions aimed at remembering, celebrating, and ritualizing the social structure (as well as reducing tension). "Instrumental" actions are "goal-seeking" actions aimed at integrating the group, setting goals, and imposing social controls.

Though all political systems are charged with setting and reaching societal goals, they do so in different ways; these we can usefully describe with the pattern variables. In the most general terms, politics starts to "modernize" in the eighteenth and nineteenth centuries, first in Europe, then in other parts of the world. In theory though not always in practice, this modernization is characterized by a shift to universalism, specificity, achievement orientation, and instrumentality. All political systems become more committed to the universalistic rule of law; to specific, and named, relations between the rulers and the ruled; and to practical problem solving (that is, instrumentality). They erase rights and preferences based on ascribed statuses and treat people equally, regardless of their sex, age, ethnicity, race, or class.

In all these respects, modern states show the ideal-typical features that Max Weber said characterize "bureaucracy," and especially a reliance on the fair and rigorous application of written rules. Modernity, in other words, is associated with rational-legal authority, with the rule of law. It is also associated with market relations: that is, with the assumption that each individual has his or her own goals, and that the purpose of the state is to protect and further the pursuit of those goals.

Modern political systems vary, over time and from one to another, in their degree of affective neutrality and collective orientation. Some states are noisily patriotic—even chauvinistic—and constantly whip up emotional fervour. Canada, by contrast, is a relatively peaceable kingdom, a model of affective neutrality. Some states protect individual rights, even at the expense of collective interests; other states protect the collective interest much more vigorously.

For example, Sweden and the other Scandinavian countries have historically promoted collectivist policies, while the US has tended to promote individualistic policies. The difference is obvious both in the tax rates (the US taxes its people at a lower rate than Scandinavian countries tax theirs) and in the provision of a social safety net: universal health care, low-cost public child care, high-quality public education. Here, the collectivist Scandinavian countries do much better than the US. In these respects, Canada is in the middle, though closer to the US by most measures.

But regardless of their stand on affective neutrality and individualism, all modern states favour the rule of law. Compare a modern elected government, such as Canada's, with what Weber would have called a "patrimonial" form of government—say, rule by a traditional king or emperor. For King Henry VIII of England in the sixteenth century or Louis XIV of France in the seventeenth, or for a Chinese or Ottoman emperor even more recently, the state was a personal possession. All the people and their property "belonged" to the ruler. He could tax them and rule them as he wished, given that he was imagined to have the divine right of kingship.

Of course, many kings and emperors went too far. Some were greedy, some were crazy, and some did nothing but make war. In time, many of these kingdoms and empires, and the royal families they supported, were swept away by revolution and war. (We do of course still have a Queen as a figurehead, and the Governor General as her representative.) But even under the best circumstances, patrimonial rule was unsustainable. Even a wise King Solomon is inadequate to the task of ruling a modern society. A large, complex, and diverse modern society needs written rules and fair, predictable application of these rules. Otherwise, all social and economic life is unpredictable; planning is impossible, economic growth will not occur, and science and technology will not flourish.

Alongside the shift from patrimonialism to rule of law and parliamentary democracy, we see the rise of "citizenship" as a social form. Citizenship, which developed (as the name suggests) out of the relative freedom of city life, is a taken-for-granted feature of modern life, but it has taken several centuries to evolve and is still evolving. Essentially, citizenship—providing equal guarantees of freedom and fairness to all people who hold the status of "citizen"—is the basis of all modern social life. The British sociologist T.H. Marshall asserted that citizenship has several different stages of development, and we are now nearing completion of the last stage: social citizenship.

Marshall argued through a historical analysis of English society that citizenship has developed in the following stages: first, civil rights; then political rights; then social rights. Further, these stages were attained during the eighteenth, nineteenth, and twentieth centuries, respectively. What is important here was his idea of social rights. Marshall claimed that a citizen is only a full citizen if he has all three kinds of rights, and that this possession of full rights is linked to social class. Let's briefly examine this important insight, as it is central to our discussion of the role of politics in integrating society.

In England, legal rights and protections were the first to develop, through professionalization of the law and an unfettered legal system. By the eighteenth century, people were being treated fairly and consistently by the courts, in both criminal and civil matters. This allowed a commercial and industrial civilization to blossom in England, and along the way, it also benefited common people. It was another century or so, however, before everyone achieved political citizenship, meaning the right to vote and hold political office. Women, of course, didn't get the right to vote until the twentieth century.

Only as the twentieth century progressed did all British people begin to acquire "social citizenship." By this we mean a social safety net, including old age pensions, unemployment insurance, welfare payments, and universal health insurance. (Actually, these innovations started earlier in the UK than the US: most date from the Liberal government before World War I, when Asquith was prime minister and Lloyd George was Chancellor of the Exchequer. Universal health insurance, on the other hand, began after World War II.) These innovations—some introduced prior to World War I, the last of them not until after World War II—enabled the population to enjoy their civil and political rights more fully. In fact, some would argue that people still don't have social citizenship, and therefore equal access to civil and political rights, unless they also have equal, guaranteed access to jobs, education, and housing. In this sense, the development of social citizenship is still far from complete. Yet no one can deny that the British—and for that matter, Canadians—are a lot closer to this "full citizenship" than two centuries ago. They are also a lot closer to it than, say, citizens of the US, Brazil, or Hong Kong: these are countries with much lower taxes, fewer social benefits, and much more measurable social inequality.

It is in this sense, then, that social citizenship is connected to the social class structure. In every society, the rich enjoy full citizenship of every kind: civil, political, and social. Only in the most advanced and progressive societies will even poor people enjoy something like full citizenship. The more unequal the class system in a society—measured, for example, by the Gini index of income inequality—the less likely are all people to enjoy full citizenship. (The Gini index, with values between 0 and 1, shows how closely the distribution of national wealth approximates perfect equality, where 1 percent of the population gets 1 percent of the income paid out, 10 percent gets 10 percent of the income paid out, and so on.) And what this means is the political system of a society is able to integrate people only when there is rough economic and social equality.

Yet what we have seen in the last decade or two is a shift away from the politics of class and from fights over economic equality in the direction of a politics of identity: that is, a shift toward fights over equal treatment for women, people of colour, disabled people, the elderly, and so on. Another important development has been the growth of environmental concern and "green politics." The political scientist Ronald Inglehart, mentioned earlier, claims that these "post-materialist" political orientations are a result of the baby boom generation having grown up in relative prosperity during the 1950s and 1960s. Conceivably, there will be a shift back toward class politics, and new fights over economic inequality.

Despite this seeming loss of focus, modern states have been surprisingly successful in helping to integrate societies. They have done this mainly by promoting social citizenship in the form of broader legal (and especially civil) rights, and through the growth of human rights legislation of various kinds. In this last part of the chapter, as we have done in earlier chapters, we will consider how these developments have contributed to the growth of "civility" and interdependence in Canada and elsewhere.

CIVILITY

The role of political institutions in bringing about civility (and through civility, instilling social integration) is influenced by a key distinction between two kinds of instruments.

Both of these have been historically important, but they are different. One, often associated with the term "civil liberties," is what we might call the award of negative freedoms: that is, freedom *from* mistreatment. Civil liberties are defined as freedoms that protect the individual against government. These freedoms would include freedom of speech, freedom of assembly, freedom of movement, and freedom of the press. So, for example, we may argue that everyone, under every circumstance, has a right to expect that they will not be arbitrarily jailed and tortured by the state or experimented on without their consent, or will not have all their property confiscated without redress.

Freedom from job discrimination because of sex, age, race, or sexual orientation might also be considered a negative freedom and a civil liberty issue, although usually it is considered a civil rights issue. Some people argue that such negative freedoms grant a special status, or advantage: for example, some argue that affirmative action for blacks in the US or employment equity for women in Canada give these two groups an advantage in the competition for jobs or admission to limited educational programs. The argument against this is that historically disadvantaged groups must, at least for some period, be given special opportunities and incentives to create in effect a newly equal set of social institutions.

The other idea of freedom, often associated with the term "civil rights" or on an international scale "human rights," is something closer to what Marshall would have meant by the notion of social citizenship. These are rights which we consider are deserved by all people under all circumstances, without regard to race, age, sex, or other personal qualities. In effect, they ensure the equal treatment of all people with protection of the law as well as the free enjoyment of their lives and property. These rights grant freedom to take part in society as an equal, with equal capacity. In effect, the goal of civil rights or human rights legislation is to set a floor—a baseline—for what people can expect from society.

These two very old concerns about political rights, probably tracing back to John Stuart Mill (if not before), are related to each other and at some point shade into each other. By tradition, people often talk about them differently. The important point is that both make an important contribution to social integration, citizenship, and civility. A culture of human rights protects people's dignity and removes degradation and humiliation, a reality common in societies with a two-tier system of rights (one set for men, another for women; one set for the rich, another for the poor; or one set for Caucasians, and another for non-whites). More than that, it affords people protection and safety under a transparent rule of law—a system of law available to everyone that treats everyone universally.

What's more, such a system rightly promotes a widespread sense of fairness and equity in the society. But it is worth noting that this is not identical with social and economic equality, which is (apparently) impossible to attain, given that no society has ever attained it. Finally, the system, where necessary, builds and preserves boundaries between communities. Here, multiculturalism is an example: it tries to protect the rights of communities (for example, ethnic communities) to preserve whatever differences they want to preserve while guaranteeing their individual members access to entry and equal treatment in all of society's key institutions: schools, housing, workplaces, law courts, and so on. Preserving the balance between community rights and individual rights is one of the most difficult challenges that states are facing today.

It is often difficult to observe societal change taking place, such as constitutional and legal transformation around people's rights and freedoms. We saw in chapter 1 that many social changes are so slow and deep as to be almost imperceptible. We must take a large, historical step backward to put them in proper perspective. Consider, for example, England before and after the Magna Carta of 1215. This document required King John of England to give up some of the monarch's rights to nobles and barons, to respect certain legal procedures, and to accept that the King's will could be bound by the law. It clearly protected certain rights of the King's subjects, whether they were free or tied by bonds of serfdom; most notably, it included the writ of *habeas corpus*, which allowed appeal against unlawful imprisonment. This momentous change is the basis of all constitutional law in English-speaking societies, and changes of this size come only rarely.

Sometimes we gain a clearer hold on important societal differences by comparing two (or more) societies at different levels of civility or constitutional development. Monarchic absolutism—we called it patrimonialism earlier—took much longer to limit and tame in other parts of the world. Often, as in France and elsewhere in Europe, a revolution was needed to bring about this change. In some parts of the world, kings, princes, and royal families still rule, largely untamed and unlimited by law or revolution; think of the House of Saud in Saudi Arabia.

It is often after revolutions (or similarly cataclysmic events) that we see a massive, public, and conscious overhaul of the system of rights and liberties. The civil rights movement in the US was one such dramatic process during the 1950s and 1960s. More recently, the overthrow of apartheid in South Africa, followed by lengthy Truth and Reconciliation hearings and much new legislation, was even more dramatic, since it was purposely more public. Unlike the US civil rights movement, the South African movement, when it succeeded, strove to make past wrongs visible.

Human rights activism, truth commissions, and juridical proceedings are powerful mechanisms for dealing with historical trauma. Further, in South Africa cultural productions, including memorials, museums, heritage sites, and public spaces of commemoration, provide another opportunity for healing. Practices of remembering and forgetting saturate the public sphere and the world of things. Spectacles of trauma and memory in the new South Africa are also influenced by global interventions including international politics, international tourism, and the activities of international NGOs concerned with development. Perhaps never before has any society been so closely watched by so many outsiders, as well as insiders, as it experiments with new freedoms and rights.

Far more often, societies as traumatized as South Africa have been unable or unwilling to look at historic wrongs, as part of the process of bringing change and making amends. The closest Canada has come to this process has been around the treatment of Aboriginal people by the residential schools, which, as we now know, abused (and sometimes killed) Aboriginal children over a period of several generations.

In many parts of South and Central America, decades of civil war and political repression—including genocide, murder, and kidnapping—were hidden from global attention. People "disappeared" if their actions appeared to go against governmental wishes. Often, outside powers like the US government were complicit in these activities and had strong motives for hiding them. Even today, the US government in many parts of the world protects governments that are grossly unfit—as is the case in Pakistan—or brutal. Sometimes they are both.

As a result, the police, the military, and local chiefs or warlords—often with the co-operation of large landowners, the Church, and multinational corporations—terrorize the local people. In countries like Colombia, continuing conflicts, counter-insurgencies, and the "war on terror" blur the boundaries between war and peace. The boundaries between combatants and civilians disappear, and everyone is plunged into an inescapable, never-ending "routinization of terror" (Gill, 2008) that regulates daily life under conditions of unending instability.

It appears that the only solution to these problems comes by a combination of both top-down and bottom-up struggle against terror and tyranny, conducted under the harsh and unrelenting public spotlight. In this sense, both global and local influences are important. Following a comparative study of social movements, Kiyoteru Tsutsui and Hwa-Ji Shin (2008) argue that

(1) global regimes empower and encourage local social movements and increase pressure on target governments from below, and

(2) local activists appeal to international forums with help from international activists to pressure the governments from above.

When the pressures from the top and the bottom converge, social movements are more likely to succeed. As well, these pressures are stronger in countries integrated into global society, and they are also stronger on issues with dominant global norms.

Consider the empirical analysis of social movements by resident Koreans in Japan supporting four types of human rights—civil, political, social/economic, and cultural. This analysis reveals that the movements produced more successes as Japan's involvement in the international human rights regime expanded since the late 1970s. In particular, activism on issues with strong global backing achieved the greatest successes. The analysis also reflects that a lack of cohesive domestic activism can undermine the chances of social movements' success, even with strong global norms on the issue.

We will have much more to say about social movements in the final chapter of this book. Here it is important to note only that political systems do not magically or automatically fix themselves, to bring themselves into "equilibrium," as the most extreme versions of functionalist theory (under Talcott Parsons) were alleged to argue.

Today, the language of civil rights, human rights, and civil liberties is extending far beyond its original concerns with universal franchise, old age pensions, and anti-hate laws. Issues are being raised about the rights of disabled—or differently abled—people, for example. What do airlines owe to obese persons? Should they get two seats for a single fare? And what constitutes reasonable accommodation for people who, one might have said, lack the capacity to do certain jobs or fill certain social roles? Would it be discriminatory if a symphony orchestra refused to hire a deaf conductor? In fact, Ludwig van Beethoven continued conducting orchestras in public even after he was completely deaf. It is reported that his concerts were a disaster and finally, with encouragement, he retired from conducting, although he did continue to compose brilliantly.

Nothing about rights and responsibilities is taken for granted anymore, in the civil realm or the political one. What this means—and all this means—is that we are in the middle of a political and legal discussion whose outcome (we hope) will probably be more inclusive and more integrative.

The world of politics is famously fractious; it is built on debate and the display of heads butting other heads. It also only rarely rises above low behaviour. There are many famous cases of political corruption (not to mention incompetence), and it seems likely that, even in Canada, a certain amount of political corruption goes on. We are still trying to determine the nature of the bargain struck between former prime minister Brian Mulroney and his German money-man, Karlheinz Schreiber. We may all be dead—our grandchildren may all be dead—before the truth on that case finally comes out.

Still, Parsons's quaint formulation of politics as a "goal attainment system"—a system that provides us with leadership and coordination—has a certain charm and even accuracy. At their best, our political leaders unite us around commonly shared values and goals. In that sense they integrate us, bring us together. When that happens, often under the most threatening national conditions, as during a war, we feel relief and a bond with our people. We make sacrifices for one another and for the country and community. This is the ideal state of politics, perhaps rarely attained. But just as Weber's notion of bureaucracy is an ideal type, rarely if ever attained in reality, and just as the perfect market is an economist's ideal type, so this notion of politics as a goal attainment system is an ideal type, reminding us of what is needed and hoped for.

Political historians will report that Napoleon Bonaparte, by his boldness, captured the French state and much of Europe, only to lose it through strategic miscalculation in the Russian winter. Sociologists will likely report that Napoleon gained his moment of prominence by rising through political murk in the wake of the French Revolution. (In this way, he was like Hitler, who rose through the political murk that followed the signing of the Treaty of Versailles.) I will also remember Napoleon for having written his beloved Josephine, "Back in three days. Don't wash!" (sometimes reported as "Will return to Paris tomorrow evening. Don't wash!"). So, on the matter of how sociology is different, it is less about great men and more about great opportunities—some won and others lost. Most important, sociology is unvarnished truth, without the simplifying spin that makes all victors into great men and all losers into fools. In effect, sociology is unwashed history. It has the smell of reality.

In the end, then, sociology is about the way people actually live: it is about the rules they live by, and the ways they make and enforce these rules. In this context, politics is a part of the larger societal picture— and sometimes only a small part. Perhaps that is what I should have told Professor Friedrich forty years ago, though probably I wouldn't have. It might have sounded impolite.

THIRTEEN

Ordinary People
Doing Ordinary Things

But what if there weren't a state to provide for goal attainment and the capital "P" Politics that political scientists like to study? What would social life be without a state? This is, of course, the founding concern of *anarchism*, which calls for the elimination of compulsory government—even for a complete absence of government.

I wondered, as I sat down to write this chapter and consider the issue of people and government: do anarchists have meetings and conferences the way sociologists do? I can imagine they practice self-management and collective decision-making. But do they have set meeting times, agendas, and rules of procedure? Is that even possible, if they shun government—the so-called goal attainment system? I checked the Internet for information about this and found an international organization committed to furthering the cause of anarchism. And apparently anarchists do have conferences. Here is what I found out about this organization, the International of Anarchist Federations, from its website:

> International of Anarchist Federations / L'Internationale des Fédérations Anarchistes (IAF-IFA) is a growing coordination of anarchist federations. It is currently made up of 9 member organisations based in Argentina, Belarus, Britain & Ireland, Bulgaria, Czech Republic & Slovakia, France & Belgium, Germany, Italy, Spain & Portugal. The website contains multi-lingual news and information about the activities of the IAF-IFA, our joint

statements and publications, discussion documents, and links to the member organisations. The IAF-IFA international secretariat welcomes contact from anarchist organisations across the world. The IFA is sometimes mistakenly (but understandably) referred to as the International Federation of Anarchists, or as IFA-IAF.

As we read further, we discover the

International of Anarchists Federation (IAF or IFA) was founded during an international anarchist conference in Carrara in 1968 by the three existing european federations of France, Italy and Spain as well as the Bulgarian federation in french exile. To counter the internationalisation of state and capitalist powers that are developing their influences ever rapidly on a global scale, the IFA has since aimed to build and improve strong and active international anarchist structures. (Note: the words "European" and "French" are not capitalized in the original; this may be intentional.)

These anarchists seem to think they can get along without government, but can they really? I recall studying Thomas Hobbes's *Leviathan* (1651) as an undergraduate and being impressed by the brilliantly nightmarish scenario Hobbes sketched. It was a shocking picture of human beings who needed to be governed, or perhaps even worse than that, a human species that needed to be saved from freedom. Hobbes's people needed a monarch and a state, no matter how cruel and clumsy, to give them lives better than those he described as "solitary, poor, nasty, brutish, and short." I wondered: does such a thing as Hobbes's "state of nature," in which people might be reduced to such depravity by the lack of a ruler and a state, really exist?

I confess I had doubts about this for several reasons. First, I was young, and young people tend to be more optimistic than Hobbes. Second, I had also read Jean-Jacques Rousseau's account of people in the so-called state of nature (written in the eighteenth century, roughly one hundred years later than Hobbes) and it was a very different account; in fact, it sounded like a rather pleasant place. For Rousseau, as for Freud, life before civilization (and repression) was nice and free. Civilization—a society with rules—was the problem, not the solution. Third, I had grown up in a socialist-communist family, with aunts and uncles who viewed the Canadian state as unjust. These members of my family did not believe that revolution was quite so bad an idea as Hobbes did. In fact, some of them had spent their lives working to make a revolution in Canada, so evidently they hadn't been persuaded by Hobbes. Overall, Hobbes's image of society seemed unrealistic, as well as pessimistic and brutal.

I continued to wonder about this matter. When thinking about a topic for my doctoral dissertation, I brought together several related themes about organization. One of my teachers, Harrison White, had already convinced me that organizations rarely if ever work the way people say they do. So figuring out the deep, hidden, or secret structure of an organization was enticing. But underneath that question lay another one: if the real structure of an organization doesn't work as it is supposed to, and all we can do is to constantly improvise, how do people in organizations actually achieve order? How do they escape the chaos Hobbes had described, to produce what society expects? In my dissertation, I planned to revisit Hobbes in a more modest, organizational setting.

The setting I chose was the Massachusetts juvenile court system. In particular, I studied two courts that were generally thought to function well. The people I talked to in fact considered these courts exemplary. I had read the Massachusetts laws governing juvenile delinquents and decided they were unworkable. They called for individualized justice, hand-tailored to every juvenile who came before the court. This sounded to me plainly impossible—impractical and chaotic at best. To carry out this well-intentioned law would need the wisdom and wealth of King Solomon, who had been dead a long time, even in 1968.

Therefore, I judged that if these courts seemed to be working well, they must be following unwritten rules. They must have developed their own rules. If so, what were these rules?

I spent a year observing the court proceedings in two Massachusetts communities, reading official records, and interviewing the court officers—the police, probation officers, parole officers, psychiatrists, social workers, judges, and lawyers. These were all lovely people, with a dedication to justice and to the welfare of the juveniles they processed. They were all helpful and kind, and often they told me the truth.

That said, my observations bore out my first hunch. The juvenile law didn't provide any structure for decision-making. Yet, surprisingly, the court officers made decisions every day in a calm and deliberate fashion. What were they doing? In short, they were chatting with each other over coffee. Typically, a police officer would have coffee with a probation officer; they would read the case reports and then chat about each kid. Occasionally, they would consider other information from the psychiatrist or truant officer. Then they would reach a decision, strike a bargain, or make a deal. Eventually, the probation officer would appear in court and quietly "sell" the deal to the judge, who fully trusted his probation officers.

Everyone found this procedure to be congenial. But how about the quality of decision-making? An analysis of my data suggested the decisions made in this way were no better than chance. Their effects on future delinquency were zero. If you followed these cases for a few years, you found that many of the juveniles would get into trouble again, regardless of the disposition they had received from the court. Kids from "good" homes would rarely get into trouble again, while kids from "bad" homes—with a parent missing or other family members in trouble with the law, for example—would usually get into trouble again, regardless of what the court decided.

In short, the written law, though kind, provided no guidance and had no effect, nor did the coffee-time decisions. The court officials had devised a benevolent decision-making structure to fill the vacuum, and they felt good about it, but I could find no evidence that the court decisions worked better than a roll of the dice. Still, I saw no Armageddon, no Hobbesian war of all against all, that resulted from this lack of imposed structure.

I put the problem of order aside for a time, but continued to think about it in various guises. Eventually, I brought the problem forward again. I became interested in disasters and disaster research. Much to my surprise, I learned that there was a whole disaster-research industry. (That's something I love about sociology: you can rarely find a topic that isn't already being studied sociologically.) So I began to wonder. During a disaster, when normal processes of law-and-order break down, do people behave like wild beasts, as Hobbes would have predicted?

This image of beastly people in disarray had been widely promoted during the 1960s and 1970s, when people took to the streets of the US and students rebelled in Europe and America. Every night on the television screen we saw cars being overturned, shops being looted, bombs being exploded, guns being fired, and rioters going head-to-head with police officers—sometimes even soldiers.

The media portrayal of black protest in the 1960s was particularly unflattering. (Rick Perlstein's 2008 book *Nixonland* deals with this brilliantly.) Often, television reports showed only blacks running through the night holding stolen TVs above their heads. The goal of such media presentations was to discredit black protest, implying that it was illegitimate, a result of inappropriate expectations or undersocialization, and a convenient excuse for noise and looting. In other words, the media presented black protest (and to some degree student protest, including anti-war protest) as Hobbesian disorder, with little or no political justification or purpose.

So in thinking about disasters, I wondered if we would see evidence of people running through the night with stolen televisions following a hurricane, a cyclone, a flood, or a bridge collapse. Hobbes would expect it; Rousseau would not. I wasn't sure. I read the literature on disasters.

A brief digression: A question something like this had been roiling about in sociology for some 150 years. The first book on a related topic—in fact, one of the first sociology books I ever owned—was *Extraordinary Popular Delusions and the Madness of Crowds* (1841) by Charles Mackay (1814–1889), to my mind a quite amazing Scottish journalist, author, and songwriter educated in London and Brussels. (One of Mackay's several hit songs, "There's a Good Time Coming," reportedly sold 400,000 copies in 1846!)

Mackay, who held a doctorate in literature and led a successful career as a journalist, wrote this book and, in so doing, launched a field that would come to be called crowd psychology. He fancied himself to be writing a history of "human folly throughout the ages," telling tales of swindles, schemes and scams, fads and delusions. His huge book is a catalogue of strange, unlikely thoughts and doings, ranging from the prophecies of Nostradamus to beliefs about comets, astrology, and practices of necromancy and magnetism, to sorcery and witchcraft.

The general theme of this book is as follows: if you bring ordinary people together, they may do nutty things. This point of view is only a slightly more amusing version of Hobbes's theory, for it postulates that people need control or, at least, close supervision by superiors.

This way of thinking about ordinary people—about the follies of crowd psychology—persisted through much of the nineteenth century. It lies at the bottom of Freudian theory (which is mainly about human irrationality) and, to some degree, it underlies Durkheim's thinking as well. Durkheim's people are not vicious like Hobbes's or sick like Freud's, but they do need a firm hand; otherwise, they will turn anomic and kill themselves. Religion, for Durkheim, is just a way of bringing people together around the campfire (or pulpit) to control one another. The notion that ordinary people might purposely and consciously come together to solve their problems without the help of a King or Duke had not yet occurred to social theorists. Though this came after the reign of Mad King Ludwig of Bavaria, it also came before the presidency of George W. Bush.

Following this logic, one might predict that after a major disaster—say, the destruction of the World Trade Center on 11 September 2001—there would be widespread looting and other crazed, pointless, and antisocial actions in New York City. This seemingly sound prediction would have been proven wrong. On 9/11, 9/12, 9/13, and long thereafter, Americans displayed bravery, regret, patriotism, and concern. And, remarkably, the research literature reports that this is also what commonly happens after natural disasters.

For example, the same thing happened following Hurricane Katrina in New Orleans. People did not—do not—become crazed, selfish, or desperate for guidance when faced with a disaster or breakdown of everyday order. Often they act sooner, and just as effectively, as the "professionals" who are charged with handling disasters. Of course, after Katrina there were the usual reports of looting (see, for example, news reports on 1 September 2005), and the mayor even called for assistance in dealing with this. Interestingly, police officers were among those apprehended for looting.

However, a more important point needs to be made. There is always theft going on in any city, and the concern about looting merely brings it to light, as part of the disaster mythology of public disorder. Also, some behaviour viewed as looting is merely a survival tactic. What's more, it may not happen at all, in the sense the media convey. In a 2008 journal article, disaster researcher Mark Constable reports that media reports of looting in New Orleans mainly repeated second-hand accounts. Says Constable, "It is likely that there was in fact *no looting in the traditional sense*. . . . A clear definition of looting is suggested for emergency managers to use in order to separate acts of survival from pure criminal acts." (Emphasis added.)

Constable notes there is a significant research literature that suggests looting during natural disasters is a myth. Propagation of the Katrina looting stories is just another case of the media's mythological reporting on disasters. Certainly, such stories are promoted by people in authority, who are looking for someone else to blame for tardy and insufficient efforts to remedy the problem.

On the contrary, ordinary people are evidently good at organizing themselves to help one another when the need arises. But they don't always do so. Sometimes they organize themselves poorly, or for bad purposes. Sometimes collective action is even harmful. What makes the difference?

Forces Pushing People Apart

It's hard to stop thinking about that Hobbesian state of nature, especially given that many powerful people on the political right—and their friends in the media—promote such a view of humanity. Consider three different examples of this Hobbesian universe, and how they can be seen differently.

Consider first the image of Western vigilantism in the US, when (according to the movies) plain people grab a rope and set out to lynch an accused wrongdoer. This theme has been treated in a hundred Hollywood films. The "mob" always seems crazy, unorganized, and infinitely suggestible. Then consider the genocidal wars in Rwanda (Hutus against Tutsis); Iraq (Shiites against Kurds); Asia (Japanese against Chinese); Germany (Nazis against Jews); Yugoslavia (Serbs against Muslims); or Canada, the US, and Australia (whites against Aboriginals). Are these also just crazy, unorganized episodes and the result of mere suggestibility?

Consider one other topic with which I am familiar: problem gambling. Currently, there is a class action lawsuit against Ontario casinos on behalf of problem gamblers. These gamblers had specifically asked to be excluded from gambling, but nevertheless, they were allowed to participate. The psychological viewpoint, heavily supported by the gambling industry (the casinos, racetracks, betting shops, and so on), is that problem gambling is a rare form of addiction or mental illness; people with a gambling problem have the responsibility to seek treatment for their problem. End of story. This convenient way to frame the issue of problem gambling lets casinos off the hook quite nicely. The guy who loses the family home or his daughter's college education fund shoulders the blame, not the casino.

A sociologist considering this topic might ask: what is it about our society, our values, and the ways we advertise gambling that makes people—especially poor, economically marginalized people—risk everything they have on cards, dice, horses, or lottery tickets? Is there something wrong with a society that, through advertising and other mass media messages, makes people feel like losers if they aren't rich, if they aren't leading the glamorous life (supposedly) associated with Las Vegas? A sociologist might ask whether the upsurge of gambling, even excessive gambling, isn't just a normal response to desperate disadvantage. Perhaps people are being taught to want more than they can possibly get, then being told that they can get it easily by gambling. A certain number of ordinary people—people like you and me—are bound to fall for that, particularly if we are feeling desperate enough.

What each of these scenarios has in common is crazy, seemingly inexplicable behaviour that, when seen in its social context, makes sense. The problem gamblers are told they can stop being losers by risking everything they have on a roll of the dice. The "ethnic cleansers" are being told they can serve their community, renew their nation's pride, or secure its future by killing traitorous "outsiders" in their midst. Members of the lynch mob are being told they have a moral responsibility to purge the community of criminals and the right to take an eye for an eye.

Each of these social scenarios has a few common features. First, each calls on people to solve a problem they are facing in a courageous and forthright way. Second, each situates the discussion of the problem and its solution in a familiar, often traditional cultural rhetoric. Third, there is always someone—a person in authority, with status or charisma, and sometimes with access to the media—who is directing this supposedly spontaneous outburst of "craziness." You can say that people are gullible and perhaps they are: P.T. Barnum, the great nineteenth-century American showman, is credited with the line, "there's a sucker born every minute." Maybe that's true. Certainly, the public acclaim for many mass advertised products and celebrities suggests that it is.

I consider far more important psychologist Stanley Milgram's interesting sociological observation that people are almost infinitely obedient to authority. People are sociable, yes, and they like to conform. More than that, they want to do the right thing, and since they don't always know what that is, they rely on experts to tell them. That's why ordinary, normal people are willing, if directed by strangers in white lab coats—supposed scientists—to administer lethal shocks to other strangers in laboratories. They want to do the "right" thing (though some *do* refuse to murder in the service of science).

This is a social behaviour, not a psychiatric symptom. When we study what appear to be fads, delusions, and manias—the seeming irrationality with dangerous outcomes—we rarely find truly inexplicable, uncontrollable behaviour by the masses. Rather, we typically find mass manipulation by the powerful, using traditional ideologies and powerful institutions (the schools, the churches, the army and police) to justify and facilitate Hobbesian brutality. At the very least, so-called irrational people are responding to socially created turmoil with socially constructed strategies.

Take rumours and panics: they can come as close as anything to producing the Hobbesian state of nature. In the summer of 1986, during a long drought, rumours spread through the Dordogne region of France that large agricultural enterprises—Spanish "tomato barons"—were to blame for the water shortage. According to the rumour, cloud seeding intended to prevent hail had malfunctioned, and this had caused the drought. These rumours were apparently similar to other rumours about the tomato barons that had surfaced in 1985 and earlier, during equally severe droughts.

Little surprise that it turned out that these rumours were based on inaccurate information. Cloud seeding may not always *produce* rain, but there is no evidence whatever that it *prevents* rain. Why the rumours? They appealed to people during a drought given their uncertainty about how weather actually works, but there are other factors as well. There is a reason the French populace blamed *Spanish* tomato barons. After all, the French and Spanish people have been military and economic rivals for over five hundred years. Moreover, the alleged wrongdoers were "barons"—people of wealth and standing, therefore perhaps rightly distrusted by the smaller farmers. Rumours often contain allegations of wrongdoing by the powerful, and in fact they are often justified.

By studying rumours, we learn something valuable about the hierarchical organization of society and about the organization of people's fantasy lives. Rumours, after all, are improvised news—news imagined and created under conditions of hardship and uncertainty. From this standpoint, a rumour is a hypothesis provided to explain an ill-defined problem. In creating a rumour, people draw on their sometimes limited stock of information, but in a purposeful manner. Rumours that convey stereotypes or archetypal images are more likely than other rumours to gain currency in the public discourse; they are also more resistant to denial. The most "successful" rumours correspond to what people hope or fear will prove to be true, rather than to what has actually happened. Usually, rumours are powerful because they make visible certain concerns that are otherwise invisible. All of this is sociological, not psychiatric.

Take another example: the snake in the greens. In Dayton, Ohio, a rumour made the rounds for a week or so in 1991 alleging that a poisonous snake had popped up in the produce section of a local supermarket and bitten an old lady, who had then died. Within three days after the rumour began, sociologist Dan Miller began interviewing rumour-bearers. In the course of his research, he found out that the rumoured event had never happened—there had been no snake and no dead lady. Otherwise, the rumour held up pretty well: unlike many rumours, it did not become more distorted or less authentic with repeated telling. (That is, it didn't become a story about five snakes and a class of second-graders.) As is usual, the rumour diffused through existing social networks of friends and acquaintances. And it stayed in people's minds: respondents remembered when they had first heard it, and then recalled also when they passed the story on.

After all, it was a good story, the basis for joking and sociability among the young men. It also stimulated chit-chat among the elderly who used the rumour as another productive topic for conversation. Third and most important, it provided everyone with a vehicle for social criticism. It allowed the poor black residents of this community to speak out against the white owners of the supermarket and against white society more generally. It was, in the end, another version of the Spanish tomato baron story.

Most people are naturally sociable. Segregation and social distance are not natural: they must be promoted. Prejudice and discrimination need to be inflamed. Suspicion and distrust require the nourishment that only rumours, lies, slanders, and veiled threats can provide. Abuse and violence are not the "state of nature" for most people; rather, they are a clear result of social breakdown, inequality and conflict, of a loss of confidence in civil society and its public institutions. Often, it is the doing of troublemakers. People behave like animals when they have been starved, frightened, and misinformed. That is not the state of nature—it is the sign of a misgoverned and manipulated society.

People are not incapable of rational co-operation, as Hobbes seemed to believe. They are not in need of just any ruler. They need *good* government, for it is bad government that creates Hobbes's state of nature.

Without interference from bad government and other malign influences, people can work out a great deal of their lives themselves. Social peace and integration are possible in a variety of forms and domains. We have already discussed some of these forms—the family; the small group; the team, band, or gang; and the community. Not one of these forms is perfect, but each develops and evolves through the efforts and investment of its members.

In the pages that follow, I will discuss a few other mechanisms through which people achieve social integration without needing despotic control or falling into a Hobbesian state of nature.

Contributions to Integration

FAMILIARITY

Some of the mechanisms that contribute to social integration rely on traditional face-to-face interactions. These include voluntary associations (say, alumni associations, charitable groups, fraternal orders, and mutual aid societies); clubs (think of golf clubs, book clubs, and church groups); and support groups (for recovering addicts, families of prisoners, and spouses of people with Alzheimer's disease).

They all draw on the usual factors that make for integration. First, they promote familiarity among members through communication and interaction. In some of these groups, intimacy, trust, and similarity develop gradually and even unexpectedly, as members work together to raise money for a charity, say, or recruit people to work on a community issue. The more people work together on a common goal, the more similar they become, and the more they find—and create—experiences that they can share with each other.

Members of voluntary associations share a common loyalty to a given goal, and they get to know one another around that shared goal. Members of support groups, on the other hand, share a common problem and become involved by helping one another directly; they may share advice and information. Members of clubs share neither a common loyalty nor a common problem; they group together for entertainment and sheer *sociability*. And that, when you think about it, is the strangest but most impressive reason for grouping together.

According to early sociologist Georg Simmel,

> Sociability is . . . the play-form of association. Since sociability in its pure form has no ulterior end, no content, and just involves the satisfaction of the impulse to sociability . . . the process remains strictly limited to its personal bearers. Therefore, the character of purely sociable association is determined by the variety of personality traits possessed by the participants.

Perhaps sociability, pure play, is the real "state of nature" for human beings. The philosopher Johan Huizinga, writing in 1938, spoke of humanity as "homo ludens"—man the game-player. According to Huizinga, play has three key features that attract people: play is free, in fact freedom; play is a departure from "ordinary" or "real" life; and play occupies its own time and place. When people really play, they are taken out of themselves and become "in the moment." Every society has play—even animals have play—and one might even say that culture itself is a form of play (consider wordplay in the form of puns and jokes). In this respect, the abstract arts like music are pure play, with no meaning beyond themselves but pleasure. Likewise, sport and other competition can be play, so long as it is not done for an ulterior motive (e.g., profit).

One of the things that makes playing with others fun is that different people bring different qualities and personalities to the event. People play cards differently, play musical instruments differently, dance differently, tell different kinds of jokes or stories. These differences make social intercourse interesting and unpredictable. Yet, as

Simmel also points out, play follows social forms; like fashion, play must be more than the mere expression of personal tastes and peculiarities. Otherwise there would be no bridge between the participants; people would be playing by themselves in parallel, like toddlers, rather than really playing *with* each other. The requirement for playing with others, according to Huizinga, is that

> the persons should not display their individualities with too much abandon. Particularly relevant here is the sense of tact, which guides the self-regulation of the individual in her/his personal relations . . . In sociability, whatever the personality has of objective importance . . . must not interfere with purely sociable interaction.

So even in play that is free and for fun (not profit), there are social norms to obey: specifically, norms of tact. These norms, related to civility, oblige us to keep a little of ourselves back even when we are being the most open and intimate. To do otherwise is to capture a play event for some other purpose: to demand attention, support, pity, or encouragement, for example.

Another interesting social form is altruism—again, not explainable within a Hobbesian framework. Altruism is common in close relations, even in communities. It can be defined as a type of giving that does not expect or require repayment. It is unselfish love for others, the show of unasked concern with other people's welfare.

Durkheim defined altruism, in the form of altruistic suicide, as "the violent and voluntary act of self-destruction for no personal benefit" and "the opposite of rational self-interest." Hobbes would not have been able to explain Palestinian suicide bombers, for example, or Japanese kamikaze pilots. Their actions make sense only in the context of a commitment to the welfare of an entire group—to the needs of society. Such altruistic behaviour defies explanation in terms of personal pleasure and this persuades Durkheim that "society" must exist outside and above the individuals who make it up. At the same time, the example set by individuals who sacrifice themselves for others also serves to keep others in line. Sainthood, such as the self-denial practiced by Mother Teresa or Albert Schweitzer, reminds us what human goodness is supposed to look like, and thereby calls us to a higher standard.

Some have expressed concern in recent years that civil society—the society that depends on play and altruism, on clubs, support groups, and voluntary associations—has gone into decline. They argue that it has succumbed to the intense pressures of work in two-earner families, pressures that reveal themselves in the practice of cocooning: going home every night and drawing the blinds against the outside world.

The classic argument on this topic was made by political scientist Robert Putnam in his book *Bowling Alone* (2000). The book argues that since 1950, there has been a general decline in the active civil engagement of Americans, most evident in strong signs of political disengagement (for example, low voter turnout and decreasing involvement with political parties). He denies that this disengagement is limited to politics, however, and claims there has been an equally strong decline in other civic participation. The decline of participation in voluntary associations like clubs and charities is a clear example. As a result, many people are "bowling alone," not joining bowling leagues as in the past. By bowling alone, people miss the interaction, engagement, and social connection that might result. Consequently, people are more isolated—atomized—than they have been in the past, and communities lose social capital and social cohesion. Putnam credits this change to the individualizing, isolating effects of modern technology, such as television, the Internet, and video game systems.

We can, however, criticize this study from several angles. First, in the most recent US election, vast numbers of people were mobilized (once again) behind Democratic Party candidates, reversing a long slide that probably began during the Vietnam War. (Of course, public opinion can change on a dime, and it is impossible to tell how Obama's presidency will unfold.) Second, earlier studies have made similar arguments about the isolating role of technology as far back as the 1920s, with the growing popularity of the radio as an example, and yet public engagement has always bounced back. Third, we may simply be less able to see sociability taking place. Traditional social ties are being replaced or augmented by less visible social ties—for example, by email and cyber-communication (of which we will say more later). These newer links do not diminish sociability, they merely delocalize it. If people aren't bowling with friends at the corner bowling alley, perhaps they are playing chess online or Grand Theft Auto with someone a thousand miles away.

Finally, there is evidence suggesting that Putnam's research may be limited to the US. Time-use diaries that covered a forty-year period from the US, Canada, the UK, and the Netherlands were examined by sociologists Robert Andersen, James Curtis, and Ed Grabb, who found evidence of the supposed decline only in the US.

In short, there is little evidence to suggest that people are naturally antisocial or irrational; they are not hard-wired to reject other people, let alone look for reasons to abuse and harm them. What's more, people have lots of reasons to depend on others and, perhaps, an increasing awareness of their interdependence.

INTERDEPENDENCE

We have argued throughout the book that one of the fundamental features of social life, and one that contributes most to social integration, is interdependence. People need one another and benefit from each other's existence. The more they realize this, the more likely they are to behave decently toward one another.

This means that people need to understand that they all have common friends and common enemies. Sharing friends and sharing enemies, as we saw in an earlier chapter, is always an important basis for social solidarity. Beyond that, people need to see the first-hand benefits of co-operation with others, both nearby and with people who are far away. This is somewhat harder to achieve, but may have become easier in the last few decades. Finally, people need to understand that they are connected together in a vast global network of exchange. The world is finite, as are its resources, and we have no choice but to share them.

The current concern with environmental issues plays to all of these themes. It is likely that one of the reasons there has been so much interest in these issues is that they are global; humanity has to unite against pollution and climate change, for example. We are all facing that problem together, regardless of sex, age, race, class, or nationality. Environmental issues give us a common foe to fight, something to talk about together (like snakes in the greens) and also something to work on together.

All of our interdependencies, which Durkheim felt would be important as sources of (organic) solidarity in an industrial society, are clearer today than they ever have been. Consider a few examples of this.

First, we all live and work in a global marketplace. Whether we live in Toronto, Edmonton, Halifax, Buenos Aires, Mumbai, or Moscow, we are all looking for the best goods and services at the lowest prices. And our jobs and incomes depend on the outcome of this process. Shifts in buying and selling, and in capital investment, shape our individual lives and national economies, and they determine the balance of global economic and political power. So when we buy and sell to one another, we are remaking the world's economy. We are also remaking world politics.

That doesn't mean that, as buyers and sellers, we all have an equal influence in this power transformation. We don't. However, we are all affected by it, and we all have choices to make: whether to buy Canadian goods or Chinese goods, North American cars or Japanese cars. More important, we can choose to elect governments that are more or less friendly to the concerns of ordinary citizens and workers, rather than investors.

The market is interesting because it shows how dyadic (i.e., two-person) relationships between buyer and seller can aggregate upward into complex networks of exchange that indirectly connect (and affect) millions of invisible, distant participants all around the globe. In one way, this is a remarkable human achievement, showing that people—through interdependence—can fulfill their needs quite nicely without the supervision of a Hobbesian despot. Recent economic events, however, have also shown the need for regulation. Markets do not and cannot regulate themselves. It is true that they can generate prices in response to changes in supply and demand. But as we have seen they are also vulnerable to distortion by insiders. Without oversight and regulation, markets can easily become fraudulent and create dangerous booms and busts. We are all currently experiencing a bust, a global financial downturn that has affected millions, if not billions, of people.

Markets respond to our human need for interdependence, and they are self-regulating in the sense that they set prices without outside political interference. This is the difference between a "free market" and a "command economy," for example. But to repeat: they require legally enforceable rules and a team of regulators to enforce them, or financial frauds will steal everyone's savings (again). Over the past thirty years, deregulation has been the prime source of increased economic instability and inequality—hollowing out the middle class and transferring wealth from the poor to the rich—in the US, and to a lesser degree in Canada.

The Internet is similar in some respects, though different in others. What is the Internet, cyberspace, but a vast information market, in which the participants establish the value and credibility of what is displayed? The most commonly used Internet institutions today (Google, eBay, Craigslist, Wikipedia, Facebook, and YouTube) are results of a market in information that is virtually unregulated. People continue to use these cyber-institutions because, in spite of the lack of regulation, they may possibly be as useful or credible as anything else available outside cyberspace. (And they are certainly convenient!) The most striking feature of cyberspace is its diversity, ranging from a seemingly infinite number of commercial websites to personal blogs and various group effusions (recall the International Anarchist website we discussed earlier).

As with all other tools, the Internet is a human invention that is revolutionizing human life through the efforts of ordinary people. As V. Gordon Childe said about the human use of tools through the ages, "man makes himself." But the making of these tools requires interdependence, just as it creates interdependence.

The Internet has continued to delocalize social interactions, a process that began much earlier with the development of high-speed transportation (trains, planes, and automobiles) and communication (the public mail service, the telegraph, and the telephone). Today we do not rely exclusively on direct face-to-face communications. Most of the time, we communicate in other, less direct and less immediate ways. This has led to the development of large social networks. In effect, society today is a network of networks. We are all embedded in large social networks, and most of these large social networks are all connected to one another, with the result that we all live in a "small world," as psychologist Stanley Milgram showed. Or, as is sometimes said, we are all connected by (only) six degrees of separation.

We know this thanks to a landmark study conducted by Stanley Milgram in 1967. The experiment grew out of a common observation that, when two strangers meet, they often struggle to find people they both know, and often they succeed. Milgram posed the following question: what is the probability that two randomly selected people would know each other? Or, put differently, in a vast social network connecting everyone to everyone else, how many links are needed to connect any two randomly chosen people?

Milgram came up with an ingenious way to approach this question. He chose individuals in two Midwestern US cities (Omaha and Wichita) to be the starting point of a search and Boston to be the end point or target. He then designated specific individuals in Boston to be the destination, target, or final recipient of a small package, and asked randomly chosen people in Omaha (or Wichita) to do their best to get the package to this Bostonian through people they knew personally, on a first-name basis.

If, say, George Smith (the source in Wichita) knew John Brown (the target in Boston) personally, he would send the package directly to him. But the odds of course were that George did not know John personally, so George's task was to think of a friend or relative he knew personally (say, Alice in New York) who was more likely to know John the Bostonian. Usually, participants focused on geographic characteristics when choosing an appropriate next person in the chain, sending the package to someone who was ever-closer to the target. So George would sign a roster of recipients, acknowledging he had received the package, then forward it to Alice. When and if the package eventually reached John in Boston, the researchers could examine the roster to see how many times it had been forwarded from person to person. And for packages that never reached the destination, the incoming postcards helped identify where and when the chain was broken.

Sometimes a package would reach the target with only one or two stops, and sometimes the trip required as many as nine or ten. Many of the packages never reached their destination at all. Of the packages that finally did reach their target, the average path length was between five and six people. Much more interesting, perhaps, was the finding reported later—sometimes called the "small world property"—that individuals with especially large and diverse networks played a particularly important role in linking people and networks.

These linking individuals have been called different names over time. When researchers first started to study social networks in the 1950s, these individuals were labelled sociometric stars. More recently, they have been called brokers, or even entrepreneurs, since their structural position, as intermediaries between individuals, organizations, and networks, allows them to provide unusually valuable connective services. They are entrepreneurs in the usual sense of go-between. They are brokers in the sense that they are agents for others. Typically, these entrepreneurs or brokers have an unusual amount of social capital, which they use to build their (and other people's) financial or political capital.

The conclusion from this fact is that it is important to network—that is, to set about forming networks by aggressively meeting new people and cultivating new relationships. While this may occasionally work as planned, we need to remember that people can choose other people to network with, but they cannot control the people *these* people will network with, and so on down the line. Attaching oneself to someone with a large network of what Mark Granovetter called weak ties—casual acquaintances—may paradoxically be much more useful than attaching oneself to someone with a (necessarily) smaller network of strong ties, close friends and blood relations. The result of this is that we cannot hope to control the size or quality of the network to which we belong. At best, we can try to insinuate ourselves into other people's large and extensive networks, if we can identify them.

So far, I have highlighted people's ability to build their own social lives, and have illustrated this with markets and cyberspace, showing that little top-down intervention is needed to achieve this interdependence and mutual benefit. I have also pointed out that, at the same time, unregulated markets are terribly dangerous. And similarly, unregulated cyberspace is also dangerous. First, there is the ever-present danger of fraudulent practices and the spread of false and distorted information. Second, there is the growing danger of identity theft and misrepresentation.

Finally, there is growing evidence that people sometimes use cyberspace to injure and threaten others. An example is cyberbullying: the use of Facebook or YouTube, for example, to spread malicious and embarrassing information about school acquaintances. It's been reported that this kind of bullying may have led to more than one incident of suicide, and it is no less serious and harmful than face-to-face schoolyard bullying. In fact, it may be worse, because bullying information travels faster and reaches larger numbers in cyberspace. And what's more, this information may never go away. No one has yet figured out how to purge false and malicious information posted by others in cyberspace.

So this too argues that there is a need for regulation and for civility in cyberspace, as there is in markets.

CIVILITY

As I think about it more, perhaps what I should have told Professor Friedrich that day so many years ago is that sociology is about ordinary people doing ordinary things with extraordinary results.

Consider the so-called demographic transition as an example. For millennia, nomadic humans had produced as many babies as they were able, and many of them died, so populations grew hardly at all. Eventually, human populations settled down in agricultural communities, food supplies increased and—despite wild swings resulting from famines, plagues, and other disasters—the population of humanity began to rise slightly. Then, in seventeenth- and eighteenth-century Europe, as public health measures improved, death rates declined and the population exploded. Suddenly, most children were surviving from infancy into adulthood. But what happened next is even more remarkable: child-bearing began to drop.

There are many theories about this. The best-known theory, called demographic transition, is a functionalist theory. Here it is, in its strictest version: society, experiencing disequilibrium through a rapid population growth, re-establishes the balance between birth rates and death rates by lowering the former to accord with the latter, re-establishing a zero growth rate. With increases in urbanization and social mobility, large families are disadvantageous. In a variant of this theory, social costs and opportunities change with industrialization, making child-bearing less profitable than when children were useful as farm labour. And as prolonged education becomes ever more necessary, children cost more and are less useful to their parents.

Two parts of this story have never been fully worked out, and they are the most interesting parts. First, the drop in child-bearing came about without any change in birth-control technology; people prevented pregnancy in the same ways they had done for thousands of years, through sexual abstinence or interruption. They had to accept some hardship to reduce their child-bearing, and suddenly, they were willing to do so. Second, the reduction in child-bearing was not only to be found in urban, industrial settings. There was a cultural wave taking place; women were hearing and talking about the wisdom of controlling their fertility, regardless of where they lived. Also, this was regardless of what the Church said and perhaps even regardless of what their husbands said. There is some evidence that midwives and so-called witches were often the carriers and spreaders of birth control knowledge, and maybe that's why they were burned.

Nonetheless, the result was an earth-shaking drop in child-bearing, starting in the early nineteenth century in France and the US, catching hold in Britain and Western Europe in the later nineteenth century, and then in the twentieth century spreading to Southern and Eastern Europe and beyond. The demographic transition has been even more rapid, though later, in many parts of Asia, Africa, and South America, and it is far from complete there. But everywhere, the initiative has come from the bottom up—from ordinary people making their own history, and in doing so, making human history.

This is what sociology is finally about: people making their own history. Most of human history is made in this quiet, almost invisible and incremental way. We make our vocabularies in this way—word by word, over the course of time. We make important discoveries when cooking, raising our children, or fixing household appliances.

Inventors build on their ordinary day-to-day experiences and lay wisdom. Folk medicine, folk art, and folk religions all come about in this slow, incremental, but no less important and persuasive way. The sheer persistence of popular beliefs, superstitions, and anxieties attests to the deep-rootedness of our lay knowledge, stored up like a slow-growing crop against some future need.

Other, more visible history is made by social movements—organized groups of people with an agenda or plan for social change to be achieved through agitation and political pressure. Usually social movements have an ideology, as we discussed in the last chapter. Equally important, often they have valuable resources: money, social contacts, access to the media, sometimes even weapons.

Some would say that the most important changes of the past century were brought about by great rulers, diplomats, and politicians. Others would argue that they were wrought by great scientists and inventors. But still others—and I am one of these others—would say that great diplomats, politicians, scientists, and inventors, as well as creative artists, philosophers, humanitarians, and saints, are all products of their time. In human history, there may have been dozens of proto-Mozarts or Einsteins or Gandhis, for example, but they all went to their death unfulfilled and unnoticed because the time wasn't right. They may not have had, as Virginia Woolf said of women artists, "a room of their own"—space and time to do what they were otherwise destined to do.

If so, this argues for the need to celebrate and nourish ordinary humanity, so that all people will fulfill their human potential. Doing so may call for new social movements to do for the still-unsung what the labour movement, the women's movement, the black movement, and the gay rights movement did for ordinary North Americans in the nineteenth and twentieth centuries. It will call for a culture of civility to ensure human rights and human dignity, equal protection under the law, and perhaps the kind of social citizenship that T.H. Marshall wanted: secure jobs, housing, and health for everyone. Everyone will need "a room of their own," if we are to find the other Mozarts and Einsteins and Gandhis.

However, far more than a political and economic shift is needed. Also needed is a cultural shift—a new etiquette of civility, which implies a reduced individualism and less savage competition. I am speaking with both hats on now: as a citizen, I want to live in a better society than the one I see and read about. As a sociologist, I know that humanity has no chance of surviving without a new basis for social cohesion and collective responsibility. I believe that will call for a new emphasis on collective versus individual goals; a careful distinction between public manners and private manners; and a recognition of the need for what Adam Smith (in 1759) called the social emotions—generosity, humanity, kindness, compassion, mutual friendship, and esteem, among others. As Smith understood, social life requires more than a marketplace. It requires social as opposed to selfish passions, and moral sentiments that correctly value our attachments to others.

Today, when people argue an optimistic point of view, especially if their argument is based on the genius of ordinary people doing ordinary things, they are likely to be called dreamers, mere utopians, or worse. This book doesn't claim to have solved the world's problems. What's more, it isn't promising a millennium of peace and happiness, according to a formula that is political, spiritual, technological, medical, religious, or otherwise.

It *is* saying that we humans can only live—survive—if we master living together, and we already know a lot about the ways people can live together safely and peacefully. We know the nature of the problem humanity faces, and (some of) the ways to solve this problem. Now we need the confidence to harness and use our knowledge.

Bibliographic Essay

The book that I sat down to write, after forty years as a sociologist, became a journey through a network of ideas, proven theories, unproven suspicions, and incomplete agendas; as such, I hope that it reflects what C. Wright Mills called the sociological imagination.

But I wanted to enjoy this journey without too much luggage, unburdened with excessive weights or evidence.

And the truth is, after all these years teaching and writing dozens of books, I cannot always pinpoint the exact origin of a given thought. Yet most of my thoughts here do have specific origins. I have prepared this essay, which comments on some key sociological works, for those who may wish to dip further into the sociological tradition.

For a more coherent and systematic presentation of the traditional material of sociology, I recommend several excellent and provocative texts: *A Poetic for Sociology* by Richard Harvey Brown, *The Origins of Scientific Sociology* by John Madge, *The Sociological Tradition* by Robert Nisbet, and *The Metaphorical Society* by Daniel Rigney. Finally, I want to put in a plug for *The Human Group* by my old teacher George Homans. A systematic review of key research on group dynamics, the book seems much more remarkable and personally significant today than it did when I first met it forty years ago. I wish I had written it!

Here, in brief pieces organized alphabetically by author's surname, I present some thoughts from my own (admittedly idiosyncratic) perspective. I have also included a little information about the authors to stir your interest.

ADORNO, THEODOR. *THE AUTHORITARIAN PERSONALITY* (1950).

Theodor Adorno (1903–1969) is considered one of Germany's most important postwar social philosophers (perhaps second only to Jürgen Habermas). Of Jewish and Catholic descent, Adorno left Germany in 1934 for Oxford and later for the United States, where he remained throughout the war. There, after the war, he led a team to study the social origins of fascism and Nazism.

Adorno's *The Authoritarian Personality* was one of five studies commissioned by the American Jewish Committee to research the roots of prejudice and anti-Semitism. This interdisciplinary volume challenged previous theories about prejudice, replacing them with a social-psychological model that centres on individual personality traits and childhood socialization experiences. The study found a close correlation between overt racism and several deep-rooted personality traits. By measuring authoritarianism using a newly made F-scale (F for "Fascism") and examining its correlates, the authors concluded that racism and anti-Semitism are associated with fascist tendencies that include political and economic conservatism, conventionality, submissiveness, homophobia, and superstition.

Their findings lead the authors to conclude that a formal condemnation of prejudice may reduce the expression of "overt hostility," since anti-democratic individuals are typically submissive. They also propose re-education to wipe out anti-Semitic ideology. And given the evidence that relates prejudice to early family history—chiefly to cold and harsh parenting—*The Authoritarian Personality* is also of interest to those who study families and children.

The most important conclusion of this large study was that Nazi-style fascism and racism can take root anywhere that the social and familial conditions permit. As the American Jewish Committee feared, the US was not without some dangerous tendencies, nor was Germany the only country in the international community in which Nazi genocide might have taken place.

The lesson for humanity, however obvious, has been ignored in one genocidal society after another.

ARMSTRONG, PAT, AND HUGH ARMSTRONG. *THE DOUBLE GHETTO* (1978; 2010).

Pat Armstrong, professor of sociology at York University, is co-author or editor of various books on gender relations, health care, and social inequality. Hugh Armstrong, her husband and co-author, teaches the political economy of poverty, welfare, and social policy at Carleton University.

The Double Ghetto describes the social disadvantages suffered by women at work and in the home. Women in Canada and other industrial capitalist societies lead isolated, ghettoized lives. In offices, factories, and shops, they experience job segregation at low rates of pay. When they come home at night, they do "women's work" in the household, without pay or recognition. The book further argues that capitalism depends upon insecure, poorly paid workers and a reserve army of unemployed or semi-employed people. Women play a valuable role in this system in several ways. First, women physically reproduce and nurture the next generation of workers. Second, they provide unpaid care and support for the paid workforce in the form of housework. Third, women move in and out of the workforce as opportunities and needs change; they are a floating labour supply. This suggests that breaking down injustice in paid work may also mean breaking down ghetto walls in unpaid work. A double ghetto means a double change is needed.

BECKER, HOWARD. *OUTSIDERS* (1966).

Born, raised, and trained in Chicago, Howard Becker (b.1928) spent most of his professional life in the Chicago area. There, he learned the characteristic Chicago-style of ethnographic sociology from Everett Hughes and other masters of the practice. As a professional jazz musician, Becker has unusual perspective into the experiences of the "outsiders"—jazz musicians and marijuana smokers—that he described in the book that made him famous.

Outsiders sets the groundwork for Becker's labelling theory, as it is known today. "Social groups create deviance by making rules whose infraction constitutes deviance," argues Becker, "and by applying these rules to particular people and labelling them as outsiders." Deviance is thus the result of a dominant group, insiders, devising and applying moral rules to less powerful groups of "outsiders." These groups often respond by further entrenching themselves in "secondary deviation," including deviant careers and deviant subcultures.

This is not a book about the reasons why people smoke marijuana or commit any other deviant act. The causes of deviance may be unknowable or unimportant compared to their consequences. Moreover, Becker wants us to focus attention instead on the social context that labels people as deviants.

A key point in *Outsiders* is that we must pay as much attention to the rule *enforcer* as we do to the rule *violator*. Instead of asking "why are they deviant?" we should consider the following: "why do we label such behaviour as deviant, and with what consequences?" Doing so removes the assumption of fault, blame, dysfunction, or illness. The pleasures of smoking marijuana or playing jazz or stealing cars may remain unclear to people who foreswear these activities. However, sociologists have to assume that the actors' motives "make sense," though we cannot necessarily understand them or identify with them.

BOTT, ELIZABETH. *FAMILY AND SOCIAL NETWORK* (1957).

Elizabeth Bott is a sociologist, anthropologist, and psychoanalyst who studies family dynamics.

Family and Social Network explores the influence of external social networks on internal family organization. Earlier research saw marital behaviour as reflecting the norms and values of the spouses. Bott, however, argues that marital behaviour reflects network membership:

"the degree of segregation in the role relationship of husband and wife varies directly with the connectedness of the family's social network."

This book challenges the traditional belief that social relationships are primarily shaped by the values of their participants. Instead it argues that outside influences play an equally important role in the functioning of a marriage.

Bott finds that in close-knit social networks characteristic of older, stable communities where everyone knows everyone else, husbands and wives lead separate lives and play different roles, spending most of their time with same-sex friends and relatives, not with their spouses. In loose-knit networks characteristic of newer, more fluid communities (for example, new suburbs), domestic roles are more likely to overlap, and spouses spend more time together and are more encouraging. This is because in close-knit networks people exchange mutual aid with friends and kin; spouses have less need for each other's help and companionship. However, when networks are loose-knit fewer friends and kin are available, so spouses must rely on each other for help, sharing domestic tasks and leisure time to an unprecedented degree. Bott's study influenced several generations of "network theorists" by showing that people adjust their behaviours, norms, and expectations to conditions outside their household and outside their control.

BOURDIEU, PIERRE. *DISTINCTION: A SOCIAL CRITIQUE OF THE JUDGMENT OF TASTE* (1966).

Pierre Bourdieu (1930–2002) grew up in southern France, the son of a postal worker and his wife—a somewhat unlikely beginning, perhaps, for a sociologist who would provide a revolutionary analysis of upper-class taste. Bourdieu studied philosophy with the radical theorist Louis Althusser and went on to conduct ethnographic research on Berbers in Algeria. Over the course of his career he produced a series of important books.

Distinction appears to run counter to common sense, which would dictate that many people are excluded from the upper classes because of their "lack of taste." Bourdieu however argues that people lack taste—or what sociologists often call "cultural capital"—because they are excluded from the upper classes. In *Distinction*, Bourdieu shows how relations of dominance in society are preserved by manipulating taste and the illusion of free choice. In other words, the class structure, or structure of social distinctions, is upheld by gradations of taste, and people are excluded from upper mobility not by sumptuary laws (as in the Middle Ages) but by their inability to "choose" the needed skills.

One of Bourdieu's main insights is that we can locate taste—or preferences for art, leisure, or hobbies—in a layered social space. Notions of good and bad taste are socially determined, as is access to the goods that display taste. The preferred activities of the dominant class often consist of the following requirements: a focus on form rather than function; the mastery of a set of skills or "acquired tastes" (for example, fine etiquette and skills in activities such as golf, bridge, and horseback riding); and an outlay of resources of time and money that are beyond the capacity of most people. Poorer people typically do not have the resources to play golf or go on skiing trips. However, when such activities eventually become more inclusive, the upper class changes its tastes, to exclude "outsiders."

This book has been celebrated for its complex writing, which is hard to understand; Bourdieu's defence is that complex language is needed to describe a complex reality. That said, the book bears a likeness to Thorstein Veblen's earlier and more readable *The Theory of the Leisure Class* (1899).

Braverman, Harry. *Labor and Monopoly Capital* (1958).

American sociologist Harry Braverman (1920–1976) began his working life as a coppersmith and worked for years in related trades. As a skilled labourer, he saw first-hand the transformation of craftwork by capitalism—a transformation that shaped what would become his union activism and writing career.

Labor and Monopoly Capital, influenced by the writing of Marx and Engels, explores the evolution of capitalist production over the last two centuries. Braverman argues that work, while demanding ever-higher levels of education and expertise, is becoming ever more mindless, bureaucratic, and alienating. It is being "degraded" as capitalists seek to increase their control over the labour process by separating execution from design in work. Despite occasional claims to the contrary, the goal of management is not to humanize work but to lower labour costs and improve a given firm's ability to compete domestically and internationally.

Contrary to the technological determinists who often argue that life and work is always improving, this book suggests that they are in fact getting worse. Although written fifty years ago, Braverman's book still reveals a great deal about our current work world. Our lives are still being made smaller and less secure by technology, which is ultimately enlisted in the service of capitalism. Many efforts are made by management to mask this truth, but they cannot deny it.

One managerial strategy, often disguised as "job enlargement" or "reorganization," involves cost-cutting staff reductions and increased work efficiency. Here, work is supposedly "humanized" by creating an "interesting," fast-paced environment in which there is "never a dull moment." Another management strategy creates the illusion of employee decision-making that gives workers a chance to "participate" by choosing among fixed, insignificant alternatives.

Separating skill from knowledge, or handwork from headwork, degrades the meaning of work. It also creates job worlds populated by two different types of worker: one that engages a few highly skilled, highly trained people whose time is "infinitely valuable," and the other that exploits a mass of indistinct workers who tend machines and whose time is judged to be worth nearly nothing. Among the latter are members of the service economy, drawn from the bottom of the working class—a new low-wage sector that is even more oppressed and exploited than the manufacturing sector.

BURNET, JEAN. *NEXT-YEAR COUNTRY* (1951).

Jean Burnet (1920–2009) grew up among Scottish working-class immigrants in Canada. In a long career that included serving as editor of the *Canadian Journal of Economics and Political Science* and the *Canadian Review of Sociology and Anthropology*, Burnet became a member of the Order of Canada in 1989.

Next-Year Country is one of three studies sponsored by the Canadian Social Science Research Council on the rise of the arch-conservative Social Credit movement in western Canada. In the summer of 1946, Burnet collected a great deal of data on Hanna, Alberta, from observations, interviews, and local newspaper articles.

Hanna had been greatly affected by the Depression and the droughts of the 1930s. Its problems of social organization were in part a result of agricultural difficulties and economic dependency on wheat markets, and in part the result of a diverse and shifting population. The residents, many of them migrants from a range of very different cultures, had brought ways of living, including farming practices that were unsuitable to the area. Their ill-adaptation to life in Hanna hindered the economic adjustment, with harmful consequences for the community and the individual households. The resulting distress supported the rise and development of the Social Credit movement there, with its religious uplift philosophy and clear goals.

Burnet's study is representative of dozens—perhaps scores—of community studies carried out in Canada and the US between the 1920s and the 1950s. While this style of research has gone out of fashion in sociology, it is worth revisiting. Two other classics of the kind, equally worthy of study, are Everett Hughes's *French Canada in Transition* (1943) and Rex Lucas's *Minetown, Milltown, Railtown* (1971).

Coleman, James. *The Adolescent Society* (1961).

James S. Coleman (1926–1995) was an influential and rigorous American sociologist in the field of education and public policy whose publications include *Introduction to Mathematical Sociology* (1964) and *The Mathematics of Collective Action* (1973).

The Adolescent Society is based on a conventional survey of Midwestern US high school students at nine schools. In a detailed study of adolescent popularity, Coleman found that for teenagers and young adults appearance takes on exaggerated importance, at times to the exclusion of all else. Without an attractive appearance, a student risks ridicule or neglect; with good looks, he or she would be more likely to be popular. Appearance, along with several other qualities such as athleticism, is evaluated according to a widely shared student code. Physical appearance—beauty in girls, handsomeness in boys, and good fashion sense in both—counts for more than academic achievement. The academically successful student not only fails to gain popularity from peers but is also resented, given that his or her achievement helps to uphold grading standards the other students are unable or unwilling to meet. Many other students view the "nerd" as selfish.

Coleman also argued that this way of thinking is deeply dysfunctional for society, failing to prepare students for a workforce in which knowledge is critical. For this reason, argues Coleman, adolescent culture not only cuts off adolescents from most parts of the adult world and fails to prepare them for adult life but it also makes them dependent on a cliquish, narrow-minded high school subculture.

Durkheim, Émile. *The Division of Labor in Society* (1893).

French sociologist Émile Durkheim (1858–1917) pursued an academic career in France instead of becoming a rabbi like his father. Some of his key works include *Suicide* (1897), *The Rules of Sociological Method* (1895), and *The Elementary Forms of Religious Life* (1912).

In *The Division of Labor in Society*, Durkheim argues that modern morals and accompanying laws are a result of society adjusting to increased numbers and communicative capacities. He identifies a fundamental difference between two types of society: those with a significant division of labour and those without. In older societies, the division of labour is slight, so people lead similar lives; they are bound together by their similarity. In societies with a high division of labour and specialization, however, people depend on others to complete their work and achieve their goals. From this mutual interdependence springs *organic solidarity*, with its greater individualism, variation, and the general recognition that diversity is necessary.

These changes come about through the growth of "density" in society, a combination of increased population, communication, and mobility, all of which increase social interaction. As density and technology increase, so does the division of labour. There are ensuing legal changes as well. In less complex (older) societies, which depend on homogeneity, repressive law is the norm and individualism is considered potentially dangerous. In modern society, however, law works through contract (not status or tradition), relying largely on compensation for harm. Since society depends on the co-operation of all, the law becomes more flexible, practical, and open to differences.

Durkheim notes that these changes do not always run smoothly, however. They tend to weaken the conscience (or consciousness) that binds people to the norms of society. Social conscience was strong in earlier societies, but modern societies have not yet created the system of morals it requires to function effectively. The result is "anomie" or normlessness (we will see this again below in Durkheim's book *Suicide*) and a greater reliance on non-traditional units of organization (e.g., occupational groups, rather than tribe or kin). In short, Durkheim says we have yet to complete this transition fully.

DURKHEIM, ÉMILE. *SUICIDE* (1897).

In many ways, Durkheim wrote *Suicide* to establish sociology as a recognized academic discipline. His approach in *Suicide* was based on what he called "the sociological method," founded on the principle that "social facts must be studied as things, as realities external to the individual." In addition, *Suicide* develops the idea of "anomie" that was first stated in *The Division of Labor in Society*, above. Durkheim argues that social change can have life-and-death outcomes for members of a given society. So can social isolation.

First, however, Durkheim must show that existing, non-sociological explanations of suicide are inadequate. He reasons that if suicide is strictly a symptom of insanity, then it should have no social patterning, since presumably insanity has no social patterning. (Sociologists have since found that this assumption is wrong.) Further, insanity does not always lead to suicide, suggesting that there are factors outside the individual that influence his or her decision to commit suicide. Here, Durkheim notes the Jewish community has the highest rate of mental illness but the lowest rate of suicide.

Durkheim then considers the "social causes and sociological types of suicide." He proposes three types of suicide, which he terms egoistic, anomic, and altruistic (the least important). *Egoistic suicide* describes individuals who commit suicide when they are isolated or excluded from the social group to which they belong, or when its bonds are weakened by excessive individualism. Here, he discusses the protective value of religion and family. In support of his theory, he shows that Protestants, with a weaker religious community than Catholics, have higher rates of suicide. Similarly, married people have lower rates of suicide than single or divorced people.

Anomic suicide describes "the suicides produced by any sudden social shock or disturbance, such as that due to economic disturbance." Here Durkheim takes the example of a financial crisis. People do not commit

suicide merely because they are poor but because, through impoverish-
ment, they have been subjected to "a painful process of social readjust-
ment" where many of their social standards are disturbed. In similar
ways, any radical and unsettling social change can have a similar effect,
increasing the risk of suicide.

ELIAS, NORBERT. *THE CIVILIZING PROCESS* (1939; 1969).

Sociologist Norbert Elias (1897–1990) grew up in Germany but as a
Jew was forced to flee Nazi Germany, first to Paris and later to England.

   The Civilizing Process consists of two volumes: *The History of
Manners* and *Power and Civility*. These two volumes demonstrate
the co-evolution of polite manners and state government. What Elias
calls the "civilizing process" brings parallel changes in both politics
and in interpersonal relations (such as table etiquette and good manners generally).

   Improved manners, according to Elias, began with the aristocracy,
spread to the bourgeoisie, and then were imposed on children, using
repression in the service of politeness. To show this, Elias examines
changes in the rules governing public behaviour. This includes—but is
not limited to—table manners (the use of utensils, for example); waste
disposal (the end to urinating and defecating in common public spaces,
for example); and increased shame and need for privacy in sexual relations. In short, people have to learn to repress their "natural" drives.
Embarrassment and shame become more common as politeness norms
spread. The spread of politeness also creates class distinctions, where
manners serve as markers. (Note here the similarity to what Bourdieu
was arguing in *Distinction*.)

   The second volume examines how social behaviours and social structures reinforce each other. In short, self-control requires the presence of
a strong state. Elias examines the changes in state organization from
feudalism to centralized state control. Over several centuries, European

states see the growth in power of central authorities (especially kings) who monopolize wealth and physical force, acquire legitimacy, and gain a following of noble supporters. The State becomes more stable and so too does the rule imposed on civilians. Citizens are expected to regulate their conduct in an increasingly predictable and acceptable manner. This spread of norms sets the groundwork for social complexity. With normative predictability, people become increasingly secure, can depend more on one another, and trust one another despite differences.

ERIKSON, KAI. *WAYWARD PURITANS* (1966).

Born in Vienna, Kai Erikson was the son of Freudian psychoanalyst Erik Erikson. Erikson's major works include *Wayward Puritans: A Study in the Sociology of Deviance* (1966), *Everything in its Path: Destruction of Community in the Buffalo Creek Flood* (1976), and *A New Species of Trouble: Explorations in Disaster, Trauma, and Community* (1994).

Wayward Puritans studies patterns of deviance in a seventeenth-century Massachusetts Puritan community. According to Erikson's study, the amount of deviance in a community remains constant over time. Communities, suggests Erikson, perhaps cannot do without deviance—not even Puritan communities with a high standard of conduct and strict controls on behaviour. It seems likely, argues Erikson, that deviance is necessary because it defines the moral boundaries of a community. Deviant behaviour, seemingly disruptive, actually promotes stability. The need to control and punish people unites the members of a community by clarifying their common values and dramatizing the costs of rule-breaking.

Erikson notes, "We are still apt to visualize deviant behaviour as the product of the situation in which it took place." But the reality is that societies—not individuals—create deviance by rules and rule-enforcement. Individuals merely perform the rule-breaking, a point similar to what Howard Becker argues.

To show that deviance remains constant over time, Erikson examines three specific "crime waves," each wave a specific turning point for the community, including the famous Salem witchcraft trials of 1692. Through court records, Erikson finds that while types of deviance change over time, the total number of people defined as deviant remained the same. When there was an increase in crimes against the Church, for example, other recorded forms of deviance decreased. Although theft, for example, may still have been taking place, the community changed its focus of concern and was more likely to ignore it. The witchcraft trials show such a change in focus amid a growing public hysteria.

FANON, FRANTZ. *THE WRETCHED OF THE EARTH* (1961).

Frantz Fanon (1925–1961) grew up in the French colony of Martinique among descendants of African slaves brought to work on the sugar plantations. Fanon left home early to serve in the Free French forces, and fought in Europe during World War II. After the war, he stayed on in France, studying medicine and psychiatry on scholarship. His first book, *Black Skin, White Masks* (1952), published at the age of twenty-seven, explored the effects of racism and colonization he had noted in the Caribbean. In 1961, while Fanon was in Ghana, he developed leukemia and died just after completing *The Wretched of the Earth*, a book addressed to the oppressed citizens of European colonies in Africa, Latin America, and Asia.

The book's title comes from the first line of *The Internationale*, the official anthem of the international Communist movement. It is a social-psychological analysis of the pathologies caused by colonial suffering. Fanon argues that by internalizing the views of the colonizers, the colonized develop a lack of self-respect and sense of perpetual inferiority, ensuring their continued economic and political subordination. Promoting self-respect and creating a sense of identity, Fanon believes, is a crucial step toward freeing colonized people. Moreover, violence is a key ingredient in achieving this.

To overcome the injustices of the past, and to equalize all races, a revolution is needed to redress the damage done by colonialism. Only by expelling colonial rulers and addressing their harm will the colonized be able to break free of their pathological ties to the colonizer. Violence is important because it proves that the oppressed are just as able to take action as the oppressors. Peaceful solutions fail to bring the self-respect necessary to "cure" the natives and convince them of their own power and sovereignty. Violence binds together the oppressed and engraves in them a national identity—a sense of common cause and collective history. Philosopher Jean-Paul Sartre wrote an introduction to the book, asserting that it is a call to revolutionary violence, but it is more than that. It is a book about race relations under conditions of severe inequality.

FOUCAULT, MICHEL. *DISCIPLINE AND PUNISH* (1975).

French sociologist Paul-Michel Foucault (1926–1984) became professor of the History of Systems of Thought at the prestigious Collège de France. Deeply influenced by Nietzsche, Foucault's studies of Western social institutions, including psychiatry and prison systems, have been widely influential.

In the earlier times, punishment was a public spectacle with careful rules dictating the specifics of torture or execution. However, the sovereign's vengeance, as it was viewed, often provoked pity for the tortured wreck. Occasionally, it led to outright revolt. This system came under criticism both because it was inhumane and because it did not significantly lessen crime. Punishment was supposed to deter, not incite, crime. In addition, punishment was supposed to match the offence and ensure the criminal did not repeat the crime.

In the late eighteenth century, these became the stated goals of imprisonment, and prison soon became the standard punishment for almost all crimes. Prison administrators came to think of their work as correctional, not punitive, and the punishment meted out there was no longer publicly visible. Few could witness the reformative process taking place.

Discipline of the body was an important part of this reformation. It was first employed in the military, where recruits were taught how to stand, walk, hold and fire a weapon, and so on. It soon extended to other areas such as schools, which taught students how to hold a pen, sit, eat, speak, and even think. This bodily discipline was enforced by a focus on micro actions, through the continual correction of slight slips, and through continued testing, recording, and examination. People in power set about to record as much information about individuals as possible, to better regulate and examine them. By creating, codifying, and amassing ever more knowledge about individuals, power could be exercised with ever more precision. The rise of knowledge—including the social sciences—went with the rise of centralized power.

The other main technique of discipline was increased surveillance. Here Foucault recounts Jeremy Bentham's idea of the *panopticon*— a prison where the guards can always see the prisoners, but prisoners cannot see the guards (so they can never be sure if they are being watched). This uncertainty leads prisoners to regulate themselves. In a disciplinary society, surveillance is everywhere. Prisons today are just one part of an extended framework of surveillance, recording, and domination. From the moment we are born, every stage of our lives is shaped by these institutions: not just prisons but schools, hospitals, workplaces, and so on. We are enforcing norms all the time and disciplining one another, whenever deviance occurs.

FREUD, SIGMUND. *CIVILIZATION AND ITS DISCONTENTS* (1930).

Sigmund Freud (1856–1939) was the founder of psychoanalysis and is often regarded as one of the greatest creative minds of the twentieth century. He is credited with revealing the importance of the unconscious, which led to new frontiers in psychology, literature, and even science. Freud was born in what is now the Czech Republic, but his family moved to Germany when he was only three, fleeing anti-Semitic oppression. Shortly after, they moved to Vienna where Freud spent most of his life. In 1902, he became a professor of neuropathology and remained at this post until 1938, when he fled to England to escape the German occupation of Austria. He died there the following year. His most central books on social theory, sometimes referred to as the "cultural books," are *The Future of an Illusion* (1927), *Civilization and Its Discontents* (1930), and *Moses and Monotheism* (1939).

Civilization and Its Discontents explores why humanity is beset with a constant sense of discontent and bitterness. He argues that civilization represses sexuality, resulting in a surplus of libidinal energy that interacts with innate aggression. This complex undercurrent constantly threatens to tear society apart. In a civilized society, aggression must be turned inward, leading to its experience as a sense of guilt and discontent.

The assumed goal of life is to seek happiness. This goal is achieved through direct, momentary pleasure and also by avoiding pain and suffering. Civilization, Freud argues, was created to ensure the latter at the expense of the former—for example, by controlling and channelling sexual drives. However, Freud sees humans in a constant battle between two instincts on which civilization rests: *Eros*, the instinct directed to life and love, and *Thanatos*, the instinct directed to death and aggression. Both, though opposed, are fundamental human instincts. Where Eros seeks to bind all humans together in society, Thanatos opposes this goal. Besides, the needs of building and upholding civilization demand limits on behaviour, and particularly on sexuality. But given that sexual control results in surplus libidinal energy, some of this is channelled into social creativity and monogamous romance.

Every advance in civilization, leading to more order, organization, and repression, produces an increase in discontent. Therefore, these social advances lead to more neurosis or deviance. Civilization fails to make us happy, yet seems to be a need, and even this imperfect need is in constant danger of collapse through wars and violence.

GOODE, WILLIAM. *WORLD REVOLUTION AND FAMILY PATTERNS* (1963).

Sociologist William Goode (1917–2003) was famous for his studies of divorce among other topics, and authored over twenty books.

World Revolution and Family Patterns evaluates alterations to family organization around the world in the first half of the twentieth century. In particular, Goode examines the relationship between changing family patterns and industrialization, focusing on several major cross-cultural trends. First, family patterns are moving toward the conjugal (nuclear) model. The family unit is smaller today, a self-sustaining unit of production and consumption, separate from the kinship group. In addition, with an increase in contraceptives and decrease in birthrate, family size has been decreasing. Role relations within the family have also changed. Individual members have more freedom; for example, parental authority over children has declined. With an increase in women's rights, husbands' patriarchal control over wives has also waned. Gradually, dowries and payment for brides have disappeared. A final example of the transformation is an increasing acceptance of changes in social morals and virtues, including the increased acceptance of divorce, the use of contraception, abortion, cohabitation, and premarital sexual relations.

According to Goode, the family model has been changing not directly because of a modern industrial system, but because this family model better fits industrial demands. Smaller family units have more freedom and flexibility to meet the changes in industry, for example. The influences of industry on family life are not one-sided, however; family demands, such as housework and child care, act as barriers to a complete industrial takeover of family life. Moreover, Goode argues that the family was subject to economic progress and political developments even before industrialization.

KANTER, ROSABETH. *MEN AND WOMEN OF THE CORPORATION* (1977).

Rosabeth Moss Kanter holds the Ernest L. Arbuckle Chair at Harvard Business School. In addition to being a sociologist, Kanter is also a famous and successful business consultant.

Kanter's classic work, *Men and Women of the Corporation*, challenges assumptions about the traditional system of merit and reward within organizations. Contrary to the common belief that women's opportunities are limited because they act differently from men, Kanter's study shows that women's lesser opportunity for promotion forces them to act "like women": subservient, devious, yet seemingly unambitious. When men and women have equal opportunities, both act in the same way. People—male or female—who suffer from blocked opportunity, powerlessness, and tokenism display less ambition and low productivity, a result of holding weak positions.

All women connected with large organizations—whether executives, secretaries, or even wives, are in a similar bind. Secretaries, however ambitious and talented, are tied to the fortunes of their often-male bosses. Their earnings rise and fall directly with those of the boss, regardless of the women's own efforts. Similarly, the wives of organizational executives, also often ambitious and talented, are tied to their spouses' fortunes. Both secretaries and wives are powerless, yet heavily dependent on men; their fates rise and fall with those of the men to whom they are linked. Moreover, as a result of this powerlessness, they behave in "typical" female fashion. These seemingly typical female performances support the male view that women, by nature, rarely make adequate executive material.

It is in an organization's interest to make the best possible use of its human capital, including its talented women. However, external relations with clients and other firms in the industry may hinder an organization's ability to change. More often than not, organizations copy one another and remain locked into patterns set up elsewhere. In addition, large organizations have an internal environment that resists change, despite the best wishes of one or more managers. They contain islands of vested interest: small domains with their own culture and power structure. And a final point worth mentioning is that often those in control will resist change.

Luxton, Meg. *More than a Labour of Love: Three Generations of Women's Work in the Home* (1980).

Meg Luxton's prolific work includes *More than a Labour of Love* (1980), considered "a core text" in Women's Studies and Gender Studies.

More than a Labour of Love examines the value of domestic work. It draws attention to the fact that, though domestic labour is clearly work, it is generally considered to be unimportant: that is, it is under-valued, unrewarded, and unnoticed. In addition, because domestic labour is not paid labour, it is accorded low status. By contrast, men's wage work takes priority given its role in the paid economy.

This study documents the lives of three generations of women living in the mining town of Flin Flon, Manitoba, over a period of fourteen months. Luxton examined the everyday lives and labours of working-class married women, and interviewed one hundred women about their domestic roles and activities.

The study reveals how capitalism organizes and shapes domestic labour, the family lives, and the work lives of wives and children. A husband's paid job is central not only to the family economy, but also to family life. The husband's needs are always met first, with meals, family time, and personal time organized around his schedule. Women are economically dependent on their husbands, and so largely power-less in their domestic roles. The domestic economy and wage economy are interdependent; economic life produces, influences, and shapes family life.

Superficially, domestic labour is synonymous with housework. However, many other duties fall under this category. They include providing meals, child care, emotional support for husbands and chil-dren, housecleaning, shopping, paying bills, organizing family sched-ules, and satisfying sexual demands. Women, far more than men in this community, are trained and expected to care for and recognize the suffering of others, to the point of denying their own needs. Take sex as an example: although for married women sex is a duty, single women are also expected to provide sexual service, as a part of dating. Women are expected to marry, get pregnant, and bear children. In these as in other capacities, women's needs are not often fully met, as sexuality is only part of a wife's "duty." The women in this study also often suf-fered domestic violence, both physical and psychological, as a result of their constrained roles.

Though Luxton's book focuses on the lives of women, the stresses men face are also (indirectly) addressed. From a sociological perspec-tive, it is important to recognize that while the patriarchal system often constrains women's legal rights and social influences, men also face social limits. While women are solely responsible for the care of the family, men are solely responsible for financially supporting the family. As a result, many men stay in unfulfilling, difficult, and stress-ful jobs. In addition, both men and women often remain in difficult, stressful marriages.

OAKLEY, ANN. *THE SOCIOLOGY OF HOUSEWORK* (1974).

Ann Oakley (b.1944) was one of the first students ever to major in sociology at Somerville College, Oxford University. Oakley published her first academic book in 1972, *Sex, Gender and Society*, followed by her most famous work, *The Sociology of Housework* (1974). Other works include *Becoming a Mother* (1979) and *The Captured Womb* (1984).

Oakley's research for *The Sociology of Housework* was based on a sample of working- and middle-class homemakers. Both middle- and working-class women reported similar (negative) attitudes about housework and a similar (high degree of) identification with their household role. Moreover, both middle- and working-class women disliked housework. However, in spite of this dislike, the role of homemaker was central to their identity. They viewed themselves as having authority and status only in the work of maintaining the house and tending to their children. Most of these women accepted their dissatisfaction with the monotony, isolation, and low social status of homemaking, especially compared with higher-status occupations.

Oakley concluded from this that women are both disempowered and imprisoned by their beliefs about the proper role of women, and especially mothers, in a modern society. Despite their unhappiness, they feel obliged by our culture to play a fundamentally alienating and frustrating role. They are socialized by a patriarchal gender ideology into accepting servitude in marriage and parenting. Housework is the visible symbol of this submission.

PORTER, JOHN. *THE VERTICAL MOSAIC* (1965).

John Porter (1921–1979) is a key figure in Canadian sociology; among other achievements he is credited with coining the widely used term "vertical mosaic," and developing the Pineo-Porter index of socioeconomic status. His publications include *The Economic Elite and the Social Structure in Canada* (1957), *Canadian Social Structure: A Statistical Profile* (1967), and *Stations and Callings: Making it Through the School System* (1982). A selection of significant sociological essays appears in his book, *The Measure of Canadian Society, Education, Equality and Opportunity* (1979).

In his classic 1965 study, Porter uses the term "vertical mosaic" to put to rest common misconceptions of Canada as a classless society. Like the United States, and contrary to popular mythology, Canadian society is vertical—a social hierarchy of wealth and power. Moreover, unlike the US (to which it is often compared), Canada is made up of a mosaic of largely unassimilated ethnic groups who hold different positions in the hierarchy of wealth and power.

Porter found that economic power is in the hands of a small group of elites who act to promote and protect one another's interests. Porter also found what he calls status inequalities in the patterns of ethnic cleavage and ethnic loyalty that separate immigrants from non-immigrants, and WASPs (White Anglo-Saxon Protestants) from non-WASPs. Elites are mainly composed of people with a WASP background (though some are French). First Nations and Inuit populations suffer the greatest disadvantage in Canada, with the least power and influence.

Porter demonstrated that ethnic differences lead to social inequality as well as variance in social mobility. Low-status groups often accept their inferior economic position while Charter groups (that is, English and French Canadians) preserve their historic advantage. They do so, in part, through monopolizing higher educational opportunities. Porter called for a transformation of the educational system to make it equally open to everyone, enabling most able people to advance occupationally and economically. He also favoured encouraging cultural assimilation. Immigrants to the US are encouraged to shed their cultural background and adopt an American identity. In contrast, immigrants entering Canada are encouraged to preserve their culture and ties to home. This creates a multi-ethnic, mosaic effect. Because of this and the lack of immigrant access to higher education, immigrants lack upward mobility and a role in the ruling elite.

ROETHLISBERGER, FRITZ J., AND WILLIAM J. DICKSON. *MANAGEMENT AND THE WORKER* (1939).

Fritz J. Roethlisberger (1898–1974) is an American industrial psychologist best known for his work on the Hawthorne experiments (see below). In 1939 he published *Management and the Worker* with William J. Dickson. Dickson (b.1904), chief of the Employee Relations Research Department of Western Electric, was also key in the Hawthorne experiments. He is also the co-author of a second book written with Roethlisberger, called *Counseling in an Organization: A Sequel to the Hawthorne Researches* (1966).

In response to poor working conditions and a wish to increase worker productivity, a series of experiments were conducted from 1924 to 1933 at the Western Electric Company's Hawthorne plant in Cicero, Illinois. The goal of these experiments was to study the factors that influence worker productivity. Eventually known as "the Hawthorne Studies," these experiments were published in 1939 as *Management and the Worker*.

Roethlisberger noted the attitudes of the employees significantly affected their productivity. Over the course of many experiments, Roethlisberger and Dickson studied over twenty thousand employees under various working conditions at the Western Electric Company. For parts of the studies, some employees were also monitored under controlled laboratory conditions, with an investigator measuring their productivity and changes in individual behaviour in response to changing work conditions.

What they found out is that, as Roethlisberger had suggested, the "person" and the "organization" cannot be compartmentalized. Within a large, formally organized system, small informal organizations form through personal interactions between individuals. These individuals create rules or norms for acceptable behaviour not formally recognized by the institution. The result, a social system that defines a worker's relation to his or her work and companions, is not the product of rational engineering but of natural human associations and sentiments.

SEELEY, JOHN. *CRESTWOOD HEIGHTS* (1956).

John R. Seeley (1913–2007) had a long and varied career in academia, as an executive officer of the Canadian Mental Health Association in 1947, and later as research director of the Alcoholism Research Foundation of Ontario. He also served as director of the Forest Hill Village Project, and published the results of that study, *Crestwood Heights*, in 1956. His publications also include *The Americanization of the Unconscious* (1967).

Crestwood Heights began as a project in 1950 to learn about the mental health of children in Canada, part of the National Mental Health Project, with the aim of promoting good mental health. Following World War II, this five-year project was initiated by the Canadian National Committee for Mental Hygiene to study the development of children living in a suburban neighbourhood.

The goal of Seeley's work was to study "the culture of the child under pressures for conformity." In other words, it was a study of education, but also a study of childhood aimed at understanding development in terms of values, goals, and problems. The study focused on the Forest Hill community in Toronto—not your typical suburban community, perhaps—where Seeley and his team studied significant institutions and the strains and conflicts in the family and the community.

To parents in this community, the child is a kind of problem in need of a range of solutions, like other problems in the managerial world. The parents in this community are a mixture of "new money" and "old money," successful and upwardly mobile people, usually in business or the professions. For these parents, careers are the priority and career success is of key importance. As well, they want their homes, appearances, and activities to look like Hollywood movies or *haute couture* magazines. They train their children to be "perfect": competitive and successful in all pursuits.

Even at a young age, children are taught to seek success in scout groups, music lessons, hockey teams, and summer camps—and of course in school. School, unlike religion, is the most important institution. Parents turn their children over to the school (and associated institutions), hoping that they will be returned in a more mature form.

Of course, this is complicated by stresses within the school itself. Some of these have to do with school organization, and some with the conflicting goals of education. On the one hand, the school is charged with training the children for "bureaucratic crawl." With the increasing bureaucratization in industrial society, child-rearing values shift from a stress on individual achievement, independence, and competition to a stress on co-operation, other-direction, and a submergence of the individual in the group. School trains the middle-class suburban child for "bureaucratic crawl," teaching the "new" techniques of co-operation and group orientation.

At the same time, school tries to teach traditional values of competition and individual effort. This creates tension for the students, parents, and teachers. The tension is worsened by the effects of bureaucratization on the jobs of teachers. Parents also press teachers for higher grades (more successes for their children)—the beginnings of grade inflation, which are still with us today. No wonder many students experience a troubled transition from high school to university, and much personal stress in both locations.

THOMAS, W.I., AND FLORIAN ZNANIECKI. *THE POLISH PEASANT IN EUROPE AND AMERICA* (1920).

William Isaac Thomas (1863–1947) was professor of sociology at the University of Tennessee and the University of Chicago, and served as President of the American Sociological Society. His first work, *Sex and Society* (1907), calls for the end of female inequality. Other publications include *The Unadjusted Girl* (1923) and *Primitive Behavior* (1937). Thomas's lifestyle was eccentric for the time, and his views often clashed with the academic community around him. Florian Znaniecki (1882–1958) was a Polish sociologist and philosopher. In Poland, he helped to organize the Polish Sociological institute and held the Chair in Sociology at the University in Poznan, but moved to the US at the outbreak of World War II. His publications include *The Method of Sociology* (1934) and *The Social Role of the Man of Knowledge* (1940).

Between 1918 and 1920, Thomas and Znaniecki published the multi-volume work, *The Polish Peasant in Europe and America*, now considered a classic study in sociological theory and immigrant history. This exploration of the social life of the peasant focuses on the process of disorganization and reorganization of peasant communities in Poland, which serve as background for the problems of adjustment that peasants face as immigrants to America.

The authors consider how and why immigrants often fail to meet new opportunities and challenges while trying to assimilate into a new culture. They begin their work with an analysis of the cultural tradition of Poland and its growing social disorganization. Partly due to macro social changes associated with urbanization and industrialization, many peasants immigrated to America with expectations of success. They brought with them the desire for new experience, recognition, mastery, and security. However, many immigrants failed to alter their social customs—a necessity if they were to assimilate into American culture and achieve economic success. Yet neither could they maintain the traditional system of life; for example, social solidarity decreased after immigration. Therefore these immigrants were neither entirely disengaged from their native land, nor fully integrated into American culture. They could not wholly identify as Polish nor could they identify as American. The results included poverty, deviance, and delinquency in children, marital conflict, and social isolation. Thomas and Znaniecki conclude that immigration demands prodigious change from the immigrant, yet society provides none of the means needed to bring this about.

The methodology used by Thomas and Znaniecki is of key significance, at times even overshadowing their conclusions. Their work developed a new methodology for sociological research and analysis, using a qualitative, empirical approach in their investigation of peasant life. They drew on a range of primary material—court documents, newspaper articles, archives of charitable societies and Polish parishes, hundreds of letters exchanged between immigrants and their connections in Poland, and a lengthy autobiography of a Polish immigrant labourer.

WALLERSTEIN, IMMANUEL. *THE MODERN WORLD-SYSTEM* (1976).

Immanuel Maurice Wallerstein (b.1930) is an American sociologist who has served as the president of the International Sociological Association. His books include *The Capitalist World-Economy* (1979), *Race, Nation, Class: Ambiguous Identities* (1992), *The End of the World As We Know It: Social Science for the Twenty-First Century* (2001), and *Unthinking Social Science: The Limits of Nineteenth-Century Paradigms* (2007).

The Modern World-System: Capitalist Agriculture and the Origins of the European World-Economy in the Sixteenth Century is the first book in a three-volume set. This book surveys economic developments in Europe from 1450 to 1640. Wallerstein's argument is that an important new social system has gradually evolved since the sixteenth century. The basic linkages are economic and the system is organized on capitalist principles. The result has been a worldwide division of labour and a worldwide system of stratification.

Prior to the sixteenth century, world economies did not exist as we know them today, nor were there world empires like the Roman Empire. The great expense of upholding the political structure of a world empire set limits to the potential for economic growth. This changed in the sixteenth century, when a world economy emerged that was based on the capitalist mode of production and did not require political rule to achieve coherence. The modern world system gradually developed as a world economy, and was not transformed into a political empire. "The techniques of modern capitalism and the technology of modern science . . . enabled this world-economy to thrive, produce, and expand without the emergence of a unified political structure." The capitalist mode of production built and strengthened the emerging world economy, while avoiding the massive losses and strains that would be associated with a world empire (as shown by the disastrous failure of the Spanish empire).

An important aspect of the model is its conception of the differentiation of the "parts" that make up the world system. Wallerstein divides the nations in this global system into core states, periphery states, and semi-periphery states. The shifting relationships among these three classes of states uphold a dynamic tension that insures the growing dominance of the system as a whole.

WEBER, MAX. *GENERAL ECONOMIC HISTORY* (1923).

Max Weber (1864–1920) was born in Erfurt, Germany, the son of a wealthy and worldly businessman/politician, and a mother who had been raised in strict Calvinist orthodoxy—facts that would influence Weber's later intellectual development.

Weber's major works span a variety of topics: politics, science, religion, law, formal organization, and economics. His most famous work is *The Protestant Ethic and the Spirit of Capitalism* (1904–5), in which he argues that religion was one of the reasons why the economies of the West and the East developed differently. Particular characteristics of ascetic Protestantism—Calvinism—stimulated and supported the development of capitalism, bureaucracy, and the rational-legal state in the West. Capitalism, then, is not a purely materialist phenomenon in Karl Marx's sense, but rather originates in religious ideas that cannot be solely explained by relations of production.

General Economic History is Weber's final work and brings together all his distinctive interpretations of economic life and change. Following a discussion of early agrarian systems (such as the manorial system and plantations), guilds, and early capitalism, it moves on to discuss the evolution of commerce, technology, and industrial organization and finishes with a discussion of the factors influencing the rise of capitalism. The book is thoroughly researched and is, perhaps, the most compact, comprehensive, and readable presentation of Weber's ideas about social change.

Whyte, William Foote. *Street Corner Society* (1943).

William Foote Whyte (1914–2000) was an American professor of sociology, who served as president of the American Sociological Association, the Society for Applied Anthropology, and the Industrial Relations Research Association.

Whyte approached the topic of delinquency as someone interested in studying "people and problems unfamiliar to [his] upper-middle-class environment." *Street Corner Society* began as a personal project to understand the social problems commonly found in congested city districts. Whyte later turned his focus to the interaction and network patterns of a working-class community in Cornerville, at the north end of Boston. Before this, there had been few real community studies of inner-city life.

Earlier efforts to study slums typically favoured social disorganization theory and campaigned for social reform, discounting the community's culture and social networks. Whyte's research, one might say, was more respectful: it saw a real community that was well organized and functioned successfully, by its own standards. This contradicted social disorganization theory, which argued that in slums there is an inadequate influence of existing social rules of behaviour on community members. Whyte found that communities such as Cornerville are built on social structures that succeed in integrating and regulating the smaller and more informal groupings of the district.

Street Corner Society, then, questions the previous definition of slums as socially disorganized neighbourhoods, revealing instead that they had multilayered social standards that were separate from the existing social rules and social groupings in middle-class society.

WILKINSON, RICHARD G. *UNHEALTHY SOCIETIES: THE AFFLICTIONS OF INEQUALITY* (1996).

Richard G. Wilkinson studied economic history at the London School of Economics and then took degrees at the University of Pennsylvania and the University of Nottingham. His books include *Poverty and Progress: An Ecological Model of Economic Development* (1973) and *The Society and Population Health Reader*, a large contributory volume edited by Ichiro Kawachi, Bruce P. Kennedy, and Richard G. Wilkinson.

In modern, industrial societies, degenerative diseases become the leading causes of death, defeating infectious diseases for this honour. Yet with this comes a new source of social inequality in death risks. In developed countries, relative poverty—the gradient between rich and poor—rather than absolute poverty has the greatest effect on mortality rates and life expectancy. This is particularly evident in the United States, where interstate differences show these inequality effects. This relationship between socio-economic status and health is found to be relatively linear, with those in the lowest classes always suffering worse health than those higher up, regardless of how well-off the lowest classes are in absolute terms.

Researchers first demonstrated this in the classic Whitehall Studies of British civil servants, where people in the lowest income categories were found to have four times the rate of death from heart disease as those in the highest income categories. This differential in health, as mentioned earlier in the book, is due to psychosocial factors, particularly chronic stress. For those lower down the ladder, fears of unemployment and poverty are constant. However, other sources of insecurity and low self-esteem are also stressful and more common in these classes. The conclusion is that we need to take preventive actions of a fundamental kind—attacking inequality as a health problem, rather than providing superficial solutions that do not work—including "more special needs classes in schools, more prisons and police, more social workers and health services, more counselors and therapists."

Works Cited

Azzam, Amy. 2007. Why students drop out. *Educational Leadership* 64, no. 7 (April): 91–93.

Bell, Daniel. 1960. Crime as an American way of life: A queer ladder of social mobility. In *The end of ideology: On the exhaustion of political ideas in the fifties*. New York: Free Press.

Braudel, Fernand. 1949. *The Mediterranean and the Mediterranean world in the age of Philip II*. 2 vols. Trans. Sian Reynolds. Berkeley: University of California Press, 1966, 1995.

Burr, Vivien. 1995. *An introduction to social constructionism*. London: Taylor and Francis.

Davis, Kingsley, and Wilbert Moore. 1945. Some principles of stratification. *American Sociological Review* 10 (April): 242–49.

Gill, Lesley. 2008. War and peace in Colombia. *Social Analysis* 52, no. 2 (September): 131–50.

Homer-Dixon, Thomas. 2002. *The ingenuity gap: Facing the economic, environmental, and other challenges of an increasingly complex and unpredictable future*. New York: Vintage Books.

Huizinga, Johan. 1938. *Homo ludens: A study of the play-element in culture*. Boston: Beacon Press, 1955.

Katz, Elihu, and Paul Felix Lazarsfeld. 1955. *Personal influence: The part played by people in the flow of mass communications*. New York: Free Press.

Lareau, Annette. 2000. *Home advantage: Social class and parental intervention in elementary education*. Rev. ed. Lanham, MD: Rowman and Littlefield.

Matsumura, Lindsay Clare, Sharon Cadman Slater, and Amy Crosson. 2008. Classroom climate, rigorous instruction and curriculum, and students' interactions in urban middle schools. *Elementary School Journal* 108, no. 4 (March): 293–312.

Merton, Robert K. 1938. Social structure and anomie. *American Sociological Review* 3, no. 5: 672–82.

Milgram, Stanley. 1967. The small world problem. *Psychology Today* 1, no. 1 (May): 60–67.

Mills, C. Wright. 1951. *White collar: The American middle classes*. New York: Oxford University Press, 1956.

Rainwater, Lee, Richard P. Coleman, and Gerald Handel. 1962. 2nd ed. *Workingman's wife: Her personality, world and lifestyle*. New York: Macfadden-Bartell.

Rojek, Chris. 2006. Sports celebrity and the civilizing process. *Sport in Society* 9, no. 4 (October): 674–90.

Rosenfield, Sarah, Julie Phillips, and Helene White. 2006. Gender, race and the self in mental health and crime. *Social Problems* 53, no. 2: 161–85.

Thornberg, Robert. 2008. A categorisation of school rules. *Educational Studies* 34 (February): 25–33.

Tsutsui, Kiyoteru, and Hwa-Ji Shin. 2008. Global norms, local activism, and social movement outcomes: Global human rights and resident Koreans in Japan. *Social Problems* 55, no. 3 (August): 391–418.

Index